BUFALINO

BUFALINO

REVELATIONS of a MAFIA FAMILY, THE TEAMSTERS, and the Final Resting Place of JIMMY HOFFA

CHARLES BUFALINO

CITADEL PRESS
Kensington Publishing Corp.
kensingtonbooks.com

CITADEL PRESS BOOKS are published by

Kensington Publishing Corp.
900 Third Avenue
New York, NY 10022

Library of Congress Control Number is available

First hardcover printing: May 2026
ISBN: 978-0-8065-4482-3

ISBN: 978-0-8065-4484-7 (e-book)

10 9 8 7 6 5 4 3 2 1

Printed in the United States of America

The authorized representative in the EU for product safety and compliance
is eucomply OU, Parnu mnt 139b-14, Apt 123
Tallinn, Berlin 11317, hello@eucompliancepartner.com

For the family

CONTENTS

CONTENTS

FOREWORD

GENERATIONS AND SCIONS

By Meyer Lansky II (with S. J. Peddie)

Charles Bufalino—scion of the Bufalino family in Pittston, Pennsylvania, and relative of Pennsylvania crime boss Russell Bufalino—has produced a strikingly intimate portrait of his family.

There is Mary Buff, his father's sister, who was like a second mother to him. Then her brother Angelo, who was known throughout his life as Yabo and admired by Charles for his physical courage and his principles. And there is Russell, who became the feared Mob boss—his "distant cousin—period."

Aunt Mary Buff was the one who gave the Bufalino children their first sips of wine, made them pizza, taught them card games, and tutored them in conversational Italian. She was extremely proud of her family but always told Charles that the members in his branch of the family were "the good Bufalinos." Maybe so, but they were fiercely loyal to their blood kin and wouldn't dream of turning them in to the law.

Coming up from humble beginnings of working the Pennsylvania coal mines, and at times clashing with the United Mine Workers, the Bufalino crime family was able to achieve its success through connections in its family's early neighborhood businesses.

The Bufalino Brothers grocery store, delicatessen, and butcher shop were the foundation that grew the family's name and reputation beyond the neighborhood, with Russell Bufalino ultimately working in step with the Five Families of New York.

The Bufalino story is a history of Italian immigrants in Pennsylvania, from the padrone system that enabled immigrants to pay for the expensive voyage to the United States to the dangerous coal mines where they found work.

When Russell Bufalino was linked to a truckload of stolen color television sets in the 1960s, Charles was embarrassed when a school chum saw the news and asked him if he could get him one of those TV sets. He asked Aunt Mary Buff if they were related to "this guy." She denied it.

That childhood experience is typical for the descendants of powerful gangsters. There are so many questions with no answers. They grow up understanding that there are secrets in their families. They know that there are many things that they don't know. They also know that there are just some things they should never ask about.

In this book, Charles has set out to uncover some of those secrets. He has spoken to family members, pored over dusty records, and reached out to experts. One day, he listened to a young scholar give a presentation on the bombings that accompanied the union strikes in coal mines in the early twentieth century. Imagine how he felt when he asked the presenter if there was any town or street that experienced more than its share of bombings.

The presenter didn't even have to consult his data. Without skipping a beat, he answered, "Railroad Street in Pittston, Pennsylvania."

Charles Bufalino's street. Or, as Charles put it, "Murder Street." Brutal, bloodthirsty violence was a part of his family history.

In the Bufalino family, Russell didn't particularly stand out. He had a gruff, tough-guy demeanor. He came to power when he was forty-seven years old. He didn't kill anyone to get to the top. He was given the top spot because the family only trusted their own and because no one else in the family wanted their children in that life. Russell Bufalino was an orphan. What had been a crippling disadvantage became his advantage.

Russell Bufalino was connected enough that he was the man who drove Vito Genovese out of the critical Apalachin summit in 1957. He was at Joe Colombo's side when he was shaking down producers of *The Godfather* when they were trying to make the movie in New York. He personally taught Marlon Brando the demeanor and behaviors of a don in the style of his own predecessors.

As much as he tried to keep a low profile, he was on the radar of federal authorities. To them, Russell Bufalino was one of the most ruthless crime bosses in the country. Because he was so strong in labor racketeering, those same authorities considered him the top suspect in the mysterious disappearance of famed Teamsters Union leader Jimmy Hoffa.

The Bufalino ties to Hoffa were part of family legend. Charles's uncle, Yabo, was a sometime bodyguard to Hoffa. His father's cousin, Bill Bufalino, was tough and smart enough to become the Teamsters' business agent. Bill actually implicated the CIA in Hoffa's disappearance.

While Bill Bufalino counseled Hoffa for more than twenty-five years on issues related to racketeering charges, sponsoring casinos in Las Vegas, and what to say under oath to Bobby Kennedy, it was Russell Bufalino who would be considered a suspect in the disappearance of Hoffa himself. The case has never been closed.

Russell, in fact, proved elusive for law enforcement. They were convinced he had a hand behind the scenes in major events. One theory that federal authorities put out there was that Russell Bufalino knew about the Mafia's role in the plot to assassinate Cuban leader Fidel Castro. They believed that he was worried about the fates of Chicago Mob bigwig Sam Giancana and Los Angeles mobster

Johnny Roselli, who were reportedly involved in the assassination attempt.

Any discussion of Cuba has to include Meyer Lansky, although he didn't show up anywhere in the theories about attempts to kill Castro. Lansky understood Cuba. He was the man who cleaned up casinos for Cuban strongman Fulgencio Batista, the man who fled Cuba after the revolution led by Castro. Lansky loved the island. No gangster understood Cuba better than he did, so much so that FBI agents sat rapt as he explained the political situation to them.

It's likely that Meyer and Russell knew each other, as their world was in reality a small one. But Lansky, like Bufalino, never talked about murder or assassination plots. Both men understood it was important to keep their own counsel.

That was absolutely the right course to take in the world they inhabited. One wrong word could get them killed. Or worse, a precious family member could be killed.

But for their families—their children, grandchildren, nieces, and nephews—the questions linger. Charles Bufalino has set out to answer those questions. In a way, his quest is not so unusual. Most families have secrets. But in families like his, the secrets are big.

It's likely that both Bufalino and Lansky would have counseled their families to leave it alone. It's best not to disturb those ghosts.

Charles Bufalino may be doing just that.

Meyer Lansky II is the grandson of Meyer Lansky and author of The Lansky Legacy: The Life and Letters of Meyer Lansky.

INTRODUCTION

A FAMILY MATTER

I began researching my family in earnest in the 2010s to disprove an unsettling belief that had become a burden. Living as I was in the Pittston homestead at the time, clearing up my mother's affairs, I had a series of interactions and made a few chance discoveries that presented a bizarre, compelling, and unsettling possibility. I came to believe that I knew something nobody was intended to know about the last chapters of the Jimmy Hoffa disappearance.

It bothered me enough that I set out to prove to myself that my theory could not possibly be true. I went beyond the oral traditions of my family into the written record to sort out the relationships we had to the larger organization, the original Pittston crime family. I traced our path from Sicily to America and the career paths of Russell Bufalino, Bill Bufalino, and a large body of uncles and aunts to see how they fit in with the events that led to Hoffa's disappearance.

I'm still stuck with my theory. You may come to agree or not. My suspicion may be disproved by some discovery in the future. All the same, even if there is some final discovery concerning Hoffa's remains, you might wish my version was the true story. But you'll need to know some Pittston family history first and get to know the players and the action in Detroit that week at the end of July 1975 when Jimmy Hoffa went missing.

The Pittston family has a double meaning to me. First, it's the Bufalino crime family. Like all the Five Families of New York, the

FBI-assigned names were applied based more on the 1950s headman than for the people who had established the gangs decades before. Before it acquired Russell's name as the Bufalino crime family, when it was plain that some organization was in charge of bootlegging and racketeering in the coalfields of Northeastern Pennsylvania, it was informally named for the center of the activity—the city of Pittston, Pennsylvania. Certainly the name "Pittston family" postdates the original Black Hand label, which was widely used across the country generically in the early 1900s to describe the immigrant Sicilian extortion rings the way we use the word *Mafia* today as the generic name for American gangsters and racketeers.

For simplicity and clarity's sake, whenever I talk about the larger organized effort headed cooperatively by Santo Volpe, Stefano "Steve" La Torre, and Calogero Bufalino (Russell's uncle), in any time from 1903 forward through Russell's tenure and beyond, I'm going to call it the Pittston family. Just know that when I do that, it's synonymous with other names, including Men of Montedoro, which was a local law enforcement label that got used in the McClellan testimony, and the Bufalino crime family, which is the FBI's final label. The FBI also used the acronym RABFAM as a name for investigations related to the "Russell (or Rosario) A. Bufalino Crime Family." But for purposes of my narrative, it's going to be the "Pittston family," a cooperative syndicate anchored early on by Calogero Bufalino—Russell Bufalino's uncle—Stefano La Torre, and Santo Volpe.

The second meaning of the Pittston family as I use it is that it's *my* family, the Bufalino Brothers family. Salvatore Bufalino, Bill's father and my granduncle, laid the groundwork for the Pittston family as one of the first sets of boots on the ground in the Pittston, Pennsylvania coalfields. My granduncle Salvatore and my grandfather Nicolo were associates of Calogero Bufalino and later business partners in his legitimate operations in the south side of Pittston.

Another granduncle, Ross (Rosario) is also part of the Bufalino Brothers but may have had less of a hand in Calogero's business. When I speak of any of them, I'll use the label "Bufalino Brothers." To clarify their relationship to the Pittston family: The men of the Bufalino Brothers were satellites of Calogero Bufalino, who was one of the founding and leading members of the Pittston crime family. Although relationships existed between the Bufalino Brothers and other members of the Pittston family, especially Santo Volpe, their primary relationship was through Calogero.

I never did adequately disprove my belief about the closing chapters of the Hoffa story. Everything I have found makes it more plausible, even poetic in a grotesque sort of way. But to understand that, you have to have some background in the relationships between Bill, Russell, a few key players in the supporting family, and the as-yet-undocumented relationships that existed between the Bufalino crime family and the Detroit Partnership.

It's also going to be helpful to understand that from the very first that the Pittston family's peculiar specialty was in union affairs, first battling against the United Mine Workers of America (UMWA), then against the International Ladies' Garment Workers Union (ILGWU), until, finally, they worked their way into the Teamsters Union. In union matters, they eventually walked both sides of the street and profited one way or another from having roles in labor and management, which they often occupied at the same time.

It's a little unsettling to put forth my theory about the last chapter of the Hoffa disappearance because I could be as wrong as everyone else is. But I can confidently set the record straight about so many ill-reported or outright false narratives about Russell Bufalino, his influence, his rise, the family of which he was a part, his relationship to Bill and the Teamsters, and more. At the very least, I can outline the history of the Pittston family from a mix of family tradition validated by press reporting.

I invite you to test the facts to see if they add up at all in support of my personal belief. Is Jimmy Hoffa hiding in plain sight in Pittston, Pennsylvania? You may well come to answer, as I do: Where else would he be?

BUFALINO

CHAPTER 1

THE BUFALINO BROTHERS

William Eugene "Bill" Bufalino—Teamsters Local 985 president and Jimmy Hoffa associate—and my father were direct contemporaries, first cousins, childhood neighbors, and children of two of the three Bufalino men whose first business was a combined grocery and deli-butcher shop in the old wooden-floor corner lot property operating under the name "Bufalino Brothers." With Bill's father Salvatore at the fore, the brothers were lauded for their industry and as examples of the rewards of hard work. By the end of the 1920s, they would own most of a solid half-block of commercial properties on Railroad Street in the anthracite (hard coal) boomtown of Pittston, Pennsylvania.

Mary Buff was Bill Bufalino's sister. She always said we were the good Bufalinos. I trusted her opinion. Born in 1908 as the third of my granduncle Salvatore's children, she chose not to marry on the death of her mother, Luigina Galante, in 1924 but rather to stay at home and help raise her younger brothers: Bill (age five), Eugene, James, and Yabo (Angelo, age eleven). From the day it was completed, Mary occupied the other half of the double-block home her father Salvatore and my grandfather Nicolo built, with money on loan from Russell's uncle Calogero, to house their families and businesses.

I was a latchkey kid in the 1960s. Mary was our next-door neighbor in the double-block brick house on Railroad Street, Pittston. I came to know her as a second mother when my parents were at work at my father's photography studio. Through measles, mumps, and a few pretend illnesses, I sat on her couch watching TV or at her table learning the Italian language, playing cards, and otherwise sharing time with a close relative. I was often in her company.

Mary was my main primary source for family lore, although other family, including my father Angelo, Mary's brother Yabo (another Angelo, my father's cousin), and various more distant uncles and aunts, contributed their parts to the picture of life at the homestead and on the street they called Murder Street. Bill Bufalino, of Hoffa fame, knew Mary more as a mother than sister from age five. Throughout his life, he sought her approval and attention. Because of that, Mary received a steady stream of mail from her sister Adeline, Bill's legal secretary, which included newspaper clippings, drafts of letters, photographs, framed cartoons from the *Detroit Free Press,* Teamsters publications, and whatever else involved Bill. I got to see them all or hear about Bill's exploits from Mary.

As for the family narrative, which became my own backstory and belief system to bring me to adulthood with a sense of family pride and self, it went like this:

Salvatore Bufalino, Mary and Bill Bufalino's father, my grandfather Nicolo Bufalino, and a third brother named Rosario were coal miners who established businesses in Pittston, Pennsylvania, starting with a butcher shop on Railroad Street. They grew to own a general store and a soda factory, both housed in the ground-floor cellar spaces of the current house. Salvatore founded the Montedoro Society and reinstituted the feast and procession of the Blessed Mother, a tradition of Sicily, among the citizens from central Sicily who lived in Pittston. A great many of Pittston's Sicilian population emigrated to the United States and settled in Pittston through Salvatore's efforts in what the family referred to as a kind of homespun travel agency.

Salvatore was literate and conversant in English, which made him an advocate for the Italian immigrants to the region, who numbered in the thousands. My own grandfather, Nicolo, was less literate and sociable. He ran a number of the family business concerns, including a speakeasy that he operated out of the Montedoro Society during Prohibition. On the basis of their father's refinement and position in the community, Mary and Yabo were not always able to maintain a certain distance between themselves and generally everyone else. But it did not rankle. It went with the territory. They led. We followed. I got it.

As far as the Mafia went, well, we shot at them. At least, my grandfather had potted off shots to prevent the bombing of property adjacent to ours. The Bufalino Brothers were a *thing* in the local newspapers, lauded for their industry and ability to bootstrap themselves into the American Dream.

It all came to an end for the Bufalino Brothers with the onset of the Great Depression, when Salvatore's willingness to extend credit at the general store and other financial and familial downturns ruined the family's fortune.

On the question of Russell's kinship, he was a distant cousin—period.

That was everything I knew about us all, until Russell passed and a number of authors started writing about the family. Until 2011, in my mind, Bill was the star, Russell the black sheep, and I was closer by far to the accomplished Teamsters attorney and labor leader Bill than I was to Russell. We *were* the good guys.

Mary passed suddenly in 1981 when I was working two jobs. She died within a dozen hours, stricken with diabetic shock, before I could even visit her in hospital. I felt guilty about having delayed my visit. So when Mary's brother Yabo returned permanently from Detroit to occupy the homestead upon his own and Bill's retirement, I pretty much haunted him, checking in on a near-daily basis.

I understood that Yabo had a certain history. I used to joke that he drove a beer truck during Prohibition (but in reality, the payload was probably whiskey). I further knew from Mary that Yabo had at one time suffered a nervous breakdown and had been briefly institutionalized. He went to Detroit with Bill in the forties, had a job as a millwright, and frequently accompanied Bill and Hoffa in their travels. He wore Hoffa's money belt when they traveled on business.

My own father's health was in decline by the time Yabo returned home. Yabo was a good sounding board for me as I started my career locally and was a big-framed bully of a man. I was happy to have him guarding the approaches across the yard to the house, even at his age. But apart from echoing many of the family narratives about his father's arrival and other stories, Yabo did not contribute much to the core knowledge about the family, and I did not pry. I wasn't writing a book, after all, and I didn't want to stir up any untoward memories, just in case they bothered Yabo because, well . . . *Yabo always seemed just a little haunted.*

I thought Russell's passing in 1994 would bring an end to the notoriety of the family name. Instead, Russell Bufalino's legend only grew with the release of Charles Brandt's *I Heard You Paint Houses,* the well-researched *Informer Journal* article titled "Men of Montedoro," and ever more publications, not all of which had their facts exactly right, so far as I could tell. I took it all in and bit my tongue rather than comment.

Then a series of closely-timed small unveilings led me to an uncomfortable belief that my family, my relaatives, had a direct role in the closing chapter of the Hoffa disappearance. I researched the family a little deeper. I compared known facts to the family oral traditions and written records, hoping to learn some counternarrative that would help me dismiss my suspicion.

I failed.

CHAPTER 2

THE MORTICIAN'S TALE

"Margaret Bufalino, you are going to heaven with your boots on."

Father Julio Serra of St. Rocco's Church in Pittston knew what he was talking about. My father was a professional portrait photographer whose candid wedding work frequently put him in St. Rocco's Church and often at odds with Father Serra. The source of the conflict was that during any given wedding celebrated by Father Serra in his own church, Serra believed that *he* was in charge of the proceedings. My father was of a contrary opinion, seeing as how his whole reputation as a popular photographer was on the line each and every time he snapped the shutter. Ladders in the church? No problem. How else was he going to get the wide shot? Need to change batteries? Call for a pause, no problem! My father's philosophy was that the bride was going to end up hating him one way or the other, either at the church or when she picked up her wedding album. He always chose the first option. It was a half-friendly, semi-respectful rivalry he had with Father Serra, and it led the priest to absolve my mother of every life sin just for having to deal with my old man.

In 2011, my mother, the last of her generation to occupy the Pittston homestead, passed away. Shortly after her passing, I had an encounter that would be the first of three related mini reveals:

conversations and chance discoveries that led me to a belief I couldn't dismiss. They occurred one shortly after the other, aligned on one theme, and concluded within a few months of her funeral.

The funeral home was well-known to my family and to many others in the closely-knit Sicilian community of Pittston, Pennsylvania. Generations of Italian and Sicilian families had been waked there, and the home itself had multiple generations of family operators. Many similar funeral homes had their start in the anthracite coal mining era, when the coal company black mariah hearses would simply deposit the scorched or torn and mangled bodies of miners on the front porch and drive away, often without so much as a knock. They were followed by enterprising funeral operators leaving business cards with the family, suggesting that "I can help you with that." In this funeral parlor I had attended the wakes of the two prior generations of Bufalinos and their related families in the close company of Russell Bufalino, his entourage, and the ever-present contingent of FBI agents who dutifully recorded, by the light of their flashlights, the license plates of every car in attendance. I had personally made the arrangements for my mother's wake, so I was not surprised when the funeral director made his way toward me in the vestibule. He directed my attention toward a mantel in the front parlor toward two rough-looking cement or concrete molded vases. "You see those two memorial vases?" I nodded toward them. "Bill Bufalino gave them to me." I was nodding in assent, listening. "He had a hobby of making memorial vases."

I was still nodding "yes" but my mind was rejecting the possibility that Bill had a hobby of making memorial vases. I could more easily have accepted the belief that Bill had the vases made by someone else to present to the family that owned the funeral parlor. But they did seem a little plain-looking for that to be the case. Of course, I could be wrong and Bill's family might to this day be shuttling cement or concrete memorial vases around their yard, using them to store garden tools. But I had legitimate reason to doubt. It ran through my mind that 'Mary would have had one. And I would have seen it somewhere in her house.' I knew standing there that, anything Bill Bufalino ever did, or accomplished, somehow ended up in Mary's house courtesy of Bill's sister, Adeline, who served as Bill's legal secretary. And whatever it was...a newspaper article about some Union matter in Texas or wherever, or the letter Bill drafted to the Italian authorities on the occasion of Russell's near-deportation, I, as Mary's cousin, charge and neighbor, would have seen it. I was frequently in Mary's company as a child and Mary held nothing back. Bill regarded Mary as his mother. He had referred to Mary in his WWII Army Last Will and Testament in just those terms. Absent the appearance of a single memorial vase or artifact of any kind made of cement at Mary's house, cellar-to-attic, I was dubious about what I was hearing, but I kept nodding to be polite. "Wow. That is very cool." The vases were obviously a treasured artifact in the family that ran the funeral home.

I knew Bill much better than I knew Russell. Even so, most of my experience of Bill was gathered during the years of Jimmy Hoffa's incarceration in Lewisburg, PA and the few years thereafter that Bill maintained a law practice below Mary's apartment. Bill would routinely, he himself said weekly, travel from Detroit to Lewisburg to consult with Hoffa in the company of either his son William Bufalino II or Yabo (Angelo), his brother. Lewisburg and its prison being just 90 minutes from Pittston, Pennsylvania, Bill would often schedule some time to visit his sister at the homestead, take care of local legal matters and just maybe commiserate with Russell in person to avoid wiretaps.

I liked Bill Buff. Most people did. You would have liked him. He was entertaining. My father, his direct contemporary, first cousin and lifelong neighbor, could never get enough of Bill talking about... well... being Bill Buff and taking on the Kennedys in a half-decade of hearings. When I think of Bill I think raconteur, wit, orator, fighter, lawyer. But craftsman? I didn't see that in him. I could be wrong.

As implausible as the funeral director's story seemed, I never thought for a second that he was making it up. He believed what he was saying and I had no reason to doubt him. Certainly Bill was well known to the mortician's family He graduated school with one of the former directors of the funeral home. The current funeral director has a full inventory of family stories involving Bill and Russell dating back generations. I took the story about the memorial vases as presented and got busy with other family business. I forgot about it.

CHAPTER 3

WHAT TO CALL THIS THING OF OURS

The New York State Police raid on the Apalachin meeting in November 1957 at Joseph Barbara's upstate New York estate exposed the existence of an active and organized underworld. The raid forced FBI Director J. Edgar Hoover to finally acknowledge what he had denied for years: that there was an organized body behind the individuals the FBI had identified as it poked around the edges of the larger organization through its Top Hoodlum Program. Russell Bufalino had been profiled by that program in the early 1950s, well before the New York State Police raid on the Apalachin meeting exposed the existence of the American Mafia.

Hoover's reluctance to pursue organized crime as a body mystified many, including his own number three man, William Sullivan, author of *The Bureau: My Thirty Years in Hoover's FBI*. In the 1950s, columnist Jack Anderson embarrassed Hoover by exposing the scope of a wide network Hoover had refused to acknowledge. The Top Hoodlum Program only skipped across the surface, but it allowed Hoover to say he was doing something in case anyone should ask.

Several sources explain Hoover's reluctance to pursue the broader organization as a personal and professional survival mechanism. That is to say, the Mob had something on Hoover that would end his career. For Michael Benson, author of *Gangsters Vs. Nazis*, it was Meyer Lansky who possessed compromising photos of Hoover and his close aide Clyde Tolson. The blogosphere adds more voices to the same opinion, but I hesitate to name the parties in case they take offense or recant their position. For my own family, I can only report the words of my father, a professional photographer who often traveled to do work for Russell in the 1950s. What inspired him to say it, I don't know. If there was a conversation that preceded his statement, I don't remember it. All I remember is my father saying, "We have pictures of Hoover in a dress." I did wonder about his use of the word "we," since *we* were the good Buffs, after all.

Now that Hoover was stuck with the existence of this apparently countrywide criminal organization, thanks to the efforts of a few New York State Police troopers, he had to call it something. "Mafia" would not do, since every time the word appeared or was uttered, it might expose his own steadfast resistance to acknowledge its existence. Some have suggested that it was Joseph Valachi's testimony that offered the term *La Cosa Nostra* as the formally accepted name of the organization overseen by The Commission. It's also possible that Valachi used the term at Hoover's request. One long-lost reference from my own research suggests that Hoover lifted the phrase from a wiretapped conversation between two individuals who spoke in Italian about "this thing of ours" in terms of a particular business venture between them.

Fringe opposition to JFK as a candidate for the presidency in 1960 was based in part on his Roman Catholicism. The most paranoid among the electorate feared, however irrationally, that a President Kennedy might turn the country over to the pope. In that atmosphere of anti-Catholic sentiment, La Cosa Nostra, with all those vowels, had the right ring to garner public and congressional support and funding for the Bureau in perpetuity, or at least through the end of Hoover's career. Moreover, it spared Hoover the embarrassment of having to admit he'd been wrong about the existence of anything like the Mafia. He used the La Cosa Nostra phrase as often as possible, even in abbreviation to title investigations of criminal activity under the umbrella acronym of LCN. Today, *La Cosa Nostra* and *American Mafia,* or just *Mafia,* are used interchangeably. Some will swear that *Cosa Nostra* is an age-old name for the Sicilian Mafia. Whatever they say. I'm just pointing out that Hoover used the term *La Cosa Nostra* to change the game on anybody who suggested he dropped the ball regarding the Mafia.

When the FBI's post-Apalachin investigations led them to evidence suggesting Russell was not a native-born citizen, the government began a deportation process against Russell, which led to appeals that lasted all through the early 1970s. The United States first sought to deport Russell either to Brazil or Italy. Evidence presented by Russell's defense included an orphan's court birth registry in Luzerne County, Pennsylvania, and school records, along with the testimony of his uncle and siblings. The government was able to answer these as being inconsequential since they had obtained a birth record from Montedoro, Sicily. Given Russell's clear lifelong ties to the United States, the government sought to strengthen its case on the basis that Russell was not a person of good moral character, which they probed by questioning Russell about his pursuits and employment.

Russell Bufalino explained his lack of a visible means of support in one of his innumerable deportation hearings by replying, "I have a rich uncle who takes care of me." They asked about his school history, his employment history, and his current profession at Penn Drape in Pittston, Pennsylvania. "What does an 'expediter' do, exactly?" One result of protracted hearings in 1965 was an eighty-two-page opinion rendered by William B. Taffet, who determined that Russell "had not been during the entire course of these proceedings a person of good moral character." He said Bufalino's testimony, during the lengthy case, had been "a maze of contradictions as to employment, occupational activities, and sources of income" (source: *The Gettysburg Times* Newspaper Archives, Friday, March 19, 1965, page 10).

Throughout the often-and-well-publicized deportation process, Russell's increasing notoriety haunted nearly everyone with the Bufalino name. It especially made for interesting times among those of us at the homestead, the Pittston contingent. We were taking Russell's heat in school, at work, at large. We waited through the 1970s to step out of the shadow of suspicion, held our breath in the 1980s as Russell moved out of circulation in newspapers, and thought it was all over at last when, in 1994, Russell passed.

Russell was not lying or being coy about having an uncle who took care of him. He really did have a rich uncle who had directed his actions and career from the earliest age. That uncle was among a few who built an empire out of gambling and bootlegging and other more legitimate pursuits that Russell would come to run in his own right and under his own name. Even Russell's nickname, "The Old Man," came to him in direct line of succession, straight from the first "Old Man," his uncle, who acquired it himself in the most natural of ways. Russell probably acquired or adopted the nickname while still relatively young, acting as his uncle's proxy during his own rise to influence in the coalfields of Northeastern Pennsylvania in the 1920s and 1930s.

Of Russell's legend and influence, Charles Brandt has been quoted as saying, "He was one of the most powerful Mob bosses of his day, if not of all time." Russell's own chosen successor, William D'Elia, has suggested that Russell's power was above that of The Commission itself. It's difficult for me, as an extended family member, to fathom all that. But the more I looked, the more I discovered that Russell had the kind of reach, influence, and support to sway and profit from human experiences from the basest to the most acculturED. He was in life and in death, a man of mystery, even—if especially—to those who thought they knew him best.

It's generally accepted that Russell had a role in the Hoffa disappearance. His own chosen successor, William D'Elia, claims in his biography, *The Life We Chose* by Matt Birkbeck, that he is as much in that belief as any other authority. As for Brandt and Sheeran's assertion that Russell Bufalino had a role in the Kennedy assassination, I'm willing to be wrong, but I'm not a buyer. I believe that my own father had a much larger role in the story of the Kennedy assassination and its aftermath than Russell did. Anyone with more than a casual knowledge of the events surrounding the assassination and its investigation has seen my father's work without knowing it. Any FBI disclosures related to wiretaps may also bear out his role.

The story of the organization Russell Bufalino headed is the story of family life and death in the very thick of what authors Robert P. Wolensky and William A. Hastie have called the Anthracite Labor Wars. The story's scope encompasses the Industrial Revolution, one entire fossil-fuel economy, several labor movements, Prohibition, the brutal politics of assassination of the 1960s, and one enduring mystery.

CHAPTER 4

THE OLD SOLDIER

"I'm not scared anymore." Yabo Bufalino (Angelo, Bill's brother) tugged at his hospital gown, straining to cover his knees. It was early 1993. He had coded the night before at the nursing home. This had been his second or third resuscitation. They had beaten him back to life, and the big man looked it. He had been fighting a congestive heart condition, stubbornly refusing to die, literally informing the Powers that he would climb up the pitchfork if he passed before he reached his eightieth year; we both knew he would not see his eighty-first. We talked the usual small talk, nothing deep: about the homestead, my mom, college, the family. He claimed a small victory. "I beat them all," he said. He had outlived all, including his wealthier and more accomplished siblings. His younger brother William, Hoffa's lawyer, had passed in 1990. His eldest brother Charles had passed years before.

I knew Yabo for about ten or twelve years toward the end of his life in the day-in-day-out relationship of a cousin and a next-door neighbor. I was so plagued with guilt over his sister Mary's sudden passing that I couldn't help but check in on him whenever I could. Sometimes it was just a "Hey, Yabo, how you doing?" and sometimes it was sharing his lunch. I helped him with chores the same as I had with Mary: pumping out his cellar, painting this or that, cleaning out Bill's downstairs office, picking up some bits of lore. I lost my own father in 1983, and Yabo, oddball that he was, was a great surrogate.

I relied on him throughout the 1980s. By 1993, I was mostly away at school, and Yabo was living his last chapter. He had entered a nursing home the year before.

When our visit finished, I left to return to grad school with a promise to visit again in a few weeks, as usual. I stopped at the nursing home on my way back to Bloomsburg. In Yabo's corner of the ward were a scattering of his possessions: There was the book I had brought him titled *Growing Up with Bootleggers, Gamblers, and Pigeons*, which reminded him of his own youth; one of his carved canes; some photographs; a few clothes; and a yellow legal pad with some furious handwriting in red felt marker. *I'm not scared anymore* was ringing in my ears. I asked to sign the 1993 equivalent of a "Do Not Resuscitate" order. Before I could keep my promise to visit, Yabo—my dad's first cousin, my longtime next-door neighbor, and the last surrogate father I would ever need—had passed.

I first met Yabo in 1963, when he and his brother Bill visited Pittston to see their sister Mary. Bill's mother had died in 1924 when he was about five years old. Mary, unwilling to marry the person she was promised to wed, opted to remain unmarried and help raise the boys instead with the assistance of their grandmother. Bill considered Mary to be more mother than sister and so, throughout Hoffa's later imprisonment in Lewisburg, when he visited Jimmy Hoffa weekly in prison, Bill would often drive the extra hour or so to Pittston to visit her at the family homestead. Licensed to practice only in Pennsylvania, Bill would later remodel Mary's downstairs, his father's former general store in the ground-floor cellar, into an office and spend a large chunk of three years in local practice to satisfy requirements to enter the State Bar of Michigan. We called Mary "Aunt Mary." She lived in the other half of the double-block building her father and my grandfather had built in 1915.

At the time of this first meeting in 1963, Yabo looked like an English gentleman fresh out of an episode of the *Avengers* TV series.

He was a well-dressed and well-groomed tree trunk of a man with a pencil-thin mustache. He was tall—over six feet—and he looked to me at age six like a giant. He smelled of Old Spice. There was the hint of a slice at the front lobe of his Roman nose that, for all I know, was the result of an acne scar. It looked more like a blade was involved. It made him look dangerous. He was holding a Franklin half dollar above my head, just out of my reach. "I'm sorry, teacher," he said for me to repeat, "but it's confidential between him and me." It was a simple lesson, a gesture of goodwill to a young cousin just about to start school, a bit of life advice that would advance Yabo to old age. When I quoted the phrase and earned the half dollar, I wanted to thank him, but at age five, I didn't know how. I tried to kiss him. You'd have thought I pulled a gun on him, and I laughed as he ran back into Mary's door. It was 1963. Kennedy was still president as I, just about to enter first grade, learned from my father's first cousin Yabo the fundamentals of *omertà*.

At Yabo's funeral, his nephew—Bill's son, William Bufalino II—eulogized him, saying, in part, "I was two or three years old and Yabo was in my house every day. I couldn't wrap my mouth around the name 'Yabo,' so I called him Uncle Wow." His voice cracked when he said it. It moved me. In the family, we called Wiliam II "Billy Boy." He was just all right.

I attended Yabo's funeral reception by invitation of his family. Dressed as I was in one or the other of a blue or copper three-piece polyester suit, I was surprised to find that I was not the most out-of-place character present. Maybe he sensed that, or maybe I just have that kind of face, but he came right over to me. He was a short man, powerfully built. He had come in from Detroit for the funeral, probably with Billy Boy. He was not unattractive per se, but there was, about the shape of his head, neck, and shoulders, a kind of cartoon mole appearance. He was wearing a black

T-shirt with slacks and a sport coat. Without introducing himself, he squared up in front of me, extended his hand, and blurted out, "Yabo was like a father to me."

The man spent the next two hours with me, and I don't know why. I was anything but bored. He shared every story Yabo had never told: about the Stork (later renamed to "Story") Club in Detroit, which Yabo and his brothers ran for Angelo Meli, the Detroit Partnership's consigliere; about working security at Cobo Hall; and about Teamsters business and travels with Hoffa. The man held nothing back to the point that I could hardly absorb any of it. But I came away understanding why the Yabo I knew never spoke about any of his life in Detroit in the same way that soldiers don't talk about war. It explained those dark shadows under his eyes. Yabo plugged along every day I knew him, took his life day-to-day and enjoyed a little horse-betting, socializing, and dancing, but privately, it seemed that something bothered him all the later years of his life.

Altogether, the meeting with the stranger was so bizarre, I don't think I even asked his name. When the reception was over, he told me he had been a technical adviser on Danny DeVito's movie *Hoffa,* which had released the year before. Then he pulled out a very old and authentic-looking Teamsters card. Written on the back was a short sentence: *Give this man anything he wants.* It was signed by Jimmy Hoffa.

Russell passed the year after Yabo, in 1994. I thought at the time that the notoriety of the family name would subside and that we could all get about having more normal lives. The flow of publications, scholarly and popular, about Russell that began with *I Heard You Paint Houses* would prove me wrong.

Martin Scorsese's *The Irishman* was released with its cast of usual suspects in Robert De Niro as Frank Sheeran, Al Pacino as Jimmy Hoffa, Joe Pesci as Russell Bufalino, and Harvey Keitel as Angelo

Bruno. Pesci floored me as Russell. Everybody did good work. I thought Ray Romano was well-cast as Bill Bufalino.

Altogether, the movie forced me to realize that Russell's notoriety would not fade within my own lifetime. It helped drive me to set some records straight.

CHAPTER 5

THE RIDDLE

Everybody knows where Jimmy Hoffa is. He's buried at Giants Stadium, in the foundation of Detroit's Renaissance Center, or he's pressed into a crushed car. He's on this or that farm, in this or that landfill in a drum full of this or that. In a handful of deathbed confessions, a select group of connected people sincerely report that they personally had been entrusted with or had direct knowledge of the disposal of a body supposedly transported from Detroit, Michigan, to locations as far away as New Jersey and Florida.

It seems that some deliberate misdirection and intentional misinformation was disseminated in the aftermath of Hoffa's disappearance. It's possible that some of the parties who honestly believe their version of events had been intentionally abused by the false leads. A person of any conscience might feel a weight on their chest to have such knowledge or belief and would, at the very least, pass it on, as they did, to the next party to deal with or reveal at some safe time. And yet, however widely held the belief that Jimmy Hoffa's body exists to be found, the idea has some notable detractors.

William D'Elia, Russell Bufalino's handpicked successor, tells a version of this story in his biography, *The Life We Chose*. The locally popular version departs from the published version but more or less expresses the same idea, and I personally like it better:

Billy D'Elia was visited by agents of the FBI while in prison. They had a lead on a burial place for Jimmy Hoffa, and they wanted to see if he would corroborate the story before they began an excavation. "He's not there," said the big man.

"Well, where is he, then?" asked the agents.

"I don't know where he is."

Then, after a pause for effect, he added: "But . . . he's not there."

Mr. D'Elia adamantly dismisses the Frank Sheeran story as related in *I Heard You Paint Houses* as an outrageous fiction. Only one element of Sheeran's narrative survives his criticism. Sheeran expressed his belief that Hoffa had been cremated. Mr. D'Elia can be heard expressing his own belief that "he's not on the farm" and that "Hoffa was cooked" in broadcast interviews.

A surprising story comes from the *Gangland Wire* podcast in 2022, when retired Leavenworth prison guard Kenneth LaMaster reported the answer he received when he asked Russell, "Hey, Bufalino, what did you do with Hoffa's body?" Let's just say Russell's answer falls in line with Sheeran and D'Elia's cremation theory.

In the past year, on the occasion of the 50th anniversary of Hoffa's disappearance, journalist Scott Burnstein hosted a symposium in Detroit with Nove Tocco and former Federal Prosecutor Richard Convertino. Burnstein has years of experience following the Hoffa case. His conclusions regarding Hoffa's fate are supported by James Hoffa, Junior. While the path Hoffa's body took was circuitous and grisly in Burnstein's rendition, it ends with cremation at the Central Sanitation incinerator.

Independently of Scott Burnstein, David W. Tubman authored a book in 2022 based on his own family's belief that they were eyewitnesses to Hoffa's abduction. Central Sanitation factors into their story as well.

And then there's the FBI. One of the Bureau's first theories sent agents to the Bagnasco Funeral Home in Detroit to explore whether Hoffa had been cremated at that location. When Bagnasco reported that they had no crematory on-site, the FBI pursued its theory to the allegedly Mob-run Central Sanitation, where they toured the incinerator and expressed an interest to return in a few months to investigate further. As luck would have it, the place burned down in the interim, and the investigation, to include a closer look at the incinerator, could not be completed.

Suppose for just a minute that Frank Sheeran's suspicion, Billy D'Elia's account, the FBI's gut belief, and Russell's professed confession are all true, that Jimmy Hoffa was cremated. Would anybody have left orders for disposal of the remains, or would they have left that detail to chance? Sprinkle them on Pikes Peak? Dump them in the ocean? The river? Throw them to the wind?

Russell Bufalino was believed to be close to Hoffa, or at least simpatico with him. They had enough in common with the loss of a parent to the coal industry to have the kernel of, at the very least, an *understanding*. Hoffa visited Pittston and was surrounded by Pittston people associated with Bill and Yabo. If Russell was reluctant to call the hit on Jimmy Hoffa, would he have memorialized him somehow?

Or, taking the opposite view and supposing that Russell was a sociopathic killer, could he have avoided making a trophy of a score as big as a world-famous national labor leader?

What would you have done with those few handfuls of dust?

CHAPTER 6

PITTSTON, COAL, AND IRON

"The copper bosses killed you, Joe. They shot you, Joe," says I.

"Takes more than guns to kill a man," says Joe. "I didn't die."

—from "Joe Hill" by Alfred Hayes

Pittston is unique among the many dozens of anthracite coal-rich cities and towns in the five-county region of Northeastern Pennsylvania. Five Pennsylvania counties have been presumed to contain 80 percent of the nation's anthracite coal. If so, Pittston in the northernmost coalfield, with its fourteen-foot "Pittston vein," held what was arguably the mother lode. Adding to its relative importance, Pittston sat until the 1830s at the northernmost terminus of a canal system that made moving goods—coal among them—profitable. When, by around 1870, railroads obsoleted the canals, both Pittston and the nearby Scranton would host important rail yards and roundhouses, continuing the area's status as a commercial hub.

As of 1838, there were eight or ten total dwellings in a place at the head end of the North Branch Division of the Pennsylvania Canal on the Susquehanna River just downstream from the Lackawanna River junction. It was called Pittston Ferry for the rope ferry passage it provided across the Susquehanna River to the vicinity of the Revolutionary War-era Fort Jenkins. Coal operations in the area had existed since the early 1800s. The mines were generally small and individually or family-owned and were still worked with black powder explosives. Apart from the "rough boat men," as Pittston's historian E. C. Johnson referred to the men who ferried coal barges along the canals, the people were American Revolutionary War stock and longtime neighbors. Johnson estimated the 1844 population of the town at 200 souls. The places uphill from the wharf still sported groves of trees and farmland. The main street was knee-deep in mud in the spring months.

In around 1850, anthracite coal proved its usefulness in powering a steam locomotive engine. While it was successfully, if not widely, used to that purpose, the long-and-hot burning qualities of the hard coal were already powering the furnaces that drove the Industrial Revolution and heating more and more homes. Railroad companies began to engender coal company offspring and to compete for mines, land, and—where necessary—mineral rights to mine the lands of others. By the turn of the twentieth century, most of the original mom-and-pop coal operations had sold out to the railroads and their child corporations, the coal companies.

Pittston began to grow as mining operations became ever more in earnest. The former Pittston Ferry was incorporated as Pittson borough in 1853. It became a city in 1894, sluffing off a lot of land in the process, which became Pittston Township. By 1894, the population of Pittston had grown from 200 souls to well over 10,000 and was on its way toward 13,000 by 1900. By 1910, 16,250 people crowded together in a land area less than two miles square.

For the longest time in between Pittston down by the river and up the steep hills was a sprawling camp of mine pits, shafts, breakers, and barns that held powder or livestock and service buildings. The houses and streets sprouted up in between the collieries. There were tracts of miner's houses that belonged to the company and streets full of larger, nicer homes built by engineers, mine owners, bankers, and others who built businesses in service to or were dependent on the mines. Turn-of-the-twentieth-century Pittston has been described as an urban coal mine.

As anthracite coal became more the fuel of the Industrial Revolution, and as mine ownership slipped from family-owned to one hundred percent corporate-owned by 1900, works became deeper, yield quotas grew higher, and accidents became more common. The corporate owners solved the safety problem throughout the northern coalfields in Pittston and beyond by hiring more workers to work their unsafe mines to replace the dead. This they did over and over until they had to search farther afield in the world to find workers because of the fool-me-once recognition of the new arrivals that the mines they worked in the Old Country were safer than the ones in the New World. The farther afield the companies searched, the more they found themselves hiring non-English-speaking workers like Russians, Poles, Slavs, and Germans, until they finally worked their way down to Sicily. Ownership being largely English, and quite imperialistically so in the 1800s, they had not much concern for non-English-speaking people of any kind. In fact, they considered them subhuman and would openly describe them in just that way.

The original miners and laborers among the population had been a lot of English, Scots-Irish, and the Welsh. Wales had anthracite coal mines, and the Welshmen had experience mining the hard coal. Overall, it was northern European stock. By the time the spinner on the English mine owner's Wheel of Human Resources landed finally on Sicily, the thirteen-or-so-thousand population of the now-city of Pittston, up from 200 in just fifty years, was a loose-gravel mix of English, Irish, Scottish, Polish, German, Slovak, Russian, Lithuanian, Greek, and Italian who all lived together in an area 1.71 miles square.

By the year 1900, Pittston had about 8,500 wildly different people per square mile. Mostly, they didn't get along. The main landing party of Sicilians hadn't even gotten on the boats yet. By 1910, the last wave made the total population about 16,250 and raised the population density to 10,400 or so per square mile. Just for comparison's sake, Hong Kong today is considered one of the most densely populated places in the world at 11,125 people per square mile. People walked four abreast on the sidewalks of Pittston's Main Street in the 1920s, according to my father.

With the increasing corporatization of industry of all kinds throughout the late 1800s, conflicts arose between labor and management and were often violent. Railroads and coal companies were among the many corporate interests in opposition to the growing union movements. To quell labor unrest and protect their property, the combined corporate interests petitioned the state of Pennsylvania to establish an irregular constabulary of "Coal and Iron Police." For a dollar apiece, the companies could acquire badges and issue them at time of need to anyone who could mount a horse, wield a club, or shoot a gun. When the Great Railroad Strike of 1887 flung Pittsburgh into riots, Pennsylvania's governor allowed the politically influential railroads to use the Pittsburgh National Guard. When the local Pittsburgh National Guard proved sympathetic to the strikers, some 600 Philadelphia National Guardsmen were brought in. In a separate action, the Homestead Strike of 1892 saw the steel companies using Pinkerton agents. They exchanged volleys of gunfire with rioters, with deaths on both sides.

Coal mines, for their part, were especially dangerous places to work. Miners and laborers were often killed by the scores in accidents ranging from rock falls to cave-ins or the more silent and deadly various forms of damp that would rob their chamber of oxygen or fill it with explosive gas. Workers, mostly immigrants, would die dozens at a time, as they did in the Twin Shaft Disaster of Pittston where fifty-eight men and boys, mostly Irish, were instantly entombed by a collapse 300 feet or more below ground as they tried to shore up a mine whose supports had been creaking for weeks.

In Avondale, near present Plymouth, Pennsylvania, a fire that consumed the breaker and ventilation system above the single mine entrance suffocated 110 predominantly Welsh miners. The resulting inquiry set standards for future safety, but coal companies paid little regard, choosing to rebuild the breaker and vent system to the original unsafe specifications. Their enormous political influence ensured no real culpability for harm caused. Successive waves of immigration ensured a steady stream of men reporting to work, and as they came increasingly from Slavic countries and spoke little English, they were considered subhuman by their employers and equally disdained by the general population. Due to the intransigence of the coal operators, especially the Pennsylvania Coal Company, the anthracite coal workers of Pittston coalfields would be among the last to successfully negotiate a contract.

By the end of the 1800s, the usual repressive tactics required to suppress union movements led to atrocities that created public relations problems and motivated miners toward a general strike. In 1897, in Lattimer, Pennsylvania, a peaceful protest of about 400 Eastern Europeans carrying an American flag ran a gauntlet of eighty-six armed deputies and many members of the Coal and Iron Police. The authorities opened fire, killing nineteen. Then, shooting into the fleeing crowd, they shot another nineteen who would later succumb to their wounds. It became known as the Lattimer Massacre. Most of the dead were shot in the back. A trial was held. The sheriff and deputies were acquitted. The UMWA, through John Mitchell, called for a general strike two years later.

The coal strike of 1902 lasted approximately five months, creating such hardship that President Roosevelt was compelled to intercede but without much effect. By the end of the strike, some thirty thousand hard coal miners had packed it in, heading west to the soft bituminous coalfields or, like my maternal grandparents, back to their respective Old Countries.

These were the opening battles of what authors Robert P. Wolensky and William A. Hastie Sr. would call the Anthracite Labor Wars, which would continue nearly as long as anthracite coal had wide industrial use. Of the coal company's usual soldiers, the Pinkerton Agency detectives cost real money. Armies of agents would not do. The Coal and Iron Police, fresh from the Lattimer massacre, proved an embarrassment at best. Their phase-out started slowly following the creation of the Pennsylvania State Police in 1905. The National Guard? That would require a strike of real magnitude, even with the coal operators' considerable political influence. Meanwhile, the Welsh, Irish, and Slavic miners were uniting despite language barriers. They flashed two fingers to each other like a victory sign, using both hands, as they passed on the way up and down the slopes into the mines, enforcing among themselves a "two men to a car and two-ton-in-and-out (daily work quota)" policy. They were dug in for a long fight.

In the above, the Pennsylvania Coal Company had problems to solve. They had a labor crisis due to the loss of 30,000 workers who vacated during the 1902 strike. They had a growing and strengthening union movement. They had a PR problem over their enforcement tactics. Yellow journalists had discovered the hardships experienced by the miners and their families and a popular distaste for coal industry labor practices was growing in the press. That says nothing of the moral dilemma presented by the practice of child labor. The "breaker boys" worked long hours straddling chutes on wooden benches, sorting coal from rock as it cascaded past them, sometimes losing a finger or two in the process. Giving in to popular opinion only when unavoidable, the coal operators would continue to thwart the expansion of unionism by all means possible.

The Pennsylvania Coal Company in particular may have made a conscious plan to solve all the above problems at once by hiring people who could a) work the mines, b) suppress union organizing, and c) break strikes by any means necessary without implicating the company in the matter. At least, that's what Dr. Robert P. Wolensky and William Hastie, authors of *Anthracite Labor Wars,* may have suspected when they asked a former coal executive: "Did you know who you were hiring?"

If that was, in fact, the coal operator's plan, they must at one point have asked themselves: *Where are we going to get people like that?*

CHAPTER 7

BRIMSTONE

She thought they were there to rob her. Instead, the party of rough-looking men who met Louise Hamilton Caico at the Caltanissetta train station in central Sicily were an armed escort sent by the Caico family to protect her on the twelve-or-so-mile stagecoach ride through the badlands of Caltanissetta Province to her new home in Montedoro, Sicily. Cesare Caico, the head of the family and overseer of the family business and fortune, had died. Eugene Caico, Louise's husband, had recently returned to Montedoro alone from an exile that Cesare had imposed upon him for the sin of marrying—at all. Marriage and inheritance, Cesare felt, were sure to dissipate the family's fortune, which he had guarded like a fairy-tale dragon. A mainstay of the Caico family wealth was in sulfur. In the mid-1800s, volcanic Sicily commanded some 80 percent of the world sulfur market, despite the early and primitive methods of extraction and refinement.

The sulfur mines of Montedoro were unpleasant places to work, to say the least. Corridors were cramped. The air was foul when not outright poisonous. It was so hot below that the men wielded their pickaxes in the nude. Hauling ore through the narrow passages required a special accommodation. Children were used to carry the excavated material from the mine on their backs. These *carusi* were sons and daughters of families in grinding, generational poverty who had sold the children as property to either the mine owners or to the miners themselves. They worked eight to ten hours a day. Their growth was stunted and their bodies distorted by the heavy loads they began carrying as early as age four. They were often abused by the men who controlled them, and their lives, like those of their parents and grandparents before them in some cases, were cut short by the burdens they carried and the dangerous conditions of their work.

If the sulfur mines of Sicily were not aflame with labor unrest, as were the anthracite mines of the United States, it may have been due to a combination of the rigid, semifeudal social structure; generational poverty and powerlessness; and the armed men who protected the persons and property and ensured the continued fortunes of the ruling families that Louise referred to as "gentlefolk."

Even as Louise stepped off the yellow-powder-caked stagecoach and onto the ground in Montedoro, the town and her family were facing the collapse of its sustaining industry. The global sulfur market was shifting away from Sicily. The Frasch process, developed in the United States, proved a superior and cleaner method of extracting sulfur from belowground without mining. By 1914, the United States would outproduce Sicily and begin taking over the global market. Italy and the United States would agree to divide the world markets between them, but many Sicilian mines would be shuttered. Meanwhile, in Pennsylvania, Pennsylvania Coal Company (PA Coal) and others were looking to replace approximately 30,000 laborers lost to the general strike of 1902.

According to published figures, Montedoro's population, which had steadily grown for the previous forty years, stagnated between 1901 and 1911, adding just thirty-four souls to reach 3,585 persons. By 1921, they would lose 600 more, their population falling to the levels of 1881. Sicily itself would lose around a million people to emigration in the years between 1901 and 1915. Ninety percent are thought to have come to America. Enough came to Pittston,

Pennsylvania, that as of 2024, the 18640 zip code was reported to contain 28.76 percent persons of Italian heritage (versus a statewide 10.82% and a national average of 4.93%).

Nothing could prepare Louise Hamilton Caico for the Montedoro of the 1890s. She was born of expatriate Irish nobility and was living the life of landowners and property renters in Florence. She was a modern, well-educated, intelligent, and progressive woman of the time. She was an accomplished photographer at a time when every aspect of the art was excruciatingly technical and unforgiving, from exposing the film through chemical development through to the final print. None of her upbringing, beliefs, or education could prepare her for Montedoro's practically medieval social structure, the generational poverty of its lower classes, or the endemic lawlessness of the region. She had been raised a Florentine.

Louise thrust herself into the life of Montedoro. She recorded in words and with her camera the funerals, festivals, and day-to-day life. She mourned with women at the funerals, recording the songs they sang and the feasts they observed. The people of the city called her "the English Woman." In the eleven years following her arrival, she made a practice of visiting surrounding areas in the company of an armed escort to visit and speak with the more dangerous characters, such as the Baron of Torretta, who was said to have a group of vagrants buried beneath a row of trees on his property. People in the region became as curious to meet the English Woman as she was to meet them.

Louise recorded her Montedoro experiences, festivals, and general "ways" in print with her own photographs, in a kind of English-language travelogue called *Sicilian Ways and Days* in 1910. It has been studied and written about widely as everything from a travelogue to a scholarly work of cultural anthropology. In my family, in Mary Buff's house, the Italian version of her book took second seat only to the Bible.

For all her efforts to ingratiate herself to the people and understand the traditions of the town, Louise seemed to relish the role of outcast in the Caico household. She seems to have genuinely disliked her brother-in-law, the mayor of Montedoro. She describes her living quarters as a traveler would record accommodations at a hotel and relishes that hour of the day when her command of a certain anteroom denied her brother-in-law, whom she only ever refers to as "the Mayor," bathroom privileges. She used the matriarch's best cooking vessels for photographic development, cordoned off the fruit store as her darkroom, and conjectured that the developer chemicals splashing onto the fruit might poison them all. The servants exasperated Louise by refusing to follow her directives about mealtime efficiency, probably on orders from the matriarch, her sister-in-law. It's a great read. Spoiler alert: The last five words of the book are, "The Mayor has been arrested!"

Of course, the mayor of Montedoro was released when all was said and done. It was 1897. A local attorney and political rival of his had been shot and severely wounded, and the mayor was considered a suspect.

An intensified manhunt began when the blame was placed where it properly belonged: the infamous Bufalino Brigand, Rosario Bufalino.

CHAPTER 8

THE BRIGAND

My grandfather Nicolo and his brother Salvatore, Bill's father, were the core of the Bufalino Brothers who established a number of businesses in Pittston, PA, in the early 1900s. Their last home was built to be an upstairs-downstairs living and working space. It housed a soda bottling plant and a general store on either side of the ground-floor cellars. Other businesses in the family included, at various times, a hotel, a saloon, and a grocery/butcher shop/deli in proximity to the house. They told their children stories of the Bufalino Brigand. My father and the other first-generation American children repeated them to us.

In the Bufalino Brothers version, the Rosario Bufalino Brigand (who is not our Rosario [Russell] Bufalino and was probably not my third granduncle Ross) was a small man, a dashing figure in the Robin Hood–style who was allowed to hide under the hooped skirts of the ladies of the town when being sought by the carabinieri. Their version of his end sounds like something out of a dime novel of the Old West:

> *The Brigand and an associate were holed up in a farmhouse in the Caltanissetta countryside when they were approached by a posse. The Brigand exited through a window in Billy-the-Kid fashion and ran toward the hills of Bompensiere in the gathering dark. His*

associate caught up with him. As the posse closed in, his associate, who was a relative, shot him in the head, killing him.

The theme of their narrative was always the same: *You can't trust anybody, not even a relative.* If Billy D'Elia's story about Russell's eventual downfall is true, it would seem Russell missed the lesson of this story.

According to the book *Memories and Traditions of Montedoro Vol. 1* by Giovanni Petix, the actual Bufalino Brigand seems to have been from a family of Bufalino from the next-door (and rival) town of Racalmuto who settled in Montedoro. His father may have been a member of a gang, and his uncle may have fallen victim to a posse of angry Montedoresi. The Brigand Rosario Bufalino wounded a relative in his youth and served a prison sentence followed by a period of military service. Released from the military when his service was complete, he briefly pursued an occupation as a cobbler but eventually chose brigandage as a profession. He became a leader of a group of men in his own right.

It was not uncommon for the more restless young men in the intractable social structure of Sicily at that time to choose a life of robbery and retribution or honor killings for hire. There were many scores to settle from the phases of Italy's reunification in the 1800s. Some of the deeper-seated vendettas were settled by murder-for-hire in the United States much later, following emigration.

Unlike most brigands, Rosario Bufalino advertised his services in the *Journal of Sicily*. According to an article in the *Buffalo Commercial* dated July 30, 1901:

"A noted character, Signor Rosario Bufalino, who lately escaped from prison in Italy, informs the public, in a paid advertisement in the Giornale di Sicilia" that he has organized a band of brigands

> *that will "administer justice according to the teachings of Holy Writ." All persons suffering from injustice of having wrongs that need avenging may apply to Signor Bufalino, who will "consider each case on its merits and mete out the death punishment where he deems fit."*

Nobody dared to consider that Mayor Caico might have engaged the Brigand to shoot his rival, and, of course, it would not have mattered. Rosario Bufalino was deemed a maniac at large and was hunted by the carabinieri, independent bounty hunters, and civil posse. In late October 1901, a group of men approached a remote farmhouse in which he was hiding. As per the family story, Bufalino exited via a farmhouse window and made for the hills of Bompensiere. Alerted by the exchanges of gunfire between Bufalino and his pursuers, a father-and-son party of the Carruba family found him. A negotiation ensued, but the son, possibly alarmed by some move on the Brigand Rosario's part, shot him in the head, killing him.

The father took credit for the killing so that his son would not be hunted. Curiously, the Carruba family were denied the bounty for the Brigand, perhaps because the authorities wanted him alive. Strangely, the hunters do not seem to have presented a body. Or, if they did, it's equally unclear that he was, or where he was, buried. To compound matters, *The Buffalo Evening News* quoted *Giornale di Sicilia* to report on January 26, 1903 that:

> *Finding their chief wounded, and being hard-pressed, the band murdered a stranger, inflicting a wound similar to that sustained by Bufalino, laid the body in one of his retreats, and having it identified by complaisant local authority and buried, removed the real Bufalino to Calabria, where he has ever since been recuperating, and being completely recovered, has resumed his brigandage.*

The more conspiracy-minded might wonder whether Bufalino's death was faked, either by himself or by some "complaisant local authority," who, for whatever reason or to protect whomever, wanted to suppress testimony about . . . *something*. The Bufalino Brigand himself is cited as a source in *History of the Mafia* by Salvatore Lupo as saying that "the expression 'send [someone] to America, buy someone a ticket to America' was an ironic way of saying 'to kill someone.'" It was the Sicilian equivalent of the later American expression "send [someone] to Australia" (i.e. "down under").

The Brigand does not seem to have returned to his old haunts or activities following his presumed death. His reported death date of October 1901 seems to be his final mention in any kind of action.

To the contrary, he was later reported in a short article the size of a classified ad in a Buffalo newspaper to be in the United States.

CHAPTER 9

SALVATORE: BILL'S FATHER

"My father arrived on the *SS Liguria*," said Mary Buff, Bill's sister, recounting a story I would hear in the near-exact same words from her brother, Yabo, at a later time, and from Angelo Tulumello, her nephew. They all told the story and almost always in the same words. "When he got off the boat, the telephone poles still had black ribbons in mourning for President McKinley." I took it for granted as true at the time. I was ten. Although they were fiercely proud of their father and their own accomplished siblings, Mary and Yabo, Salvatore's children, shared few stories about Salvatore. Maybe he was not the kind of personality that generated stories. He expressed at one point his satisfaction that the Pittston School District offered a course in Italian by saying, "Ah . . . *la lengua di Dante*." That's one of the three stories I ever heard about him. And it's complete.

Salvatore Bufalino, my granduncle, is by all family and independent accounts the first of our family to arrive in the United States. A family of Sciandra had come and gone for Buffalo by the time he arrived. There were others as well. There was a Bufalino named Alexander in Pittston in the 1890s. But the last great wave of immigration, the Sicilian-Italian wave, was just picking up steam by the time he arrived. According to the family narrative, his arrival was in a time frame near to, but definitely after, President McKinley's death on September 14, 1901. The president had been shot on the grounds of the Pan-American Exhibition in the Temple of Music in Buffalo, New York, a little over a week earlier, on September 6, 1901.

When I began my own research, I found that my grandfather, Nicolo, Salvatore's brother, had (also?) arrived on the *SS Liguria* but a year later than Salvatore. I was unable, however, to find any arrival date for my granduncle Salvatore. I was not alone. In their exhaustively researched "Men of Montedoro" article for *Informer Journal*, Thomas Hunt and Michael A. Tona are also unable to find Salvatore's entry records. But they do cite his naturalization records in a footnote: *Salvatore reported that he had reached New York City aboard the* SS Liguria *on September 6, 1901. Some details of his arrival appear to be in error.*

Salvatore's official naturalization declaration states that he arrived on the *very day* McKinley was shot and more than a week before he passed, but the family story about the black crepe adornments on the telephone poles in honor of President McKinley suggests a later date, beginning at least in the late middle of September, 1901.

Black crepe or silk is reported to have appeared everywhere between Buffalo, New York, the point of departure of the president's funeral train on September 16, 1901, and its arrival in Washington and eventual return to Canton, Ohio, on September 18. The funeral train itself was draped in black, and churches and memorial services all along its route were similarly decorated. How long the adornments would have remained is not clear, and it's not clear just how widespread the practice of placing mourning crepe on telephone poles would have been.

If indeed black crepe decorated telephone poles anywhere, would it have been the poles near the train station where the funeral train made its departure, in Buffalo? Did Salvatore Bufalino appropriate my own grandfather's arrival story? Was his flavorful addition about the decorative crepe a telling kernel of truth in an otherwise fabricated story? Did he come into the United States as so many others did at the time, on the quiet, via Canada, through Buffalo?

Salvatore's Montedoresi backstory has never been completely clear. His grandson Angelo Tulumello, who was just a young boy when Salvatore passed in 1936, once told me that Salvatore had been a captain of artillery in the Italian Army, which I took to account for his regal bearing, leadership skills, and the discipline and bearing his children inherited. Some mandatory military service *was* required of young men following the Unification of Italy. According to Angelo Tulumello, Salvatore was referred to by the nickname of "Artilliere" among the locals. That could all very well be. Bill Bufalino's take on his father's backstory was that he had been a sulfur miner at the Gibellini mine and a teacher in Montedoro. Salvatore's own mother-in-law was a teacher. Either of those activities, or his own father Calogero's trade of butcher and the location of his shop in relation to the Caico compound, might have put Salvatore in the company of Cesare Caico and his treasured store of classical books.

Whatever his backstory, Salvatore Bufalino was obviously a well-educated and motivated individual as well as the lead actor in the Bufalino Brothers' many enterprises, all of which, one way or another, met the needs of a population of Sicilian and Italian immigrants that grew yearly through his efforts. He arrived in Pittston in late summer, September 1901, on the simmering brink of an anthracite labor strike that would last 163 days from May to October 1902, which even the intervention of the new president, Theodore Roosevelt, could barely resolve.

Almost immediately upon securing work and lodging, he began to receive a long list of arriving Montedoresi men and their families. The railroads and their child corporations, the coal companies, actively encouraged immigration from Sicily to offset strikers and eventually replace some 30,000 mine labor positions left vacant by the strike of 1902. Several of the families who sponsored the travel and placement of ten or more immigrant families were awarded by the company with a framed rendering of a pheasant presented as a kind of heraldic or badge of honor.

Bill Bufalino granted an interview to *The Detroit News* in 1976 in which he described his father's work in relation to his actions as a travel agency: "He would send steamship tickets to others in Montedoro and elsewhere in Italy so they could come to this country. Then he would get them jobs in the mines so they could pay him back for the tickets, and he would give them credit in his store."

What Bill described is the padrone system, which was one way immigrants could manage the high cost of the voyage—thirty-five to fifty dollars a ticket at a time when bread was a few cents a loaf. The padrone funded the voyage and found work for the client, who then paid the padrone back out of his wages, shopped at his stores, and often lodged in his accommodations. The system was technically outlawed and was rife with abuse in the form of inflated prices for travel, housing, and food. Padrones were sometimes paid both by the company and the worker for their services, and some workers never stopped paying a portion of their wages to the padrone. Given Bill's own description of his father's endeavors, plus physical evidence in Mary's home and the associations made between Salvatore and other padrones, Salvatore does seem to have served in the role of a padrone. Some of his efforts may have been on behalf of the Pennsylvania Coal Company (PA Coal). Since Santo Volpe and Steve La Torre also seem to have individually sponsored families of their own, enough to be formally lauded by the mine operators, he may also have assisted Volpe and La Torre in making travel arrangements for hundreds more families.

As padrones go, Salvatore was considered fair by the people he brought into the country. By 1911, the Bufalino Brothers family businesses included a deli/ butcher shop, a hotel to lodge and feed immigrants, and a bar to serve their refreshment needs, from soda to liquor. By 1915–16, the general store also sold tools and supplies to miners and laborers in the way of the old "company store." As long as immigration lasted and the mines remained active, Salvatore and my grandfather Nicolo, his brother, prospered in their businesses. They each had large families.

In September 1904, Salvatore suffered a mine explosion that burned his body and broke both of his legs and one arm, according to Bill. He worked through it, probably still in the travel brokerage role, and returned to the mines after several months. His first son, Charles, would be born about the time he returned to work. In that same year, he would open the grocery and butcher shop on Railroad Street in Pittston. He would continue making several out-and-back trips to Sicily until World War I suppressed oceangoing travel in the Atlantic.

Salvatore's impact and influence on the growing community of Pittston's Montedoro immigrants was nothing short of profound. He was energetic, to say the least. He ran several businesses. He advocated for the more violent youthful transgressors among his families with the authorities, arranged travel and fare for countless immigrants, and, as things became more settled in the teens, arranged for pageants of a civil and religious but also political nature. He seems to have ingratiated himself with the monied class of mine and business owners because he could liaise multilingually between labor and management.

The *Wilkes-Barre Record* announced his birthday on November 23, 1926 as follows:

> *Salvatore T. Bufalino, one of Pittston's foremost Italian-American citizens, is today celebrating the fifty-eighth anniversary of his birth. Mr. Bufalino was born in Montedoro, Sicily, November 23, 1868. After many hardships in his native land, at the age of thirty-three years he sailed for America, establishing his home on*

> *Railroad Street, Pittston. From a modest start, due to his splendid personality and ability, he forged to the front and is to-day perhaps one of the most prominent and influential business men in the community and has innumerable friends among Italian and American residents. People from his native land arriving in this country found him most hospitable and always helping them until they established themselves here. Among his fellow citizens he is held in high esteem and has been the recipient of many splendid testimonials. For many years, he has been president of the Montedoro Society of Pittston, and his fellow members appreciate his splendid efforts in the society. He is president of the committee of Italian-Americans who recently installed the beautiful statue of Christopher Columbus in the Broad Street Park. He is proprietor of one of the largest general stores, 47 East Railroad Street, and of the bottling works adjoining. His home is located over his store, where he enjoys the company of five young sons and four daughters.*

Socially, Salvatore was connected to the mine ownership class from early on and was a frequent guest, if not an outright member, at a posh Wilkes-Barre social club due to his role as a labor broker for the mining interests.

As a final footnote to Salvatore's local fame and reputation, I'll share a personal story from 2022. In that year, I took part in the procession of the Feast of the Blessed Mother. Salvatore had been the founder and first president of the Montedoro Society of Pittston. The procession of the Blessed Mother through the streets of the city was a Montedoro tradition that Salvatore and his Montedoro Society associates worked to import into the local community to preserve Montedoresi cultural identity. It involves a procession of the statue of Mother Mary along a parade route, accompanied by a brass band. It is as much a social as it is a religious affair, still tying local families to each other and their Sicilian roots. As for myself, I am not well-known locally. Most of my career has been spent away from Pittston, so I marched anonymously in 2022 with a friend, as a spectator. We were walking and talking in the front and to the side of the procession, with a crowd of fifty or so marchers and the band behind us. When we came abreast of Salvatore's house, above his old general store, there was a murmur behind us. People knew the property. They tell stories about it locally. Someone in the crowd said, "Genuflect." They were not talking about the statue of Mother Mary.

Over time, among the many other immigrants, Salvatore received four other Bufalino men, some of whose declared relationships to him would change over time. Two of the four were the static members of the family, my known-and-acknowledged relatives and granduncles: Nicolo Bufalino (my grandfather) and a Rosario Bufalino (my granduncle Ross, who was probably not the Brigand and certainly not our Russell). The other two Bufalinos' relationship to us is more mysterious, as they declared or were attributed over time to be Salvatore's brothers, cousins, nephews, and, finally, the survivor of the two was deemed a completely unrelated adversary. But always until the relationship's bitter end after twenty-five years, the men were business partners in a number of enterprises.

To touch on the question of kinship, some quick facts. My grandfather Nicolo had some boys: Charles, Salvatore, and Angelo Bufalino (my father). My granduncle Ross's sons were Charles, Angelo, Samuel (possibly Salvatore?), Joseph, and James. My granduncle Salvatore's sons were Charles, Angelo (Yabo), James, Eugene, and William Eugene (Bill Buff, of Hoffa fame). The full first-generation genealogy is outlined in an Appendix to this book. Everybody has a Charles. Everybody has an Angelo. Salvatore appears often, but before Salvatore would name anyone after himself, he chose the name Eugene. Twice. After a sponsor, perhaps? A benefactor? Eugene Caico (Don Eugenio)?

By the time of Yabo's passing in 1993, my understanding of the Bufalino progenitors of my family stopped at the three brothers: Salvatore, who was Bill's father; Rosario; and Nicolo, my own grandfather. Based on the above, if you had challenged me to name two granduncles I never knew existed, I might have answered, "I don't know . . . Angelo and Charles?"

CHAPTER 10

THE PHANTOM BROTHERS

Angelo and Charles (anglicized from Calogero) Bufalino arrived via the *Cita Di Napoli* on July 9, 1903. Brothers themselves, they stated their destination as *their brother Salvatore's* apartment on Main Street, Pittston. Of course, they might have lied about their relationship to Salvatore to expedite their processing. Their unofficial and presumed relationships to the Bufalino Brothers, my direct family, would change over time depending on circumstance and the person doing the reporting. But for starters, there on arrival, they declared themselves to be my grandfather's and granduncle's two phantom brothers.

Angelo was Russell Bufalino's father. Calogero was Russell's uncle. Contrary to the narrative of some of Russell's presumptive biographers and confirmed by William "Big Billy" D'Elia and Russell both, Calogero became Russell's guardian after his brother Angelo's death.

To the best of my knowledge, by 1903 the ages of the five first-arrived Bufalino men were as follows: Angelo (Russell's father), thirty-nine; Salvatore, thirty-five; Rosario, thirty-one; Nicolo (my grandfather), twenty-seven; and Calogero, twenty-five.

The youngest of the group, Russell's uncle, Calogero, was known as "The Old Man." The name *Calogero* derives from a Greek expression meaning either "good old" or "beautiful old" to describe a figure from antiquity for whom the name Calogero was originated. Sicily's San Calogero was a black-skinned hermit who became a local deity and was then incorporated into the local canon as a saint associated with the harvest. The Feast of San Calogero is still celebrated in Montedoro every July.

Calogero Bufalino eventually anglicized his name to Charles to either (or both) conceal his past or further his business interests by avoiding anti-Italian sentiment. The nickname of "The Old Man" would eventually be applied to Russell during the 1930s as, one by one, Russell assumed Calogero's roles by acting as his proxy in various businesses and pursuits that were either Calogero's own or part of the larger Pittston family.

Calogero Bufalino has been characterized by the authors of *Informer Journal*'s "Men of Montedoro" article to be someone who would "stick a knife into you as soon as look at you." I can't argue with that characterization. The first-generation children, my uncles and cousins, describe him as dark and angry. A convicted and imprisoned Black Hand extortionist, he was someone with a violent temper that you did not want to cross.

Calogero was the silent partner behind a number of the family's business ventures, all of which occupied a single half-block of Railroad Street. The first of these was the combined grocery/butcher shop and deli at 43 Railroad Street, a double-block wood-frame structure with apartments above and business space below. It served as the first family home and place of business for Salvatore and Nicolo. It was known as the Bufalino Brothers Store and was a gathering spot for the family and people in their circle. At night, the men would gamble in the space, which was a common practice for locals through the 1980s. The men would drop coins for my Aunt Julia to find as she swept up after closing.

The next business was a saloon, the Bufalino Saloon at 57 (and later 55) Railroad Street, whose liquor license was in Salvatore's name. In fact, Salvatore was considered the titled owner of most of these properties and enterprises, perhaps due to some limitation on Calogero related to his legal problems or simply because he didn't want his name on anything. During Prohibition, the saloon was reorganized into a social club, which was probably the genesis of the Montedoro Society (social club). While the Montedoro Society fostered community involvement in pageants and events—religious, political, and social—the building that housed the society operated as a speakeasy or "Blind Pig" during Prohibition. My grandfather Nicolo tended bar. Following Prohibition, under unknown ownership, it continued to operate through most of the 1970s as the Montedoro Society.

Immediately next to the Montedoro Society at 57 Railroad Street was the Bufalino Hotel, a joint enterprise operated by Calogero and my grandfather. It was a narrow building with a barroom ground floor and rooms above to serve new arrivals from overseas and other travelers. It was opened in 1911. When immigration settled down after World War I, this business was repurposed into Bufalino Hall and was used as a social hall, yet still with rooms to rent. Its liquor license was transferred to the Bufalino Saloon in about 1915, after which it continued to rent rooms but also served as a hall to hold rallies of a political nature or events like banquets and was occasionally rented out as a store. The hotel at number 57 and the bar at number 55 were connected through internal doorways and possibly via a passageway that existed under the back porch slab of the Montedoro Society at 55 Railroad Street. Bufalino Hall burned in the 1930s during the Depression.

The last property, built in 1915, became the final residence of Salvatore and Nicolo and their families. A double-block three-story brick structure, it housed the S&R Bottling Company. Later renamed as the Gazzosa Manufacturing Company, it was a soda bottling business that Salvatore co-owned with his brother Rosario

(Ross), who rented the space below our half of the house from my grandfather. We still call the first-floor cellar "the soda factory." On Salvatore's half of the house, at 47 Railroad Street, the ground floor was used as a general store.

The Bufalino Brothers and their first-generation American children were an enterprising bunch. For a time in the 1910s and 1920s, the grocery butcher shop, bottling plant, general store, hotel, and saloon were all running concurrently with the help of the children in the family. Butcher duty, general storekeeping, bartending, and rooms for rent were the men's jobs. The women and children baked cookies for the deli to serve the banquet tables at Bufalino Hall and other venues. They operated the general store. They ran soda bottling equipment, drove trucks for deliveries, and in the very early days, tended the horses at a stable in the back alley.

It's certain that Calogero funded the construction of the homestead at 47-49 Railroad Street, because I have the receipt book and the satisfaction piece. It's likely that he was a silent partner behind all the other ventures as well, especially the first, the Bufalino Brothers Store, given the state the family was in when it was purchased in 1905. Moreover, Calogero was *present* in a day-to-day way and known to the children of the family, not so much in a familial or friendly way but rather as a strong and commanding presence. The grocery/butcher shop and deli that was the Bufalino Brothers Store was a kind of hangout for children and adult neighbors in the men's circle, all of whom were known to the children and some of whom were frankly dangerous. On a hot day, they would all be sipping a cold Gazzosa soda together, talking the business of the day. If the men got bored, they might decide to test the mettle of the children. Pairing two boys off against each other, the men would say: *"Affiate!"* ("Fight!")

Mostly when the first-generation children spoke of Uncle Calogero, it was concerning some stern business, but my own uncle Sam had the better of him one day. Sam (Salvatore), first-generation son of Nicolo, born in 1912, was driving the Gazzosa soda delivery truck in the 1920s. Seeing the men gathered in front of Bufalino Brothers Store, he blared the horn and careened the truck to a stop within feet of them, still blaring away on the horn. Calogero, certain it was a hit, did the only thing he could think of, which was to pull out a handful of silver dollars from his pocket and throw them at the windshield of the truck, cracking it, all the while cursing violently in a state of angered excitement.

Calogero's role in the Bufalino Brothers was part financier, part enforcer, collecting for Santo Volpe and others on the obligations of the immigrant workers brought in under patronage. Salvatore's exclusive province was to continue the influx of workers from Sicily, but he also worked the mines and the family businesses concurrently. Nicolo and Ross's role was to keep the businesses functioning to serve their clientele among the transplanted Sicilians. They worked hard at all of that, and so did their children, but they all lived well until the Great Depression and the big falling-out among the men. Any question of actual kinship between Russell (Calogero's nephew and charge) and William E. Bufalino or any member of the extended family becomes moot in light of the fact that the first five Bufalino men, whatever their actual kinship relationship, formed a tight-knit clan. Later, when the remaining of the first five Buffs fell out, their first-generation children remained close. Some, like Bill and Russ, kept even closer, as you may see.

Still, it's important for me to point out the following: Angelo's, Calogero's, and by extension Russell Bufalino's relationship to any member of my family or Salvatore's has been the point of many court proceedings and has been legally disproven and popularly disclaimed by parties, including William E. Bufalino. I will not attempt to contradict any such ruling or suggest anything to further the popular belief that Russell and Bill were blood cousins or relations. They were probably not, but the question of blood relationship is completely beside the point. It served to obfuscate the reality of their close relationship. The first five Bufalino men could not have been more involved in each other's affairs for a quarter of a century, no matter how distant their actual family ties.

I never met Calogero, who passed in 1960. But I can't escape the feeling that I've heard his voice. It boomed out of my uncle Sam and out of my father, and its tone and inflection was present to some extent in all of the first-generation Americans in the family, most especially when they were angry or being emphatic. It was the angry, baleful tone of expressions like *yew sonofabitch* and *you tell that sonofabitch* (this or that). Not unlike the voice of the character Moroney in the movie *Johnny Dangerously*, his speech was full of threatening invective and always power, power, power.

The squinty one eye came with the package. Bill had it. You can see it, just not quite as strongly as when he was younger, in the interview he granted to *A Current Affair* TV show in the 1980s. It was the squinty eye that grabbed you by the throat and let on that the speaker knew way more about a subject than he was saying. Mary had it too. My brothers found a way to mock the Old Man, by mocking something my own father had said to them in response to some perceived misbehavior. He explained that in this household, he was "the General."

So, for all my life when I met my brothers, just for fun, we all tilted our head forward, cocked one eye, dropped our tone, and said, "I'm the General, yeeeew sonofabitch" in mock tribute to the much larger-than-life first-generation Buffs.

CHAPTER 11

ANGELO: RUSSELL'S FATHER

The government and the press had Russell square in their sights in the 1960s. The post-Apalachin deportation furor lasted over a decade. The family name was all over the news, especially in the Luzerne County, Pennsylvania, press. It was embarrassing to a young schoolboy like me, but never more so than when Russell got into a misadventure with a truckload of stolen color televisions, the 1960s equivalent of the latest smartphone in terms of popular technology. Even the FBI were embarrassed for him. Their unofficial position was something like, "Russ, come *on*! You're *better* than this." So, when my friend Chucky Chiumento asked if I could get him a color TV as a joke, I had to find out where we fit into all of Russell's business. I went back to the source. I asked Mary Buff.

"Are we *related* to that guy?"

Mary was at her gas stove. She let out her trademark husky, suppressed laugh. "No. But he grew up here."

The look on my face must have suggested a question.

"His father was killed in the mine explosion that crippled my father."

I could have queried further, but I didn't. I assumed that some kind of kinship obligation was involved, enough to help an infant survive. Good enough. I was free to become somebody apart from Russell. When it was time, I found Russell's father with just a few keystrokes, all thanks to Mary.

Angelo Bufalino, Russell's father, died in 1904 in an explosion of gas at Pennsylvania Coal Company (PA Coal) Shaft 14 on September 22, 1904. *Reports of the Inspector of Coal Mines of the Anthracite Coal Issue 1* reports as an item: "[Salvadore Bufalino was] *severely burned by an explosion of gas. His brother Angelo and Lokon Diskis were burned at the same time and died of their burns.* Angelo, Russell Bufalino's father, is also listed as a spreadsheet line item, though his last name is misspelled as *Bufaline* (in Italy, we are the Bufalini), directly above Salvatore in the *Pennsylvania Registers of Mine Accidents, Anthracite 1899–1913*. An inquest was held to determine to what extent the mine was responsible for the deaths and injuries. The fire boss reported he had instructed the men not to enter the chamber, and that was that. Their deaths were on their own heads. There would be no compensation.

Maria Cristina Buccoleri, Angelo's wife, had arrived in New York for the first time nine months before her husband Angelo's death. She arrived on December 21, 1903, listing her destination as her husband in Pittston. In tow are the four children: Rosario (an infant), Cristina (age two), Calogero (listed as a laborer at age five), and Giuseppa (age six). It seems that, as later testimony in *Bufalino v. Holland* will suggest, the family had most of a year in Pittston before Angelo's death, which precipitated their return to Montedoro for a period of a year.

Apart from supporting the argument that Russell was born in the United States, Russell's sister Giuseppa's (Josephine's) testimony is probably correct with respect to the details of their many travels as children between Sicily and the United States. Her testimony is recapped in *Bufalino vs. Holland*, as follows:

> *She came to this country in 1902 or 1903 accompanied by her parents, sister, and brother Calogero; that her father died in 1904; that thereafter her mother took all four children back to Italy; that*

> *about a year later* [January 13, 1906] *she returned to this country with her mother and two brothers . . . ; that after her mother died in 1910, she and the appellant* [Russell] *returned to Italy from which they and their sister (Cristina) returned to the United States in 1914.*

She does seem to misremember her father as being with them on the first crossing in 1903 (he is not on the manifest) and misspeaks about Russell not being present on the trip despite his appearing on the manifest. As for Russell's lodging after the 1914 return, she reported that Russell and her sister lived with her and her husband after her own 1914 marriage. The review board was dubious about the Buffalo school records that were presented as evidence of Russell's attendance. When they asked Giuseppa who enrolled him, her reply was, "Maybe he enrolled himself."

Travel records through Ellis Island support all the incoming itinerary contained in Josephine's narrative, if not the persons present on the 1903 crossing. Records of the outbound to Sicily trips are harder to come by. Altogether, it's impossible to know a few things: a) the dates and details of their departures *to* Sicily, and b) their actual destination on the 1906 return to the United States. The ship manifest suggests that their professed destination in 1906 was Elizabeth Street (presumed by some authors to be the street in Little Italy, New York City). But a close look at the records of that voyage show that most travelers were bound for Elizabeth Street as well, suggesting sloppy, batch-style bookkeeping on the part of the recordkeeper.

Maria Cristina would have needed a support system on that return trip in 1906. An ample system was available in Pittston, where Salvatore's wife was still nursing her firstborn, Charles. But Maria Cristina may have had family in New York City, and Russell has at least one school record there in 1910. The information provided by the special inquiry officer, as presented before the appeals court in *Bufalino vs. Holland,* included an item stating: "The record of a New York City school for 1910 shows his birth date as September 27, 1903, and that he was removing to Pittston." For how long? When did he and his sister leave for Montedoro? It's not clear.

Nevertheless, there is good testimonial support for the argument that Russell grew up in Pittston—or spent considerable time there growing up—not just in his early years but also later. The most recent support for the claim comes from William D'Elia, Russell's own chosen successor, who knew Russell as well as anyone could. According to Mr. D'Elia, Russell was raised—or at least mentored—following his mother's death, by his uncle, Calogero Bufalino. Mr. D'Elia further correctly states that Russell was injured in a car crash on Pittston's Water Street Bridge in 1924, some four years before any prior biographer placed him in town. Russell's stated address at the time of his accident was 55 Railroad Street, which was a building that his uncle owned and that housed the Montedoro Society. If he did not actually live there, it was at least an address that his uncle would frequently cite as his own address for business and travel purposes, a building in town that he owned, two doors up from Salvatore's home, businesses, and family.

Buffalo, New York, does have some legitimate claim to Russell. He does appear to have school records that suggest some presence there between 1914 and 1918. Russell took his first job in Buffalo in 1920 driving a taxi for John Montana, who would later be called before the McClellan Committee following his identification at Apalachin. Russell himself owned a commercial garage in Buffalo (but kept one in Pittston as well). One of his biographers pointed to arrest records in Buffalo without citing specifics. Newspaper accounts suggest that the entire 1934–37 Pittston police arrest records, along with Russell's lifelong local record, vanished shortly after Apalachin. Claims about Russell coming up under Stefano

Magaddino or Joseph Barbara, though he may have known them, even worked in association with them seem beside the point. If Russell needed any exemplars of how to run an organization that would propel him to a position of importance superior to The Commission, as Bill D'Elia states Russell was, he had no less than two and possibly three top-tier first-generation Sicilian Black Hand extortionists to emulate, not the least of which was his own uncle, Calogero.

Calogero's influence over Russell may be underestimated and their relationship misunderstood. Russell's mother Maria Cristina's many trips back and forth to Sicily were costly. Steerage tickets ran from thirty-five to fifty dollars a head (though children two years of age and under traveled for free). This was at a time when a loaf of bread cost two to three cents, and a miner's daily pay was around a dollar. Salvatore and/or Calogero may each have been in a financial position to finance Maria Cristina and her children's many trips and might have done so out of family obligation. Salvatore was laid up for months following the explosion that killed Russell's father. He may only have just recovered by the time his son Charles arrived in 1905.

Based on the fact that Russell ended up as Calogero's ward, it's likely Calogero did the heavy financial lifting of Maria's several trips back and forth to Sicily. He's not remembered as a charitable man. It's not impossible that Russell's relationship to Calogero was the same relationship the *carusi* children in the sulfur mines had with their assigned miner.

As wrong as it may sound to the modern ear, nephew or not, Calogero just might have owned Russell outright.

CHAPTER 12

THE PADRONES

Stefano "Steve" La Torre arrived in Pittston in 1903. He is reported to have saved money to import other individuals and families, including Santo Volpe, who arrived in 1906. Steve La Torre, Santo Volpe, and probably Calogero Bufalino were all actively assisting other families to join them in America and fill the many laborer positions in the mine left vacant by the thousands of laborers who simply quit the field or moved back to the Old Country during the 1902 strike.

Salvatore Bufalino may have been acting as a padrone himself or may have been acting as a travel broker and lodging coordinator for the padrones among the Pittston family. The railroads and coal companies themselves fostered this activity. Any family that sponsored ten or more families of immigrants was recognized by the company. Ten families per year for ten years earned you special recognition, and you were presented with a framed portrait of a pheasant as a kind of heraldic representing abundance and good fortune. Volpe and La Torre were both honored by the receipt of such an award from the coal companies. I can't say for certain that Salvatore was so honored, but it's my recollection from Mary's apartment that he was.

Whether Salvatore himself was or was not a padrone, the businesses in the family, from the grocery to the deli to the hotel to the saloon, would have served to support an influx of immigrants, regardless of their sponsorship. His service as a travel broker, hotelier, grocer, merchant, and bar owner would have also served the needs of a padrone class.

Immigration from Montedoro peaked just before the start of World War I. Today's Italian population in Pittston exceeds 20 percent as of the 2020 census, many times the national average. The transatlantic crossing via steamship would have proved prohibitively expensive for most of the Montedorese immigrants. They would have relied on funding from either a broker or from one of Pittston's padrones to make the trip. It's possible that the principals of the Pittston family, Santo Volpe, Steve LaTorre and Calogero Bufalino acted in concert from early on to form a padrone system. It's possible also that Salvatore and my grandfather Nicolo, as the Bufalino Brothers, serviced the material needs of the new immigrants through their various businesses as a condition of the padrone's contract with the new arrivals.

The padrone system was one avenue by which people without means could cross the ocean. The other was by way of "banks" of labor brokers who promised emigrating families good jobs across the water but often placed them into situations where they would be little more than what Pittston historian E. C. Johnson described as "Mafia-bonded slaves" The onset of World War I with its U-boat campaign hampered immigration, stemming the flow of immigrant families for the labor brokers in Sicily and for the padrones. After World War I, immigration was formally restricted out of fears of importing foreign anarchists. By 1930, the padrone system in the United States was effectively dead.

Some time ago, before I began any real research, I came across a miner's remembrance on a genealogy board. The writer claimed that "everyone wanted to work for Santo [Volpe] because he paid." But sitting at the cafeteria table just outside the paymaster's booth sat Calogero Bufalino, twirling a revolver around the tabletop.

The collector was *in*.

CHAPTER 13

A ROUGH START

A document titled *Partial List of Acts of Violence or Intimidation During the Anthracite Strike of 1902* records nine deaths and many more serious injuries in a report seventy-plus pages long detailing daily acts of mayhem throughout the anthracite region in the May through October anthracite strike of 1902. Pittston and its surrounding communities between Wilkes-Barre and Scranton are well represented among the accounts of intimidations, shootings, effigy hangings, beatings, threats, dynamite bombings, and general anarchy that occurred throughout the Pennsylvania anthracite counties of Schuylkill, Carbon, Lackawanna, Susquehanna, and Northumberland.

The Montedoro Sicilians and other Italians who were the first arrivals in to fill job vacancies or cross picket lines had to start their working careers as scabs, confronted by the angry predecessor Welsh, Irish, Scottish, German, Russian, and Slavic miners and laborers who had made up the previous waves of immigration to the coalfields. Many of the Sicilian newcomers had little choice, as they were under contract to a padrone who had financed their crossing and who was expecting a regular percentage out of their wages. So even before the cultural clashes could begin in earnest, the stage was set for hostility over the right to work.

The Italians arrived in 1902 and later generally populated the south side of the small city, displacing the Welsh and Presbyterian population at first gradually and then suddenly as simmering tensions erupted into street violence.

On Saturday, June 13, 1908, a party of six young married men—Evans, Vaughn, Charles and Joseph Alford; Park Clelland; and a Mr. Vandenburg—were walking home from work, traveling up Railroad Street away from the corner at Main. Just past the Laurel Line railroad trestle, about forty yards up Railroad from Main Street, a much larger gang of young Italian men blocked the sidewalk. Vandenburg, one of the six citizens, himself a city councilman, asked the larger group to make way on the sidewalk. They would not. He started to elbow his way through when someone pulled a stiletto. Seeing it, he made a jump for the street, but several of the gang set upon him, knives drawn. His friends, family men with wives and children, were overwhelmed and started to run up the street. One of the gang pulled a revolver and shot Park Clelland twice from behind, killing him.

The shooter ran into a nearby grocer's shop to hide. When the grocer objected, the young man showed the gun and stayed waiting for the crowd to disperse. The shooter escaped. The grocer was arrested. Subjected to the third degree, he broke down and told them what he knew about the shooter. There were property searches and immediate arrests, but the roundup of gang members was not completed until three days later, on June 16.

On the evening of the shooting, among the citizenry, all hell broke loose in Pittston. Shooting victim Park Clelland, a harmless clerk at Evans Brothers local grocery, had been well-known and well liked. A crowd of citizens numbering close to a thousand gathered around the police station as the suspects were brought in. They seized one of the men, intending to beat him to death. Mayor Gillespie, who had been assisting the police with the roundup, is said to have stunned the crowd with a brief address, imploring them not to descend into mob rule, all the while working his way toward the man on the ground. He rescued him from the crowd. Briefly subdued, the crowd again began to murmur and press on the police station, calling for a lynching. Gillespie called the state police, and a party of mounted horsemen arrived at a gallop to engage the crowd after a ride of just three miles. While the crowd finally quieted and dispersed, many stayed behind in vigil.

On the Tuesday of the following week, the citizens of Pittston met at the local armory, voicing demands that the city offer better protection to the citizens and a crackdown on weapons. Local dignitaries chaired the meeting, and the clergy and the mayor were there. Mayor Gillespie promised no street would be paved and no sewer dug until his promise to make the streets safe was fulfilled. The dignitaries and clergy in attendance reiterated the mayor's plea to let law and order prevail. The assembly settled on the commitment of five of its members to assisting the police and the city in every possible way to restore order.

Just down the road and at the same time, the Italian community had its own meeting at Bianco Brothers bank. They passed among themselves resolutions to assist the authorities in every way. On the evening of the meeting, the police search in the Italian section resumed. Eighteen people were taken into custody in total. In accounts that I have seen, Salvatore Bufalino took on the role of advocating for several of the young suspects among the angered citizens on Railroad Street.

Ultimately, two men were charged in Clelland's murder and four for carrying concealed weapons. Murder indictments were issued against Chanto Carmello and Luigi Attardo. Four others were held on weapons charges, and two, including the grocer, were held as witnesses.

By the time of the hearing, three more arrests produced the names of more participants. It was supposed that one or more of the gang returned to Sicily to escape capture or prosecution. Italy had not historically supported the death penalty and would not extradite suspected murderers to the United States for that reason.

Carmello does not seem to have been convicted in the Clelland murder. The local newspapers of the day mangled ethnic names too horribly to tell. Luigi Attardo seems also to have escaped conviction. It's likely the true shooter did flee to Sicily. If Mayor Gillespie held true to his pledge, it would be a long time before roads were paved or sewers dug, at least—if not especially—on Railroad Street.

The Pennsylvania State Police came into being in 1905, following a legislative push begun during the 1902 strike, to establish a regular constabulary with better resources and wider authority than the local police. Initially the state police were regarded by coal workers warily as straight-up replacements for the Coal and Iron Police, who were considered to be merely thugs and head breakers. You may find references to the mounted troopers of the Pennsylvania State Police being described as "American Cossacks" in an American Civil Liberties Union (ACLU) filing from the 1920s. The thing—if there was just one thing—that set them apart from the Coal and Iron Police was professionalism. Add training, discipline, and protocols to the mix for good measure. On one undated occasion, they proved themselves much more than just company thugs.

In a book called *Justice to All: The Story of the Pennsylvania State Police,* author Katherine Mayo describes the nature of the conflict between the English-speaking population and the newcomers, if prejudicially, via an incident in a community just across a boundary line from Pittston.

> *Hughestown is a miners' settlement, near Pittston, Luzerne County. Hughestown possessed its share of decent, orderly, English-speaking miner folk, and it also possessed a gang of Italian banditti more brazen and bloody here than they had dreamed of being in their own Sicilian hills. These outlaws had not jumped from the immigrant*

> *trains full-fledged in boldness, but, step by step, had worked themselves up, through experiment in immunity, to the impudence that they now enjoyed. Fully aware of their freedom with knife and gun, of their daily shootings, stabbings, and robberies, the community had been content at first to say: "Small harm, for they only kill each other."*
>
> *And when, as was bound to happen, the bandits, tiring of limited game, began to reach afield, each citizen yet unmolested still gave thanks that he himself had not been the one to suffer, half deploring, half enjoying his neighbors' "bad luck."*

The Italian youths haunted the Hughestown streets at night. They assaulted the women, robbed the men, and threatened the lives of the officials who knew full well they were capable of following through.

One August evening, four young girls walking in the street were seized and held by some of the gang. One girl broke free and ran into the arms of Officer Schmaltz. Thomas Loftus helped identify and arrest her assailant.

A week later, while Thomas and his father were at work, Mrs. Loftus answered a knock on her door. The visitor coolly told her that her son would not come home alive since they planned to kill him that night. Afterward, they would deal with the rest of her family at their pleasure. The messenger left, and the house then sustained a prolonged bombardment of rocks. Mrs. Loftus hid in fear during the assault. When darkness fell, she gathered her daughters and fled into the town center. They were followed. They begged the first person they met to send for the state police.

The state police dispatched three troopers—Privates Garland, Adelson, and Butler—to the Loftus house. They found it surrounded by Italians. They dispersed the mob but were fired upon from the street. Turning to the sound with their clubs, they were fired upon from all directions by what must have been an exaggerated report of fifty Italians. The troopers were still wielding clubs when Garland took a bullet to his lung. When they drew their revolvers, Adelson was shot through the body. Butler took the offensive and rushed the gang, still on his mount, which dispersed the gang, leaving one man behind, struggling in his grip.

Back at the station, Butler sent out a call for help and the barracks dispatched Sergeant Wilhelm and ten troopers to suppress what had now become a general riot. Mounted troopers and horses quelled the crowd. With that accomplished, Butler led the sergeant to the houses suspected of hiding the men who shot Garland and Adelson. The whole town was watching as the troopers carried out a miniature siege. They kicked in doors, ransacked houses, pulled men out from under beds, up from cellars, and down from lofts until they felt they had most of the gang. Some went to a hospital; some were marched off to jail.

Mrs. Loftus begged for protection, and a guard was placed at her house for the night. Sergeant Wilhelm also set a guard over the Italian quarter. It remained, it was said, until peace was restored to the town. Altogether, the episode impressed the population of Hughestown to no end. Before that day, people expected little more of the state police than to be the state-sponsored replacements for Coal and Iron Police thugs. Katherine Mayo summarized the outcome by herself quoting another source, the *Pittston Gazette*:

> *There has been noticeable on the street since last evening a most remarkable change of opinion in regard to the State Troopers. Since the recent strike trouble, there has been considerable prejudice against the troopers, but last night no one could be found who did not have a word of praise for them. It was the most serious local action the Troop has yet encountered, and they bore themselves in such soldierly fashion as to deserve praise on all sides.*

Finally, Katherine Mayo puts a footnote onto the whole affair that attempts to rationalize the violence of the coalfields in the aftermath of the 1902 strike: "Let it be marked, however, that not only Thomas Loftus, but all his male relatives beside, were members of the United Mine Workers of America, of which Mr. John Mitchell was president."

As an outcome of the bitter 1902 strike, the UMWA coal workers of Northeast Pennsylvania won concessions from PA Coal in terms of a raise, limits on work hours, and an arbitration process, but they were still operating without a contract and would continue to do so for years.

Katherine Mayo was wondering out loud whether the assault on Loftus and his family was a union-busting action in disguise. It's a fair question.

CHAPTER 14

THE RACE RIOT AT PA COAL #6

On Thursday, October 4, 1906, at the PA Coal #6 colliery, a small group of five or six Lithuanian miners and laborers were set upon by a much larger number of Italian workers. Reports vary widely, but the Lithuanians may have been outnumbered by anywhere from five to one to twenty to one.

It started innocently enough. Five or six Lithuanian men were seated in a circle at the powder house, waiting to receive their supplies for the day's work, when an unnamed Italian approached one of them, sliding playfully into the lap of a Mr. Smeltzer. He was pushed off to the lap of the next man, and the next. Suddenly there was a melee. Colliery tools were wielded in the form of sprags, wrenches, and files. Stilettos were pulled.

The Smeltzer brothers took the worst of it, with Anthony reported to be dying from a wound to his right side and bruises about his head and body and his brother Matthias suffering six stab wounds. The remaining Lithuanians broke to make a run for the mule barn. Seeing the disturbance, the barn occupants shut the doors in time to stop the crowd in pursuit. The mine detective, arriving after the fact, rode to the state police barracks some three miles away and returned with a party of state troopers, who set out to find the participants.

The *Wilkes-Barre Times* reported that a Calogero Bufalino reported having been struck by Smeltzer with the wrench of a rock machine, requiring five stitches. Another Calogero Bufalino, reported to be a cousin of the previous, sustained deep cuts on his head caused by flying stones. One or the other of these men was Russell's uncle Calogero. The same newspaper source identified a family member as having plunged the sharp end of a mine file into Smeltzer's side.

By Saturday of that week, an unnamed state trooper visited Alderman Barrett to issue warrants for Nicolo Bufalino (my grandfather), Calogero Bufalino, and the other known participants in the fight. By the evening of the same day, Salvatore Bufalino appeared before the Alderman to request warrants be issued against the Smeltzer brothers and others of the Lithuanian combatants.

It is near impossible to tell the further outcome of the riot from any news source due to the gross misspelling of virtually every immigrant name, with the names ranging from "Buffaloni" to "Smellster." It's not clear whether Anthony Smeltzer did in fact die from his wounds, as expected. There does not seem to be any follow-up reporting in the next week.

Why do the Smeltzer brothers look like the targets of some organized action? Were the others allowed to escape? Did the coal company get what it wanted out of the affair? Was some union organizing curtailed? The *Pittston Gazette,* a company paper whose 1850 volume 1, issue number 1, announced itself as the *Pittston Gazette and Susquehanna Anthracite Journal,* dismissed the matter as "the culmination of long-standing jealousy between the races." And that was that.

PA Coal #6 colliery will appear frequently in relation to union troubles that led to violence, and several of the city's unsolved murders will have a #6 connection. That is true in the above, and it's all the more true after the Pittston family members became coal contractors in their own right.

CHAPTER 15

THE PITTSTON FAMILY

The expression "Men of Montedoro" was new to me when I first heard it in reference to the Pittston family's first-generation founders. It was a name that local law enforcement used that was later invoked before the McClellan Committee, formerly known as the United States Senate Select Committee on Improper Activities in Labor and Management. If it ever had wide use as a label, it would be quickly supplanted by the FBI's assigned label, which named it after Russell: the Bufalino crime family.

The original Pittston family leadership was embodied in the persons of three men: Santo Volpe, Steve La Torre, and Calogero Bufalino, all of whom arrived to the anthracite, or hard coal, region between 1903 and 1906 and would continue to operate as a triumvirate of centralized coal region power across the early 1930s through ownership and conduct of businesses and activities, legitimate and otherwise.

The Pittston family may have grown out of the Iron Head Society, which established early dominance and later notoriety when it became widely known during the Black Hand trial of 1907. There were many Black Hand societies operating in the anthracite coal region in the early 1900s. The Strong Arm Society, the Iron Head Society. and other Black Hand extortion networks vied with each other for territorial and predation rights among the Italian population.

Calogero Bufalino arrived in Pittston in 1903 with Russell's father Angelo. The ship manifest records that they were destined for "their brother Salvatore's" home in Pittston. Calogero's own arrest and conviction in the Black Hand trial of 1907 supports my belief that he was conducting Black Hand activities in the area almost from his arrival forward. His leadership of the Iron Head Society predates the arrival of Santo Volpe by three years. It's possible then that the Iron Head Society (of the Black Hand) provided the structural template for what later became the Pittston family, making the Bufalino crime family unique among named organized crime families in that it was both started by and later named for a member of the Bufalinos. It's at least possible that Salvatore Bufalino, who had arrived two years before, in 1901, had an organizational role in assembling the players. It's clear from newspaper accounts that he and my own grandfather Nicolo, his brother, were active participants in early disturbances. By 1904, however, Salvatore was injured in the mine accident that killed Russell's father. He was laid up for some time, walking with a cane thereafter and not suited for vigorous exertion. By 1909 he and my grandfather Nicolo and their children became more the mercantile branch of the Pittston Family's many enterprises.

Steve La Torre is also supposed to have arrived in Pittston in 1903 and is also considered by many to have founded the Pittston family. When he arrived at age seventeen, he was already a trained assassin, which made him a good fit for the enforcement needs of the Pennsylvania Coal Company. In the Black Hand roundup of 1907, Steve, his brother-in-law Sam Lucchino, and Calogero Bufalino were arrested in relation to a terror attack initiated on behalf of a different society, possibly the Strong Arm Society. In time, the "Luchino faction," as police called it, and the "Consagro faction," which was closely aligned with Calogero, would be at odds over turf. Steve's first allegiance might have been to his brother-in-law, Sam Lucchino, which might have put him in opposition to Consagro and Bufalino.

The net of all that is that one or the other of these Black Hand societies, the Iron Head Society or the Strong Arm Society, was the basis of the Pittston family, and either Steve La Torre or Calogero Bufalino was an import into the entity that became this organized crime borgata. Whether Steve or Calogero were the initiators of the Pittston family, Santo Volpe arrived in 1906 and soon assumed the preeminent position, probably because La Torre and Calogero were taken off the streets from April 1907 through April 1908 by force of a conviction we'll discuss shortly. The three men—Santo Volpe, Steve La Torre, and Calogero Bufalino—enjoyed a long run of operations that made them all wealthy and dominant over coal and other businesses, legitimate and otherwise, in Northeastern Pennsylvania.

Volpe was older than La Torre but was roughly the same age as Calogero Bufalino. It's most likely that he was the most politically or socially conscious among the founding members. In contrast to both La Torre and Bufalino, Santo Volpe made for a good front man. He stood first in line to receive a contract when the Pennsylvania Coal Company reinstituted the contract system in 1913. His work as a coal contractor alone made him, and eventually all of them, wealthy, making the Pittston family unique in its control of the coal mines, the principal industry of its region.

Santo was able through force of personality, raw wealth, and eventually alcohol to cultivate relationships with high society, especially political and legal figures. It may become clear when we talk about marriages and events in his family that he relished the "Big Man" role. By the time he passed away in 1958, his honorary pallbearers included two former governors of Pennsylvania, a PA Supreme Court justice, Congressman Dan Flood, UMWA President John L. Lewis, state senators, and other luminaries. Santo Volpe was a *very* big deal. When the grizzled and gruff coal miners of my youth even dared to speak his name, they seemed to do so in their baby voice, as if for fear that he might appear on call in a puff of coal dust.

The family still refers to him as "King," short for his title, "King of the Night."

As to where the Pittston family "fit" in the organizational structure of the Five Families or the other borgatas around the country, it has never been completely clear. The later presence of Joseph Barbara in the structure of the organization has led some to assert that the Pittston family was some satellite of the Magaddino organization. Some have even suggested that Russell "came up" under Magaddino, which is wrong, or that Russell was Barbara's underboss, which is also wrong. There is no doubt at all that there were strong family and business ties among the Buffalo, Endicott, and Pittston families. Salvatore himself may have come down through Buffalo, or at the direction of someone in Buffalo. Joseph Barbara was a local who worked his way from the coalfields into Endicott, New York. His wife was from an Endicott family. John Sciandra, a Montedoresi related through marriage, would return from Buffalo to join the Pittson family in the early 1920s. He would be trusted to fill in at the top spot when the old guard stepped out of the limelight in the 1930s.

All the same, the Pittston family was associated with the Genovese family from the early 1900s, as will be seen. Russell was found to be driving Don Vito Genovese himself out of the Apalachin meeting in 1957. Russell made the arrangements with attendees from around the world to act as Genovese's facilitator in the meeting, where Genovese thought they would disband the Five Families and crown him king.

It's more likely that neither Buffalo nor the New York families owned or controlled or leased rights to the Northeast Pennsylvania rackets. It may even be, as Russell's handpicked successor William D'Elia has said, that Russell himself was or at least came to be regarded as "above The Commission."

What is certain is that the Pittston family had broad regional autonomy. It settled a turf war between itself and Lupo-Morello, the nascent Genovese family, very early on, sending a brutal "hands-off" message to would-be infiltrators from New York City via the corpse of Luciano Perrino.

CHAPTER 16

NOT ONE OF US

Luciano Perrino (a.k.a. Tomasso Petto), is supposed by some to have been a high-level Black Hand operative, and on that basis, some claim he was the first head of what became the Bufalino crime family. The lateness of his 1905 arrival and his brief local tenure do not much support that belief. Calogero Bufalino and Steve La Torre were already active in their respective Black Hand societies by the time Perrino arrived. While his Black Hand chops may be valid, nothing about Pittston's history or Perrino's story suggests that any of the Black Hand societies in town recognized his authority over their activities.

Perrino had been detained by New York City authorities after a pawn ticket found in his jacket pocket led to the personal effects of a murder victim. Perrino ran with the Lupo-Morello gang, headed by Ignazio "the Wolf" Lupo and Giuseppe "the Clutch Hand" Morello, the founders of the crime families that would much later be named for Carlo Gambino and Vito Genovese, respectively. He was a suspect in the 1905 murder of Benedetto Madonia, a case that became known as the Barrel Murder or the Barrel Mystery. Benedetto had been murdered in a brutal fashion, his remains left in a sugar barrel and placed on a street corner. Not a very tall but a very strong man, Perrino was known as "the Ox."

Released after months in the Tombs for lack of evidence that would lead to a conviction in the Barrel Mystery, Perrino moved first to Scranton, Pennsylvania, where he was arrested for robbery; then briefly to Virginia, where he ran into trouble over selling cigars not bearing the proper stamp; then to Pittston, Pennsylvania. In the summer of 1905, he opened a grocery store downtown, which he abandoned for a butcher shop in an area just outside the city in Pittston Township, which was populated by a wealthier class of Italian immigrants. His side-hustle huckstering acquainted him with the residents, who politely accepted his company and that of his friends from New York City. Shortly after such visits, letters began to arrive to the unsuspecting residents of Pittston Township demanding large sums of money and threatening violence that included physical harm or bombing. When the residents consulted with Perrino about the letters, his response was to suggest that they give him just half the requested amount, and he would make it all right with the actors behind the letters.

Perrino's career came to an end on October 21, 1905, as he walked to his home on Lincoln Street in Pittston Township around 10:30 p.m. His wife had told him in the days before that the house was being watched. People were running through the yard. The trespassers were making her uneasy. He traveled armed with a .38-caliber revolver. As he approached his door, three or four assailants set upon him. At least one had either a shotgun or muzzleloader filled with shot. Someone else had a larger-caliber rifle whose slug tore straight across him, severing his spine and leaving an exit wound below his left arm the size of a teacup. His gun hand and pistol were too badly damaged for him to return fire. His wife found him in the yard. He asked for a glass of water. He died before she could bring it. In an account to a paper of the day, his wife reported having seen someone dressed in white (the attire of a padrone) in the vicinity after the shooting.

The ferocity of the attack suggested to law enforcement that this was an act of vengeance. Possibly his associates in the Lupo-Morello gang considered him to be too greedy or not forthcoming with the extortion money. It was also suggested that Giuseppe de Primo, the brother-in-law of the man found in the barrel, had, over time, orchestrated Perrino's murder as well as those of others related to the case both in the United States and in Italy. Those responsible for Perrino's murder were never found. The local police chose not to investigate. There were too many potential suspects among his victims, too many waterlogged mine pits the weapons may have been cast into, and plenty enough other grief in the coal region to keep the police busy.

They dropped the case. Perrino, they may have felt, was someone who would not be missed. His murder had been the sixth of a recent spate of murders in the city. It may have been too early in Pittston's own Black Hand era for police to have made the connection, or the authorities might have chosen to ignore the local Black Hand threat since it may have led them to a third, less-comfortable thesis about the killers.

They might have failed to consider that Perrino's Black Hand extortion racket may have been in too-direct competition with the Black Hand societies that existed among the Sicilian residents in Pittston, which, in a very short time, would make national news of their own.

CHAPTER 17

THE BLACK HAND AND THE IRON HEAD

In February 1907, Russell Bufalino's uncle Calogero, and if I'm honest, my grandfather Nicolo Bufalino and his brother, my granduncle Salvatore, were arrested in the largest Black Hand nationwide bust of its time for an act of terrorism that took place in Pittston, Pennsylvania. Twenty-three or twenty-four (the numbers vary) Black Hand extortionists were arrested by the Pennsylvania State Police in conjunction with a gang assault against the home of the Rizzo brothers. Thirteen would be held over for trial on charges that included dynamiting, robbery, and obtaining money by force or threats and conspiracy.

The event that precipitated the bust was an all-out assault on the home of the Rizzo brothers. The house was peppered with rifle fire, and, it was reported, took over fifty hits. The Black Hand societies involved believed that the Rizzo brothers were running card games and possibly other games of chance out of their house. This was never either proved or disproved, as it did not matter. The gang's belief led them to want *in* on the profits from the suspected enterprise. Representatives of more than one of the gangs may have been among those arrested, but it was the Iron Head Society that, from the initial roundup by the authorities until the day of the trial, let loose a stream of threatening letters targeted at the police, the prosecution, and even the court. It may have been a coincidence, but a judge from outside the area was chosen to hear the case.

The harassment of the Rizzo brothers had taken place over many months. Initially, the brothers agreed to pay the gang a sum of money to be left alone, but the demands persisted in the form of five or more threatening letters delivered by Steve La Torre and his brother-in-law Sam Lucchino. As the Rizzo brothers continued to resist the demands, their home became the occasional target of gunfire.

On Christmas Eve, 1905, their house was dynamited. Usually, this was done in such a way that a porch would be blown off, but the structure would remain standing. The point of the dynamiting was to inflict terror, and the aim was to secure payment. In 1906, the Rizzos' house was shot up. The brothers took two of the extortion letters to Pittston Police Chief Loftus.

In the ensuing months, the Black Hand extortionists, including Lucchino, attempted to get the letters they had delivered back from the Rizzos. The Rizzos had to say they had burned the two they delivered to the police. The gang's suspicions were further piqued when they became aware that the city and the Rizzo brothers set a trap for the extortionists at a scheduled pickup, complete with officers carrying repeating rifles.

On January 24, 1907, the Rizzo house was targeted for a mass shooting. One of the Rizzo brothers was reported to have shot back with a scattergun at the receding crowd of thirty assailants. A few, who had been hit by shot, lay in the street when the shooting stopped. A few days after the action subsided, according to the *Wilkes-Barre Times*, Sam Lucchino showed up at the Rizzo house to say, "Now see what you have done. One of the men is dead and another near dead. Now we have to add five hundred dollars for expenses."

Russell Bufalino, Angelo Bufalino, and Yabo Bufalino on the electric mule at PA Coal #6. *Bufalino Studio.*

n coal mine workers, early 1900s.
no Studio.

Pittston, Pennsylvania, 1906.

Russell Bufalino po
Bufalino S

Nicolo Bufalino and family, 1914.

and Giuseppina Bufalino
Pina) with children, 1927.

Salvatore Bufalino, Pittston Italian community and business leader, founder of the Montedoro Society. Top: Wilkes-Barre newspaper photo, 1926.
Times Leader.

Stefano "Steve" La Torre, Pittston family founding member in the early 1900s, after emigrating from Montedoro, Sicily.

Santo Volpe, "King of the Night," who led organized crime in Pennsylvania until the 1930s in association with Montedoresi ass… Steve La Torre and Calogero Bufalino.

Tomasso "The Ox" Petto, Morello gang member from New York, prime suspect in the 1903 Barrel Murder, and murder victim himself after moving to Pittston and operating as a Black Hander.

Giuseppe "The Clutch Hand" Morello, first boss of what eventually became the Genovese family in New York.

Lupo "The Wolf" Ignazio, Morello's fellow counterfeiter and racketeer. He would eventually form his own borgata, which became the Gambino family.

Angelo (Yabo) Bufalino, c. 1928.

Yabo Bufalino, Bill's brother,
Pittston, Pennsylvania, c. 1937.

Yabo, the family outdoo

Feast of the Blessed Mother,
Pittston, Pennsylvania, c. 1937.
Angelo and Nicolo Bufalino
are center left, near the truck.

lo Bufalino, Bill's cousin,
r's father.

Angelo and his wife Margaret Bufalino.

Angelo, standing with glasses, in grade school.

Yabo Bufalino, Bill's b
Detroit portrait, c.
J. J. K

Nicolo Bufalino in his later years—at Santo Volpe's PA Coal #6, c. 1937, in the bottom right photo.

Mary Bufalino, c. 1927.

Mary Bufalino, c. 1964.
Bufalino Studio.

The Stork Club
(later the Story Club)
in Detroit, Michigan.
Joe Clark, HBSS.

Yabo pours a drink
for Gene at the
Stork Club, c. 1946.

Gene behind the bar, c. 1946. *Joe Clark, HBSS.*

Gene regards his Wurlitzer jukebox at the Stork Club, c. 1946. *Joe Clark, HBSS.*

Eugene (Gene) Bufalino.

Gene in the Navy.

Bill and Gene in uniform during World War II.

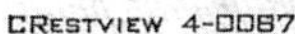

Gene Bufalino
VICE PRESIDENT

DISTILLERY, RECTIFYING, WINE
AND ALLIED WORKERS
INTERNATIONAL UNION OF AMERICA
AFL-CIO

9015 WILSHIRE BLVD.
BEVERLY HILLS, CALIF.
108

Gene's union, founded by Bill.

(right) with friends. It's speculated
J. Edgar Hoover in the middle.

Gene goes to Washington, DC.

Author's father, Angelo Bufalino, in his Army uniform.

Angelo's portrait.

ɔ and Margaret Bufalino
town.

Angelo and Margaret's wedding.

William E. (Bill) Bufalino, Army portrait, c. 1942.

Bill at his Army desk.

The Rizzos went to the police and the matter was put before the district attorney, prompting the state police to arrest the gang, many of whom lived just across the city line from Pittston in the Brandy Patch section of Pittston Township.

Thirteen of the arrested gang members were held over for a trial en masse. Nicolo and Salvatore Bufalino were not among the men held over for trial, since they were not recognized as participants in the attack that precipitated the roundup. Local people were watching the trial to see some extreme justice carried out. Hangings were still a common occurrence on the Luzerne County Court House lawn. The frightened local population knew the stories of Black Hand victims being hunted and murdered an hour away from home for failing to pay up or remain silent. People were confident in a grave outcome for those arrested. They started to talk to the press about things they had witnessed or overheard. One man recounted seeing Steve La Torre going up the street with a wheelbarrow and two accomplices. Like a scene out of *Young Frankenstein,* protruding from the barrow was a pair of feet in work boots. The gang swore to kill the family of the witness if he talked about it. But with the gang in jail, and about to hang, well . . . people began to talk.

The Black Hand being a countrywide menace at the time, the trial attracted reporters from Philadelphia, Ohio, and elsewhere. The brief trial was concluded by April 1907. The judge disappointed the crowd of witnesses, who all had many stories to tell of Black Hand outrages, by restricting the scope of the trial to hear testimony and make a ruling only concerning the attack on the Rizzo brothers. The maximum allowable penalty for each of the defendants under such restrictions would have been a two-year prison sentence. When the verdicts came back guilty for eleven of the thirteen defendants, the judge announced his ruling. He referred to the defendants as "strangers in a strange land" and delivered a sentence that shocked even the defense in its leniency.

Eleven of the thirteen were sentenced to a year each in prison, to be isolated from other inmates in solitary confinement. Among them were Russell's uncle, Calogero, Steve La Torre, and his brother-in-law Sam Lucchino, as well as others who will factor into the later narrative. A Salvatore Volpe was alone acquitted of involvement and released. Many authors assume that Salvatore Volpe was Santo Volpe. It was likely not. In any case, Salvatore Volpe was acquitted and remained on the street when the convicted Black Handers went to prison. A Mr. Paternoster was acquitted but held over on other charges. Santo Volpe remained to run the show in their absence. It's likely during that 1907–08 period that Santo attained the top seat in the Pittston family. He would never relinquish it. Calogero would never have wanted it, in any case. He preferred to be in the background. Steve La Torre seems not to have minded either, and the relationship among the three men was good for years to come.

According to an article in the *Wilkes-Barre Times* dated February 26, 1907, the Iron Head Society, which peppered the prosecution and law enforcement with threats during the trial, was headquartered in Paterson, New Jersey, and a Jim Jormonia was the local coordinator in charge of fundraising for the defense of those arrested in association with the attack on the Rizzo brothers. That may or may not be accurate. Jormonia was arrested by a Luzerne County detective on grounds that he had participated in the extortion against the Rizzos, but his name is not among those docketed for trial, because he was not identified as an antagonist by the Rizzos.

As for what the Iron Head Society was and who its own Iron Head was, Louise Caico's narrative *Sicilian Ways and Days* tells that the pole-mounted effigy of a certain saint in Montedoro was made of iron rather than the usual paper mâché to avoid being damaged as it scraped against buildings on the parade route during the saint's feast day. San Calogero, the black-skinned hermit, was thus "the saint with the iron head."

Based on that, I'd bet that, whatever his last name was and wherever he was, the first name of the leader of the Iron Head Society was Calogero. Others have suggested it was Calogero Bufalino.

That is likely correct.

CHAPTER 18

AN ANCIENT WRONG TO RIGHT

From the beginning, the Pittston family in Pennsylvania had strong connections to the Genovese family in New York. These bonds were forged at the turn of the twentieth century, in the days when the Black Hand served as a precursor to the organized crime model of the American Mafia. Roots had been planted over the decades, developing independently, albeit nationwide, across the urban landscape through a common Sicilian origin and hierarchical structure that stretched all the way back to ancient Rome.

Sam Lucchino had been among the eleven convicted Black Hand extortionists sentenced to a year of solitary confinement following the Black Hand trial in April 1907. He led a complicated and dangerous life. His sister was Steve La Torre's wife, and Steve was or would be among the leaders of the Pittston family. Steve was also convicted of Black Hand activities and served time related to the Rizzo house attack. Lucchino was godfather to one of Charles Consagro's children. Consagro had been a suspect in the murder of a Joseph Castellino in 1905, and was aligned with Calogero Bufalino in a competing Black Hand society.

In the business that led to the Black Hand bust and convictions, Lucchino himself had been dispatched to the Rizzo brothers to deliver several threatening letters demanding funds. The Rizzo testimony was that they followed the group to a meeting in the woods, listening in fear because the party was too large to take on themselves. They had overheard Lucchino at the meeting, boasting that he had thirty men under his control (by way of collecting tribute from them). Other voices in the crowd, according to the Rizzo testimony, suggested that thirty was not a number to brag about.

Following the gang's conviction, yearlong imprisonment, and eventual release, Sam Lucchino was courted in early 1909 to turn state's evidence by William Flynn, the Bulldog Detective and future chief of the United States Secret Service. Flynn may or not have had Sam at his advantage on a counterfeiting charge for exchanging bad money. Flynn himself does not allude to any such thing in his book detailing his prosecution of Ignazio "the Wolf" Lupo and Giuseppe "the Clutch Hand" Morello, which he titled *The Barrel Mystery*. Rather, he lauds Lucchino (whose name he misspells as "Locino") for his participation in the trial and convictions of Lupo, Morello, and other members of the Lupo-Morello gang on a counterfeiting charge in New York City.

The full text of Flynn's *The Barrel Mystery* was digitized by the Internet Archive in 2007 with funding from Microsoft and is available to read online. Flynn was bulldogging the Lupo-Morello gang in New York, the gang behind the Barrel Murder. A pawn ticket found in Luciano Perrino's pocket had led to the effects of the man in the barrel. Lupo and Morello were running a counterfeiting operation with another party named Cecala. Secret Service Agent Flynn had got wind that a Black Hander named Boscarini had been to Pittston and was willing to sell counterfeit two- and five-dollar bills into the city at thirty-five cents on the dollar. Flynn asked Sam Lucchino to procure samples from Boscarini by mail, which he agreed to do. The samples secured under strictest measures of traceable surveillance, Flynn pressed Lucchino to meet with Boscarini at Mulberry and Prince Streets in downtown New York City to buy a hundred dollars' worth of counterfeit currency using marked good money.

The exchange was made under the gaze of the Secret Service. Flynn eventually had what he needed to make a case. Now he needed Lucchino's testimony. Flynn writes about the process:

> *Locino was perfectly well aware what it meant to go on the witness stand and "squeal." He had heard of the man in the barrel. After some weeks of thinking the matter over, Locino loosened up and declared that he had an ancient wrong to right! He never explained to me further just what his grievance against the "Black Handers" was. He finally made up his mind to take the stand and tell what he knew.*

The aftermath of Lucchino's association with the United States Secret Service was that Boscarini was sentenced to fifteen years at a federal penitentiary in Atlanta, Georgia in 1909. Lupo and Morello went to trial with six associates in January 1910 and were sentenced to fifteen years' hard labor, handing their borgatas over to a string of successor bosses (see *The First Family* by Mike Dash for a comprehensive account). This was not going to sit well with elements in the city of Pittston that had aligned themselves with the Lupo-Morello gang and profited from counterfeiting. It was an association that would remain strong even in later years as the gang weathered the Joe Masseria, Lucky Luciano, Frank Costello and Vito Genovese reigns.

The course of Lucchino's life had taken a dangerous and irreversible turn. After helping the Secret Service convict the New York City associates of his own Black Hand family and neighbors, he would never again have their trust. He would continue to be married to the sister of a prominent Black Hander, one of the top-echelon members of the triumvirate Pittston family organization that would rule the coalfields of Pittston and the surrounding region. He was a resident of a street and a section and a city utterly under Black Hand control. In time, he would become a Pittston police detective.

Within a year of the Lupo-Morello sentencing, the first of several attempts on Lucchino's life was made in 1911. There would be at least three failed attempts over a decade before the last successful assault. They would all take place on Railroad Street.

CHAPTER 19

MURDER STREET

Murder Street. That's strictly the local and unofficial name for it. Railroad Street's black-eye nickname. For certain, the name is known to everyone of a certain age in South Pittston, even if they can't recount any of the spectacular murders that earned the street its grisly moniker. Railroad Street is just a long, three-block street from Main Street to the city line. It continues as Railroad Street into Pittston Township at the Brandy Patch, the clustered streets of miners' houses where the who's who of gangsters and racketeers took up their first residence on arrival in town. You may find Railroad Street in Pittston referenced as "machine-gun alley" in some sources. That name is old, too, and dates from the Prohibition years when Pittston itself was known as "Little Chicago" for the free-flowing liquor trade and its attendant George-Raft-movie-style machine-gun violence. In the 1960s a political campaign used the name "Pistol City" as a platform on which to offer change and revamp the overall image of the city from its rich history of dark deeds that made national attention.

Walter Winchell, the news-ticker radio host of the 1930s through the 1950s, once informed his twenty-million-strong audience of Mr. and Mrs. America and all the ships at sea that anyone who wanted to commit the perfect crime should go to Pittston, Pennsylvania. It wasn't so much the sheer *number* of murders in the city that contributed to the reputation Winchel reported. It was the sixty-plus *unsolved* murders that led to the quip. Quite often, murders like Perrino's and others, while they may have been solvable enough, were not followed up on or the identified killers could not be brought to conviction, even when authorities felt certain they had a strong case. Pittston being a company town, and the region itself coal-industry-dependent, made some wonder whether the murderers in many cases were simply too valuable to the company to be taken off the board.

It has been said that more money has been made from mining coal than was ever made mining gold. Whether that's true or not, Pittston rivaled any Old West mining outpost you can name in terms of sheer violence. While some of the miners and laborers were family people, a lot were young men looking to earn enough of a living to continue supporting the habits that drove them from card game to tippling house to brothel. There were legal drinking establishments by the dozen, and for every one of those, someone else was running a bar out of their home. And a card game.

Mining was a dangerous business. People literally died by the dozens, sometimes scores at a time in explosions, cave-ins, or through asphyxiation. With a bar for every roughly 160 or so people in town, a miner could forget his worries pretty quickly. All over town were shootings, stabbings, fistfights, gunfights, and mayhem of every sort. A gunshot murder at a bar on Tedrick Street (at the end of Railroad, at the Brandy Patch) was said to have been incited over the cost of a nickel beer. That says nothing of the labor unrest such as the mayhem prevalent in the region during the 1902 strike. It's possible that the name Murder Street dates back to the time before the Sicilians arrived, but if it was used before, the Sicilian wave of immigration following the 1902 strike would give the name a whole new meaning, starting with the murder of Frank Cullaro.

A culm bank is a stories-high hill of waste rock and slate or slag that had been hand-separated out from the mined coal in a coal breaker. The mound can reach over a hundred feet tall and become very broad at its base. Several mounds can combine into a local geography with navigable paths between hills. Before someone invented a gasification process that could recycle the waste rock, the area was dotted with, and still sports a few, culm banks. People still bike paths along the remaining culm banks today and use the trails through them as shortcuts, just the way the workers did on the morning of June 6, 1905, when John Swift, walking to work at a working portion of the old Fernwood colliery, found the body of Frank Cullaro at an abandoned part of the workings.

The body was found on June 6, 1905, in a shallow depression on the side of a culm bank in an area where Pittston, Cork Lane, and Browntown converged. The culm bank in question was in an abandoned section, even at that time, a closed-off part of the Butler complex known popularly as the Cork-and-Bottle. Lying next to the body was a .45 revolver. The pockets of his clean, semiformal traveling clothes contained incidental silver change amounting to two dollars and ten cents, a razor, a few pocketknives, some ammunition, and some cheap stogie cigars. The body was discovered about 400 feet from the sealed-off shaft of the Cork-and-Bottle mine. The best guess of the police first arriving on scene was that the head, which was nowhere to be seen, would be found in the mine shaft. Inspectors found the wooden structure protecting the shaft from entry was broken open in a few places, and the timbers showed signs of blood and strands of hair. The authorities looked for a volunteer to be lowered into the shaft to retrieve the head. Ferdinand Mecadon took the dare and earned twenty-five dollars for bringing the head up in a sack.

Cullaro's brother identified his body and provided the police with backstory. The murdered man had been a local for years operating a store at the top of Broad Street. He had recently moved to Rochester, New York, to open another business with his wife and two children. There, his wife Santo Cullaro met John Cacciatore, fell in love with him, and eloped, leaving her children behind with the father in Rochester. The murdered man packed up and sold off his store and returned to the area to leave his children with his mother-in-law in the nearby town of Luzerne while he searched for his wife. John Cullaro added one more detail. His brother traveled with his full worth on his person, which he estimated between $2,000 and $3,000. This led police to craft a circumstantial case and issue warrants against Cullaro's wife and Cacciatore.

Deputy Sherriff Vincent J. Masi followed the leads to the mother-in-law in Luzerne and came up with a competing theory. Cullaro had not traveled alone from Rochester. In his company was Ignazio Tuzzolino, whose several brothers resided in Pittston on Railroad Street. Tuzzolino had been present at dinner with the mother-in-law when particulars of money were discussed. He knew Cullaro had money on him. Cullaro left the house to return to Pittston to retrieve his luggage from storage at the train station and to ask his former neighbors in town for leads regarding Cacciatore. He may also have been seeking to enlist some help in subduing his rival. Tuzzolino stayed behind until evening in Luzerne. Then he announced he was heading back to Rochester.

The Tuzzolino brothers of Railroad Street were known to have operated a tippling house, or unlicensed drinking establishment. Joe Tuzzolino was reported to have been one of Santo Volpe's enforcers at the Pennsylvania Coal (PA Coal) Company workings. At least one other theory was considered: that Tuzzolino directed Cullaro to visit his brothers to enlist their aid, and the job of robbing and beheading was done in the basement of their Railroad Street house.

Masi did not find that Tuzzolino himself had visited his family while in town and presumed him to be in Rochester. He believed that Mrs. Cullaro and Cacciatore were in Rochester as well. He offered to pursue and capture for questioning one or all three on his own time if the county would cover the expense. The county had no desire to solve the matter. One official reported that the Luzerne County detective was already overworked and had no time to devote to the case. Although a Scranton newspaper put up funds to cover expenses, Deputy Sherriff Masi did not want to buck authority by pursuing the case without official sanction.

The county would have let it drop, but Masi *did* apparently travel to Rochester on June 15 to drag Tuzzolino back to Wilkes-Barre under arrest in the murder of Cullaro. This was much to the chagrin of Rochester authorities, who had not been consulted in the matter and who suggested that Masi was guilty of a felony in the conduct of what he considered his duty.

The *Wilkes-Barre Semi-Weekly Record* reported on June 16 that Tuzzolino (found here as Tuzzaloni, elsewhere as Trosselini and any number of other iterations) complied willingly with Masi in an effort to clear his name and provided a solid alibi for his whereabouts at the time of the murder. The case does not appear to have been solved.

The Cave Hole Mystery presents a second beheading whose details are confused with the above, though the two happened five years apart. The story of this murder illustrates the factions that existed between different Black Hand groups and generally explains the blood feud that would conclude with the deaths of two key members of the warring factions.

On June 2, 1910, Browntown residents James O'Donnell and John Connors followed a dog to the berm of a deep mine depression in the ground behind the Pittston Odd Fellows Cemetery. In the hole they saw what looked like a body covered over with branches. They summoned the police, who extracted the body using a leather harness. The head had been half sawed through, and the broken and chipped blade of a straight razor still protruded from the wound.

The murder victim was later identified as Peter Salvaggio, a resident of the nearby community of Luzerne.

Initial reports in the newspaper offered competing theoretical motives for the murder. The first was that Salvaggio had been the witness in the murder case of a friend who had been extorted by two brothers named Cacciatore. The brothers were presently in prison awaiting a grand jury verdict in the matter. The second theory was that a relative had followed him with murderous intent from Sicily after being released from prison for shooting Salvaggio in the arm some twelve years before. Neither of the leads would bear fruit. It's not clear that the killers were ever properly identified and punished. Before the matter finally died in the press, two identified Black Hand factions in Pittston, represented by Sam Lucchino (for the Strong Arm Society) and Charles Consagro (for the Iron Head Society), would take turns implicating each other for the act, setting the stage for bloody conflict down the line.

In March 1911, Salvaggio's widow took the stand to tell what she knew. In 1907, she and her husband Peter had been living in Bernice, over an hour from Pittston. Two men came to the house and summoned Peter to a meeting in the woods with a group of men who apparently tried to extort him. One of them shot at him, but he ran. The others fired as well, but he managed to get away. In a few days, one of the gang, Charlie Bertolino, came to the house and wanted Peter to go with him to Pittston. The man said he would pay his way for the hour trip. In Pittston, Bertolino took him drinking and then to a Polish cemetery, probably St. Casimir's, to meet with Sam Lucchino, Joe Sciandra, and Charles Montagna. Lucchino prevented his companions from shooting Peter at that time. It seems clear that Peter was hiding details of the encounters from his wife.

At around the end of 1909, Peter Salvaggio and his wife moved from Bernice to Luzerne, Pennsylvania, just eight or so miles south of Pittston. On a day in December 1909, David Bertolino told Peter's brother-in-law that he had beheaded their dog and planned to do the same to Peter. Peter seemed to have gained some antagonists after his move. He once told his wife that if he was ever killed, it would be by the two Bertolinos, Charlie Montagna, Tuzzolino, and Joe Sciandra. She had heard Luigi Randazzo threaten Peter herself, saying he would kill him if he did not receive the money Peter owed.

You might think that would have done it for the defendants, but in May 1911, Sam Lucchino, his brother Peter, and Steve La Torre were arrested and imprisoned and charged with the murder of Salvaggio. Lucchino himself had offered testimony implicating the Bertolino brothers and others in the case.

Charles Consagro and Angelo M., whose name has been too badly mangled by every journalist for a positive identification, had testified against Lucchino and friends. The newspaper article of the day pointed out that Consagro and Lucchino represented two warring Black Hand factions. The hatred between them existed for a number of reasons, the most personal and deepest felt probably based on the fact that Consagro himself and Angelo M. had both spent months in jail over the Salvaggio murder already. It was already in Consagro's mind to kill Lucchino out of concern that Lucchino's new habit of being an informer, as he was in the Lupo-Morello trial, would result in local convictions—even, perhaps, his own.

To complicate matters, it was at the very same hearing that Lucchino testified as to the events of the first two attempts on his life, which had just been carried out in the prior six months, and used the floor to implicate Angelo M. and his brother Ferdinand and Charles Consagro in that matter. It's not clear that the actual murderers of Peter Salvaggio were ever correctly identified or punished, but Lucchino's arrest would do him no harm. He would be a Pittston police detective before the year was out, thus Charles Consagro would realize his worst fears.

Each decade had its own list of murders: Park Clelland, Joseph Castellino, Paolo Guidice, Calogero Calamera, and many others. Mary Buff used to point out her window to the streetlamp at the corner and say that's where a Mr. Lynch jumped in fright at the sight of his own shadow one evening. Most of what the Railroad Street murders had in common were union matters and officially unsolved status. The police rounded people up well enough, but witnesses were hard to come by, and convictions even more so.

CHAPTER 20

THE SECOND DECADE: WINDFALLS AND GROWTH

The 1910s were a period of growth in multiple directions by the Bufalino Brothers in concert with Calogero Bufalino and the larger Pittston family. It was in this period that the big three Pittston family leaders would come into a huge revenue stream as coal contractors, and it was the decade that saw the Bufalino properties and legitimate enterprises, all satellites of Calogero, enter full flower.

By 1913, the Pennsylvania Coal Company was reporting a healthy profit on its coal operations. Its shafts, breakers, and other works were so numerous they were identified by company, type, and number in official documents, such as "PA Coal #14 Shaft." Profits were in the 30 percent range, despite the company's repeated whining that 90 percent of what came out of the ground was unusable rock, slate, or otherwise unburnable material. It's not clear why they chose to reinstitute a contract system allowing individual operators to run their works and employ their own gangs of miners and laborers. It is also unclear what criteria one would have to meet to be awarded such a contract. But it was a timely decision considering the tide of public opinion regarding the general condition of poverty endured by miners in every minority patch town and the many abuses of the industry which included the use and treatment of breaker boys in places like Pittston. Barely a year later in 1914, a tent colony of striking miners in Ludlow, Colorado, caught fire under withering machine gun fire of a local militia. The flames suffocated and burned two women and eleven children. Another child was killed directly by gunfire.

Public relations notwithstanding, PA Coal may simply have made a business decision to turn their corporate energies toward oil. Oil was just clearing the horizon for use in military applications and would eventually power trains and trucks and heat homes in place of coal. Under the new contract system, PA Coal paid the contractors a negotiated amount for the tonnage produced, and the contractors would pay their work gangs out of that. Increased mechanization made the work profitable. Union troubles and PR boondoggles would no longer be corporate's problem.

Among the first to receive a contract to operate a mine under his own authority as a contractor was Santo Volpe. Santo may already have been "a rock man" in his previous work for PA Coal. At least, he would be referred to as such in the 1920s. The rock man's job was to perform the work of blasting through the rock walls that separated the undulating coal and rock seams in order to expose the coal seams for miners and laborers to work. Santo would eventually become a major coal contractor, working thirty-plus contracts, a number second only to Luigi Pagnotti. Calogero Bufalino (who was himself a rock man with his own crews) and Steve La Torre were awarded mining contracts themselves in that decade.

Whether the contracts were awarded based on some recognition the men received for running the mine operations, or controlling striking workers, or filling the mines with ready laborers by sponsoring families to come to Pittston is not clear. Certainly, there were many other contracts awarded to people of other nationalities. Volpe, La Torre, and Calogero Bufalino shared a partnership of common cause. The contract system made them all rich men through legitimately conducting business. They might all have gone straight then and there but for the lucre that gambling and other vices continued to pull in and the opportunity that Prohibition would present in the coming decade.

In 1914, Russell Bufalino made his last inbound trip as a youth to the United States aboard the *SS Venezia* and in the company of his sister Giuseppa and her intended husband. They traveled in the company of an aunt. Russell's mother had passed in 1910, and that may have precipitated their return to Montedoro for another brief period of time. Later, authorities would reject Russell's Buffalo, New York, school records as fraudulent. Just in case, Russell had had local Pittston authorities also prepare a set of school records for him. These were kept for a long time in the attic of a woman who had been a secretary to a local school superintendent. Russell's defense chose the Buffalo records to present to authorities. It's possible that through this period, Russell stayed primarily with his uncle Calogero, as his ward. That would have put him in the near-daily company of accused and convicted Black Hand extortionists and the children of the ever-growing Bufalino family at the Bufalino Brothers Store. If that were not the case, Mary, who was born in 1908, would have been too young to remember Russell, much less report later that he "grew up here."

By 1911, mass immigration was just peaking when the Bufalino Hotel at 57 Railroad Street came into service for the new arrivals and regular transients who came to work the mines. At that time, the hotel was the second business in the family. It was owned by Calogero and run by Nicolo, my grandfather. The ground floor served as a sort of saloon. Salvatore owned the liquor license. It was a family concern, along with the butcher shop and deli on the far corner at number 53. By 1915, a dedicated saloon was constructed in a building immediately adjacent to the hotel at 57 Railroad Street.

When the new Bufalino Saloon opened in 1915, Salvatore moved the liquor license from the hotel at 57 to the Bufalino Saloon at 55 Railroad Street, and the hotel became Bufalino Hall. Connected by door to the saloon, Bufalino Hall would be used for every purpose from political meetings to receptions and even, for a while, as a showroom for the sale of phonograph machines. Last, in 1915, the new brick family house was begun at 47-49, which would house the soda bottling factory and a general store below.

It was in the latter half of this decade, 1918 plus or minus, that Salvatore's son William Eugene (Bill) Bufalino, my own father Angelo, and my granduncle Rosario's (Ross's) son Jimmy were born. They were among the last-born of Salvatore, Nicolo, and Ross. They were direct contemporaries in school, graduating in 1935.

While they were still infants at the time, Russell took his first job for John Montana as a taxi driver in Buffalo, New York. Nevertheless, through the 1920s Russell continued to be in Pittston and in the family's company on a regular basis. My father, William, and Jimmy all came to know Russell as well as they knew Calogero. They had and enjoyed continued, repeated contact with Russell most of their lives.

CHAPTER 21

NICOLO: BILL'S UNCLE

One of my father's favorite stories was the story of Franco Mellovatsu. It was told to him by my grandfather, Nicolo. As my grandfather related it, a friend of his was hiding from the authorities in our house, on the flat roof near the little coop on top, shielded from the street view by the parapet in front of the building. His meals were delivered to him via the roof access. When it came time to make a break for freedom, he came down from the rooftop perch and made for the Laurel Line train to leave town. He was stopped at the train by police, who asked his name.

"Franco Mellovatsu," the man said.

"Okay, Franco," said the officer. "You can go."

That's the part of the story where everybody laughs because the phrase *franco mellovatsu* in the Montedoresi dialect means "to the tell you the truth, I'm on the lam," or as my father would say in his more alliterative decomposition of the phrase: "To be frank, I'm flying to freedom."

It was a story staple the first-generation men liked to tell because it showed them being more clever than the "Menicana" authorities. I've heard the story any number of times from my father, and it's always the same. But when Yabo told the story to my brother Nick, he added detail to suggest that Franco was my grandfather, Nicolo.

In Yabo's version, my grandfather had done something rash in defense of one of the girls and was walking across the Water Street

Bridge on the way to Calogero's house in Wyoming, Pennsylvania, some three miles distant, near the state police barracks, to give him details and ask advice, since the action took place at one of Calogero's places of business.

When the police stopped him, he excitedly began to say: "To tell you the truth, I'm on the run. I [committed some act], and to be honest, I'd do it again, and you would, too, under the same circumstances." All of this he said in a fluent Montedoresi dialect, since he had little English.

So, they stopped him at the "Franco Mellovatsu" part and said, "Okay, Franco, you can go. But don't leave town."

My grandfather and the Bufalino Saloon bartender Charles Betrio were the first on the scene on February 9, 1916, when Paolo Guidice (a.k.a. Paul George) was shot to death on his way to work as he left his home at 57 Railroad Street. He was headed to PA Coal #6 but never made it past his back door. My grandfather had been awakened, he said, by two shots around 6:00 a.m. From the window of our living room, he could see the back door of the Bufalino Saloon just across the neighbor's yard. The shots had come from that direction. He collected the bartender to check out the saloon with him, and they discovered Guidice's body next door to the saloon, on the back porch of 57 Railroad Street. My grandfather phoned police from the saloon at 55 Railroad Street.

The police determined that the man had died nearly instantly from one or more shotgun blasts. A loaded .32-caliber Springfield revolver was found near the body. It seems a friend and coworker of his at PA Coal #6 had been murdered recently, and Paolo was on guard for his life. Authorities guessed based on the scene of the shooting that the shooters had been waiting concealed behind a small cook shanty at the property. It was, in their opinion, a Mafia hit.

Salvatore and Nicolo both testified at the inquest as to Guidice's last night, since he had spent it in the Bufalino Saloon in their company. Salvatore reported there had been no problem with Guidice, nor was there ever among Guidice and the eight or so other patrons present. The bar closed at 11:30 p.m. the night before, he said, and Guidice had left around 9:00 p.m. They provided the names of the other eight patrons at the bar to the police, but the expressed opinion at the inquest was that their testimony was otherwise not material. The case was unsolved. Someone might have noticed or mentioned that the address provided as being the victim's home was the Bufalino Hotel/Bufalino Hall at 57 Railroad Street. But that was never mentioned.

My father practically worshipped Papa Nick. He spent time with him, helping him with the chore of preparing the wine for sale at the Montedoro Society during its speakeasy days. Into the bathtub the wine keg was emptied . . . then in went water, sugar, and grain alcohol to stretch the product for sale to a clientele of social club guests that included, by that time, Irish as well as Italian patrons.

One day, as the sugar-sweet concoction was almost ready, my grandfather looked at my father and said in his broken English, "You see dot? I knock out alla dere teeth, I never t'row wunna punch."

Nicolo was not known for being a doting parent. My father's special attention may have been due to his runt status. The rest of Nicolo's children knew Nicolo more as a disciplinarian who was not overly demonstrative. My uncle Sam, his oldest boy, born 1912, was a physical prodigy and a live-wire athlete that Nicolo couldn't really tame to any degree. He was a wild kid known for being a great pitcher. He would play for the Scranton Red Sox and the Majors wanted him. At the same time, he played violin in a quartet on WBRE Radio during a stint with the Civilian Conservation Corps. In his youth, Sam was pretty wayward, spending the money for his violin lessons at the pool hall.

One day, Sam was walking up Market Street on the sneak when he should have been at lessons and walked straight into Nicolo coming the other way with a friend. He didn't know what to do, so he hailed him in a respectful manner, with the standard blessing: *"Si benedica."* Whenever Sam told the story later in life, he would recall that Nicolo, torn between maintaining his composure and killing Sam, merely grunted back at him "like a pig."

My granduncle Ross's son James told me how Nicolo tried to discourage Sam from playing baseball. Sam was literally that kid from *Bad News Bears* who drove his motorcycle onto the playing field to take his place at the mound. Walking around Pittston in the 1980s, forty-plus years after he'd left town, people would walk up to him on the street and say, "You're the pitcher." One day, Nicolo went to West Park to drag him home and saw how well he pitched and how people were reacting to him. "That's my boy," said Papa Nick to anyone who got near, and he never bothered him about baseball again. But there was never anything like love between them that Sam would acknowledge. Even the girls in the family said they respected Nicolo, but that was all.

Yabo, however, thought the world of Nicolo. It was Nicolo who taught Yabo woodcraft and hunting skills that Yabo exercised as often as he could his entire life. Yabo told stories of how fair Nicolo was to the traveling Roma who rented space and modern facilities of the store from the family every Thanksgiving at a price so reasonable that they left the premises clean and unmolested when finished out of respect for my grandfather.

Nicolo's own career path aside, his crowning achievement as a parent was that none of his own children would have a role in the Pittston family. They did not all go to college, my father being the business college associate degree exception, but they all worked in trades and ended up doing well. Long after the Bufalino Brothers split with Calogero, Nicolo passed in 1939. Any bad feeling aside among the first-generation men, Russell was among the family members that bore his pall.

CHAPTER 22

CALOGERO SHOOTS AND MISSES

Throughout the 1910s, Railroad Street continued to earn its reputation for murder and mayhem. Charles Consagro ranks high among the principals identified, arrested, and eventually tried and released in a series of murders. Authorities failed to convict Charles Consagro of the murder of Joseph Castellino in 1905, an attempt on Lucchino's life in 1911, and by 1917, the shooting murder of Charles Attardo.

The events of the Attardo shootings present the only specific reference to Calogero Bufalino's direct involvement in Consagro's business and offers a clear turning point in the professed relationship among the Bufalino Brothers or, at least, the relationship between Salvatore and Calogero Bufalino.

On November 11, 1917, Charles Attardo was talking to his brother Louis near the city line on Railroad, just feet from the spot where the first attempt on Sam Lucchino's life had taken place in 1911. Charles Attardo had been shot at and wounded in the past by Charles Consagro, but the latter was never brought to trial. On this night, he was just standing outside his house, talking with his brother Louis. Charles was shot and mortally wounded by someone wielding a shotgun. Falling to the ground, he told his brother, "Charles and Louis Consagro got me." Charles's later autopsy revealed eighteen holes in his body, which County Detective Connoly attributed to a .22-caliber revolver and not a shotgun as reported.

The younger Attardo ran after the shooters and identified them under the light of a streetlamp as Charles and Louis Consagro. The brothers were arrested by two county detectives, a police sergeant, and the chief of police and held over for arraignment the next day. Also arrested as material witnesses were Angelo and Ignazio Carruba, who had been visiting the Consagro brothers.

Challenged to recount the events of the night before at hearing, Louis Attardo faltered in identifying Consagro, perhaps owing to Consagro's fearsome reputation for violence and out of fear for his own life. A pair of women recounted seeing two men fleeing from the scene, which then tended to shift blame to the Carruba brothers. These brothers explained their presence at the Consagro house to see their sister marry Louis Consagro. They produced a marriage license to verify their story.

The Pittston police knew Consagro well for his many past involvements with them. And nobody wanted Consagro more than Detective Lucchino, who believed Consagro had set him up for murder in 1911. Police theorized that the murder of Attardo was committed out of revenge by the Consagros and that the Carrubas knew more about the crime than they would reveal. It was also thought that possibly they came to Pittston to aid in the crime. The mother of the murder victim was outraged. The family complained that all of the witnesses had not been heard from. The Attardo family insisted there was a romantic jealousy angle to the murder that had not been explored. But without the consistent testimony of a solid witness as to who pulled the trigger, the police had to let everyone go, then consoled the family by saying they could be rearrested upon the presentation of compelling new evidence.

Louis Attardo asked for police protection, which was granted. On the 21st of November, the Consagro brothers had their final hearing and were released. Louis Attardo accompanied Chief Newcomb and Detective Sam Lucchino to the train station to put the

Carruba brothers onto a train for Wilkes-Barre to connect to New York. Chief Newcomb was acquiring the tickets when, according to newspaper reports, "several of the Bufalinos and their friends approached." Calogero Bufalino offered cigars to the Carruba brothers. Louis Attardo, still impassioned over the murder of his brother, could not help but point out in front of the police that Calogero Bufalino was treating the Carrubas "pretty good." Calogero drew another cigar from his pocket. "No more than you," he said, offering the cigar to Louis. Louis told him where to stick it.

There followed an "exchange of words" in which Louis Attardo threatened to hit Calogero on his horns, making as he did the sign and proclaiming Calogero to be a *cornuto,* the cuckoo bird, a cuckold. It's the ultimate in throw-down language for an Italian. Calogero leaped at Attardo. Suddenly Calogero and Louis were all arms and legs over each other, exchanging threats and blows. Lucchino had to throw himself in between them. Chief Newcomb threw his own body into the mix. Attardo was warned that he was going to end up like his brother, a warning in Italian that Lucchino alone might have understood.

Two days later, on Friday, November 23, Louis Attardo was visiting his brother-in-law at Dominick's Store, on the ground floor of a street address you may by now remember: 57 Railroad Street. The Bufalino Hotel's ground floor was operating as Dominick's (a family surname) Store at the time. Calogero Bufalino, if he was not the titled owner, put up the money to purchase or erect both buildings. And this was Murder Street, after all. So it was dark, and Louis Attardo was not just on Murder Street but was in Calogero's building while Calogero was at the saloon next door. Calogero poked his head in the door of the store and angrily demanded: "Come out here, you spy!" Everybody in the store tried to prevent him, but Louis made for the door, followed by the storekeeper and an upstairs tenant, a Mrs. Licata.

Out in the street was another exchange of words between Calogero and Attardo. Mrs. Licata came through the door just as Calogero was pulling his gun. She managed to divert his attention just enough that the single shot he fired missed its mark, and he retreated back into the Bufalino Saloon next door. Louis Attardo took off running, "hatless" for the police station a little over a quarter-mile away.

By the time Chief Newcomb had been summoned, Salvatore had arrived to surrender "his nephew" Calogero. Attorney W. H. Gillespie, the former and future mayor of Pittston, was in their company. Six witnesses came to testify to the shooting, but not all were heard. As Attardo testified, a throng of supporters in the hallway shouted "Liar!" Calogero jumped to his feet to attack his accuser. The hearing continued when he was subdued. Justice Loftus offered bail of a thousand dollars. Salvatore provided surety for the bond, showing deeds to extensive property holdings on Railroad Street as proof of his ability to pay.

Ironically, Calogero certainly financed the construction of Salvatore's current residence and place of business at the general store and had probably financed others of the properties whose deeds Salvatore produced as surety. The police department objected to Calogero's release, fearing further violence. By that time, there was just one "strong faction" in South Pittston, and it was the Consagro/Bufalino faction. Police were concerned that the Attardo clan would rise to defend Louis and create a state of siege in the area not seen since the first attempt on Lucchino's life in April 1911.

That seemed to be the end of the Attardo affair. It may have been the beginning of something with further-reaching impact with respect to the professed relationship between Salvatore and Calogero Bufalino. Heretofore, in the early 1900s, the men had openly expressed, correctly or not, that they were brothers at times when, for example, the press reported on the bombing of the Bufalino Hotel in 1913. Now, in the hearing related to the Attardo affair, Salvatore dropped hint that Calogero was more his hotspur nephew.

Salvatore and Calogero could not have been more different. Salvatore cultivated an image as a community leader and a businessman, someone people could rely on to say and do the right things. He advocated for people before the authorities in English. He assisted many people in settling and finding jobs locally. He probably was a padrone, with a right to expect a tithe of earnings, but he was also someone who let out a little too much credit for his own good to his customers. He led community affairs and produced and engaged in pageants for feast days relevant to the Montedoro Sicilians in the south of Pittston. He created the Montedoro Society and reinstated the practice of the procession of the Blessed Mother, a homeland tradition. To put it concisely, he was a "big man" locally but renowned for fairness and not so much for criminality.

And then there was Calogero, the Caliban. His reputation as a "man who would stick a knife into you as soon as look at you" was well earned, and this instance with the young Attardo showed him, murderously angry and unchained, to be the antithesis of Salvatore. They were matter and antimatter, but they still needed each other. For a while yet, at least.

CHAPTER 23

VENDETTA

"It all started with the murder of Lucchino," my father said, pointing to the street corner at Railroad Street as he handed my mother another bag of groceries from the trunk of the car. I never heard the start or the end of that conversation. I was outbound to the car to pick up another load, so I never came to know what the "it" was that started with Lucchino's death. It might have been any one of the traumatic events that shaped my father's childhood, such as a spate of gangland murders including Lucchino's or the series of events that led to the ultimate breakup of the first five Bufalino relatives. But ultimately, the "it" was probably my father's early childhood. Lucchino's murder, fifty or so feet down the street, might have been among his first memories in life on the street the locals called Murder Street.

The first attempt on Lucchino's life occurred in January 1911, in a time frame closely following Lucchino's testimony in the New York trial that sent Lupo, Morello, and associates—the forerunners of the Genovese crime family—to extended prison terms for counterfeiting.

Lucchino and Consagro had personal history. Lucchino was himself the godfather of Consagro's son. Charles Consagro, for his part, was not feeling the love any longer between himself and Lucchino. Lucchino had obviously broken faith with his former associates by testifying against people in New York who were in business relationships with the Black Handers in Pittston. Consagro was convinced Lucchino's role as an informant would generalize and threaten the local gangs.

He was right.

By 1911, Consagro himself was under the microscope for the shooting death of Joseph Castellino some years before. The man who owned the handgun used in the shooting was on the spot to answer for the fact, so he was talking to the police about having loaned Consagro his gun. Further, he was sharing conversations he had with Consagro in front of the Bufalino Brothers Store in which Consagro clearly expressed intent to murder Lucchino for having turned state's evidence.

On a day in January 1911, a few months before Consagro's hearing in the shooting case, Lucchino was walking Railroad Street with Charles Consagro. Lucchino was on alert because Consagro seemed to be lengthening the conversation, pressing an argument to keep them walking and talking near the city line. That was when one or more assailants approached the two and shot Lucchino. One bullet caromed off his skull and another went straight through his neck. It felt, he said, like his shirt collar was on fire as he went down, bleeding, but he was fully conscious and would later report that he heard every word Consagro said as he lay on the pavement.

Lucchino survived the shooting, the bullet having just grazed him, missing the major arteries and his spine. After a very short convalescence, a period of months, he was scheduled to testify on a hearing related to his own shooting and on another matter. The other matter was related to another grisly cutthroat murder, whose supposed perpetrators, including Consagro, implicated Lucchino in the killing. Lucchino never had any doubt that Consagro was behind the attempt on his life. Consagro would later be convicted of conspiracy in the matter of Lucchino's shooting but nothing more.

Luigi Consagro (Charles's brother), Ferdinando Manero, and David Bertolino were convicted of felonious wounding in the shooting of Lucchino.

In the weeks before Luchhino's testimony in the above, a second attempt was made on his life. One evening, a relative appeared at his door, saying he had been followed to the house and that there were people lurking outside. Lucchino armed himself and returned outside with the relative. The relative was attacked and his coat sliced by a knife or razor wielded by someone dressed in women's clothing (that is to say, all black from head-to-toe, including a face covering. The oldest-order Sicilian women dressed as though in mourning). The assailants then gave up the attack and fled.

By the time of that second attack, Lucchino was still living in an area called the Brandy Patch, just over the township line from Pittston, three blocks up from Main Street. In the ten years following his testimony in New York, while employed as a detective by the Pittston police, he would move his residence three times. His last three addresses would place him in a house directly next to the Bufalino Brothers Store, then at a property directly across the street from it, and finally at a property two doors closer to Main Street (two doors downhill and across a street from the store but on the same side of Railroad Street).

It may look like he had a particular interest in the Bufalino family or perhaps the kind of men that made the store their gathering place. That's possible, but it's equally possible he wanted to be near to and keep eyes on Charles Consagro, whose own house was just catercorner to the Bufalino Brothers Store on the other side of Railroad Street and scarcely two doors farther up the street from Main. Lucchino had, as he reported to Secret Service Agent Flynn, "an ancient wrong to right" when he agreed to testify against the Lupo-Morello family. It's just possible that the wrong he referred to, the score he had to settle, was against Consagro.

The third attempt on Lucchino, following the pretrial assault at his house, happened in the overnight hours of July 7, 1915, during the construction phase of the Bufalino Brothers' final double-block brick property just next to Bufalino Brothers Store. The new brick building would house a general store, soda factory, and apartments above as living quarters for the family. Lucchino was living directly across the street from that property at that time and sleeping on the ground-floor level on the evening of the shooting, perhaps not to rouse his family. He was making a trip to Buffalo in the morning.

At 2:30 a.m., he awoke and turned on a lamp. A gunshot broke his window, but the bullet missed him. His assailant was behind a pallet of bricks outside the construction site across the street. At the first shot, a police officer named Munley started running from Main Street one block up Railroad Street toward the noise. Then followed an almost-comical exchange with the gunman, who fired a time or two more at the house, then ran up Railroad Street, away from Main, with the officer in chase. The gunman turned left at the first corner and made another left at the next corner with the officer still behind him.

At the next block, he turned left again and then left another time at the next block. Four left turns put him right back in front of Lucchino's house, where he stopped again to shoot a few more times at the house before Officer Munley appeared at the corner. Then he ran off again up Railroad Street. The young man, a Sciandra, was captured at length exiting the rear-facing window, as the newspaper reported, of "a property behind 55 Railroad Street." That is to say, the apartment above the Bufalino Saloon/Montedoro Society, two doors farther up Railroad from Main. Calogero's place.

In July 1920, Sam Lucchino was investigating Consagro's mine practices as workers for PA Coal began what would be a successful twelve-week strike against PA Coal and its contractors regarding the contract system. On July 21, 1920, at about 10:30 in the evening,

Sam Lucchino was just arriving home from work. He was shot from behind by an unknown assailant and succumbed to his wounds after a short time. Assisted to the hospital by police, he was reported to say that "strangers shot me" to officers variously described as Chief Tierney and others.

In other reports, I have heard it said that Lucchino implicated Consagro in the shooting, saying words to the effect: *I don't know who pulled the trigger, but they pulled it for Consagro.* Police suspected that the two men they arrested for the shooting following their investigation, Peter Enrico and Tony Puntariro, had been hired to do the job by a third party with funds amounting to $3,500 that had, in fact, come from Consagro.

Charles Consagro was implicated in a statement provided to police by Sabatina Rombolla. Rombolla said that Puntariro had told him Consagro put up $3,500 to pay the men to do the killing. Faced by Consagro at a hearing, Rombolla recanted his sworn statement and ended up serving time himself for perjury. Consagro walked free. Peter Enrico and Tony Puntariro were found guilty and sentenced to death by electrocution.

CHAPTER 24

DIG TWO GRAVES

Charles Consagro was a nearby neighbor and a friend of my grandfather, Nicolo Bufalino, and a close associate of Calogero Bufalino. They pretty clearly belonged to the same society, which Calogero headed. Consagro was a regular-enough visitor to the new house or the businesses of the Bufalino Brothers Store that my very young father knew him. At least, he knew him well enough to ask my grandfather, at the age of five or six, whatever happened to him.

My grandfather's association with Consagro dated back to before the Black Hand arrests of 1907 and probably went all the way to Montedoro. Charles Consagro was suspected but never convicted in relation to of a number of killings, including the shooting of Giuseppe Castellino, one of two decapitating murders in the city, and the shotgun slaying of Charles Attardo in 1917. Moreover, he was always, at least in Lucchino's mind, the principal suspect in three of the four attacks levied against him and was probably the financier, if not the author, of the last successful attack.

Peter Enrico and Tony Puntariro, the men accused of Lucchino's murder, were electrocuted in the Rockview Penitentiary in 1922. The two men were obviously despondent about their situation in prison and despairing of any help. When asked if they had any special request regarding the disposition of their bodies after their impending deaths, they responded that they had no family or friends. They simply didn't care.

Charles Consagro went missing sometime just before the executions of Peter Enrico and Tony Puntariro in 1922. His disappearance from Pittston was sudden, but he does seem to have left and traveled under his own power and brought with him money and effects to take up someplace else. Sightings of him were reported in Buffalo. At some point, clothing of his was found on the shores of Lake Erie, and after that, nothing. The police suspected that friends of Peter Enrico and Tony Puntariro were dissatisfied with the lackluster defense presented at their trial, a defense Consagro was to have funded.

At some point, my father asked his father Nicolo why Charles Consagro was not coming around anymore. My grandfather gave a most unusual response considering my father's very young age. My father was not quite four when Consagro went missing. It's unclear when he asked about him. Either Nicolo knew of Consagro's fate and wanted to conceal his knowledge, or he had a dream about Consagro after his disappearance, or maybe my father was walking the halls at night and my grandfather wanted to put a stop to that. Or possibly, he learned of Consagro's fate in just the supernatural way he said he did: "His ghost appeared to me in the landing at the top of the stairs to the street. He said: 'They killed me in Buffalo.'"

After my father related the story to me, I can report for certain that my own nightly trips down the hall grew fewer in number. I respect that staircase after dark to this day. Lucchino's murder and its aftermath were my father's first lesson in the mechanisms of assassination. By the time he reached age eighteen, he would have at least two more.

CHAPTER 25

THE BUFFALO CONNECTION

In the early 1900s, Buffalo, New York, had a large enough population of Montedoresi Sicilians to support its own Montedoro Society. It also had a club called the Pittston Club. Family ties, the Lehigh Valley Railroad, and business interests legitimate and otherwise connected the two cities. John Montana, considered by some to be a relative of Salvatore Bufalino, was for some time president of Buffalo's chapter of the Montedoro Society. John Montana was frequently present in Pittston for family events such as a testimonial dinner in 1926 for a Dr. Mantione, at Salvatore's son Charles Bufalino's prenuptial dinner in 1930, and doubtless other occasions.

Arrested in 1957 at Apalachin along with a who's who of America's organized crime figures, John Montana would tell the McClellan Committee he had been on his way to New York City and had a planned stop in Pittston at the time to check on a compressor he had left at Medico Industries in the Pittston area. Car troubles in the form of a faulty wiper blade and/or brake trouble in a pouring rain led him to Barbara's estate. He was looking for Russell, his own onetime employee, who worked for Joseph Barbara—on paper anyway—as a mechanic. The owner of a taxi company in Buffalo, Montana had given Russell his first job as a driver and mechanic for his fleet of cabs in a time very close to the beginning of Prohibition, which took effect on January 16, 1920.

While one of Russell's presumptive biographers has suggested Russell was raised in Buffalo, Russell's own successor, "Big Billy" D'Elia, has claimed, correctly, that Russell came up under his uncle Calogero Bufalino and was raised in the company of the Bufalino families in Pittston. Although Russell presented school records from Buffalo at a deportation hearing, the court itself was dubious based on their own research. In any case, with the number of trips he made in his youth between Pittston and Montedoro, it's hard to believe he had much formal education at all. So why was his first job for a taxi company owned by John Montana in Buffalo?

Buffalo, just across the Niagara River from Canada, was a hot spot for illegal liquor trafficking into the United States during Prohibition years, and was also known for illegal immigration across the Canadian border. Smuggling in good liquor from across the border was Stefano Magaddino's specialty. As most NASCAR fans know, stock car racing began as mechanics in the Prohibition era began souping up otherwise "stock" cars to evade police. Russell had just the right job as a mechanic, at just the right time, and all the right contacts to run good Canadian whiskey into the finer speakeasies in the coal region, which included one rumored to have been on the grounds of the Pennsylvania State Capitol in Harrisburg.

Residents of Pittston who rode with Russell as passengers or who hung around his Pittston garage said he was pretty crazy behind a wheel as a young man. Russell's job in Buffalo notwithstanding, he was as much a dual resident in his youth as he was in the 1960s, his time divided between upstate New York and Luzerne County, Pennsylvania.

In 1924, at age twenty-two, his driving style caught up with him when he wrecked a new Dodge sedan while traversing the very narrow two-lane Water Street Bridge in Pittston. He was trying to pass two trucks in a row on the short quarter-mile span of the bridge when a bus approached from the opposite direction. He skidded his car and crashed toward the sidewalk, wedging the car between two steel girders. The car was a total loss. Russell was helped out of the car and rushed to Pittston Hospital, bleeding profusely from a gash over his right eye; he also had a deep laceration on his forehead as well as a severed ear. The *Pittston Gazette* had an arrangement with an insurance company. They were selling insurance through the newspaper. Russell was reported by them to be the first beneficiary of their policy. He was awarded ten dollars a week during his convalescence. It's not clear that this accident was the genesis of his lazy eye. It was reported in the press that Russell was living in Pittston at 55 Railroad Street, which was the street address of the Bufalino Saloon/Montedoro Society, the building his uncle Calogero owned.

Whether Russell continued the trips between Buffalo or not after his accident is not clear. By 1928, he took up permanent residence in Luzerne County, in West Pittston across the river, with his new bride, Carrie Sciandra, a cousin of Giovanni "John" Sciandra. John Sciandra was already in town since 1921 and would be invited to run the Pittston family in the 1930s following a tumultuous set of events that placed Santo Volpe and Calogero Bufalino under scrutiny.

Sciandra's tenure lasted from 1933 to 1949. It was in this period that Russell's grooming for the larger role of head of the family would be completed.

CHAPTER 26

TO THE MATTRESSES

My father's memory of the explosion was that the family had been warned in advance. My grandfather advised his children to place mattresses against the windows to mitigate the usual expected blast damage, which often resulted in flying glass. He then posted himself in the narrow, darkened doorway street-side, shaded from the streetlamp on one side in the cramped, three-foot recessed walkway. He was armed with two pistols. He heard a car climbing the shallow hill from Main Street and noted how they cut the motor to coast past our house to the intended target just doors away. Seeing an individual leaving the car with a fused bomb, he started shooting, to the effect that the bomber dropped his package and ran back for the car as the motor kicked on, and it sped up the street.

The bomb fell short. The explosion shattered windows on both sides of the street and may have been the one that cracked the half-inch plate glass in the storefront of the soda factory in our ground-floor cellar. The concussion knocked my father out of his bed in the second-floor bedroom above the factory. "I came up cross-eyed," he would say, as the shock of either the blast or the fall tore a muscle in his eye that never would be surgically repaired. Instead, he would keep his two eyes straight and level by a steady application of will when he was awake. You could always tell later on how tired he was by whether his right eye was drifting toward his nose or not.

Oddly enough, this signature handicap probably advantaged him in feats requiring hand-eye coordination. He said he had been a third-service command Ping-Pong champion during World War II. It was easy enough to believe if you watched him take on all comers at La Torre's Rec in the postwar years. Playing with abandon, stripped naked to the waist, the old man was unstoppable. When the Chinese table tennis team participated in an exhibition match at the 1972 Olympics, my father exclaimed, "They stole my grip!" And there on the screen, the handles of their paddles pointed skyward and the paddles cupped against their palm, it seemed as though they had. The other thing his ocular handicap brought him was a profession. He studied under the world-famous Severo Antonelli on the GI Bill after World War II to become a professional photographer.

My father reported that the target of the blast had been Charles Consagro's house. It may have been, but the only official reporting regarding a bombing at that house was in 1918, the year my father was born. So either the bombing he reported was a second, undocumented occurrence at Consagro's house (which is unlikely) or instead an amalgam of the several documented bombings within a few dozen feet of the house on Railroad Street between 1913 and 1927. More likely, the bombing in question was the last one, at the Montedoro Society when he was nine years of age. There were bombings enough to choose from, after all.

There is no shortage of explosives in a mining camp. From even before the monthslong general strike in 1902 and onward, sticks of dynamite were wielded as weapons and instruments of terror by everyone from coal miners to garden-variety anarchists to militant members of the Industrial Workers of the World (IWW) union (popularly known as the Wobblies) and Black Hand extortionists. Extortionists blew up porches simply to terrify the victim into paying up. Other explosives were planted by other parties with more deadly intent.

Once a year in January, the Anthracite Heritage Foundation, in association with local historical societies and universities, holds a series of events at Northeast Pennsylvania venues concerning coal mining, union affairs, and organized crime as they shaped the Wyoming Valley of Pennsylvania in the twentieth century. One of the presenters in 2022 was a young scholar who made it his business to document the various explosions that peppered the region during the years of what Dr. Robert Wolensky has called the anthracite labor wars in a book he coauthored with Robert Hastie by the same title.

I attended the presentation with my friend and Pittston native Lou DeGrose. I took the opportunity to ask whether there was any one town—or street, for example—that experienced more than its share of bombings. The presenter did not pause to consult his presentation or view a data sheet. His answer was instant and unequivocal: "Yes. Railroad Street in Pittston." My street. Murder Street. Three blocks from Main to the city line at Tedrick saw more bombings than any other location in the five-county region. At least three of the bombings I know of took place within a hundred feet or so of the house, and a fourth some two hundred feet away toward Main. Two of the first three were targeted against Calogero (and as such, businesses in the family) by unknown parties and a third against Charles Consagro. I'll treat them in order of occurrence, but first, just a note about the lay of the street.

The properties and businesses in the Bufalino family covered one side of half of a city block of Railroad Street with numbered street addresses from 43 Railroad to 57 Railroad with just two skips, numbers 51 and 53—which represented a single property sandwiched in between the soda factory at number 49 and the Montedoro Society at number 55. Charles Consagro's house was not quite directly across from number 55. At that spot, at number 55, the road makes a shallow bend, like the inside angle of a boomerang.

Calogero Bufalino's properties at number 55 and number 57 and Salvatore's at number 47 are like the inside ends of the boomerang. Consagro's house was the inside apex of the angle. All of that is to say that the shock of any bomb set off at any of the three properties was likely to rebound and break windows at the other two just by simple reflection. At least, they always seemed to, starting in 1913 with the bombing of the Bufalino Hotel.

The Bufalino Hotel bombing at 57 Railroad Street is the first of four. It occurred in 1913, just three doors up the street on the same side. I learned about the bombing from an article in the *Pottsville Republican* (an hour distant on today's roads). The hotel had somehow escaped being mentioned in any of the family lore, but the story of the fire that took it down was recounted by Mary Buff as a fire that killed the arsonist who set the blaze during the Depression. The building's purpose was to lodge and otherwise accommodate with meals and drinks the incoming arrivals from Sicily prior to World War I.

The bombing occurred in the overnight hours of September 8, 1913. Neighbors reported hearing footfalls in the street beforehand. The charge that was placed on the stoop blew a hole into the first-floor barroom and subcellar of the property and knocked a man and child out of bed in the upper-story apartments above.

The newspaper accounts I read referred to Salvatore, Nicolo, and Calogero as the Bufalino Brothers and partners in the business. None of the men could account for a motive in the bombing. The newspaper postulated that the bombing may have been related to the Black Hand, since the Bufalino Brothers had been so instrumental in fighting the Black Hand during the 1907 trial six years before. The problems with their theory included an absence of threatening letters and the fact that Calogero served a year sentence for being a Black Hander himself.

By 1913, the Pittston family was moving into contract ownership of the mines. Calogero was among the several accused and/

or convicted Black Hand conspirators who became, in effect, mine owners through the contract system. It's possible the miners were trying to send a message.

The Bufalino Hotel was repurposed a number of times, perhaps after immigration settled down by 1914, to a store, a reception hall under the name of Bufalino Hall, and even, for a while, a showroom for the sale of Victrola record players. It later was used by the politically active family to mobilize support for candidates they favored and to host civic and private events and pageants for the large Montedoresi contingent that made up much of South Pittston.

The second of four bombings was at the house of Charles Consagro in 1918. Consagro, coal contractor and notorious Black Hander, was a friend and associate of Calogero Bufalino and my grandfather, Nicolo. He was our catercorner neighbor on Railroad Street, on the inside angle of the boomerang-like bend in the road.

Family members were sleeping in the rear rooms of the house at the time of the explosion and were thrown from their beds. The front porch was badly damaged and the windows in the front of the house were smashed. Several windows in the Bufalino home nearby were also broken by the concussion. The interior of the house was not damaged to any extent. Mr. Consagro told the police that two months before, he discovered seven sticks of dynamite that had been placed under his porch, which he turned over to the police after the explosion.

The time period of this bombing, April 29, 1918, was a few months after Consagro and his brother were acquitted in the murder of Charles Attardo. Consagro figured as the primary police suspect in a number of killings, including the first attempt on Sam Lucchino's life. Police had been concerned that there would be blowback among the Attardo and Consagro factions at the time, considering that Charles Attardo had been shot just the year before, with Consagro as the accused shooter.

It is also possible that unrest among miners over the contract system was the cause of the bombing. Following several other bombing attempts, one against the La Torre family, miners' belongings and lunch pails were subjected to search upon leaving mine premises, just in case.

The third of four on-street bombings was half a block away in 1923, down toward Main Street and just along the far side of the railroad trestle, whose superstructure is gone but whose footings still form the basis of walls that run perpendicular to Railroad Street. I learned of this bombing first from my own uncle and his traveling companion in the 1980s.

One Friday night at 2:00 a.m., I woke to a loud, persistent knock on the back porch door. I snapped on the light as I threw back the curtain, ready for anything. I wasn't expecting my uncle Sam Buff and his friend, Tony M. My uncle Sam painted houses. (With paint.) He was a wealthy painting contractor in California. By then, he was in his mid-seventies, as was his traveling companion. He and other relatives of his own beat generation would frequently visit Pittston whenever an excuse would justify a three-day one-way red-eye drive. He and Tony had come to visit relatives for what they estimated would be their last time. It was their Thelma and Louise tour.

Tony was pretty formidable-looking for an older man, stringy and tough with a big barrel chest thrust so far forward at his collarbone that it was a hair away from looking like a deformity. Together the men stayed in the two front rooms of my mother's apartment for most of two weeks as they traveled throughout the valley to visit relatives and friends from Wilkes-Barre to Scranton. One night, they sat around the kitchen table with my mother and myself. I tried to be entertaining and to engage them in conversation. I asked my uncle Sam why he left Pittston. Then I asked the same of Tony.

"Aw, I left some trouble back here," he said. It was a *How 'bout them Yankees, huh?* moment.

I took the cue and changed the subject. Nobody had to tell me there were bodies involved. My uncle Sam and Tony M. finished their stay and left after a few weeks. A year later in the *Sunday Dispatch*, my godfather Pidge Watson's newspaper, came a story under the headline "Tragic Events in Pittston's Past."

Members of the Lovullo family operated a butcher shop at 9 Railroad Street. It was separated by a narrow alley from the Laurel Line trestle, barely sixty feet up Railroad Street off Main Street. It was October 1923. A recent spate of terror bombings had erupted in the city with targets among and apart from coal contractors. The butcher had been receiving Black Hand letters demanding a payment of $2,000 lest he suffer the loss of his eyes and hands. He resisted. A charge blew the front off the butcher shop, above which slept the family.

The brother-in-law of the butcher enlisted his own son and armed him to stand watch in the gathering crowd for people who took unusual interest or seemed out of place. The brother-in-law had a shotgun. His son had a pistol. They were looking for the bombers who they expected might come to see their handiwork. They found them at the corner of Main, crowing that that's what happens when you ignore the threats from the Black Hand.

They attacked the men. The younger man may have shot a Mr. Martello, who fell through a store window and died at the scene. The uncle pursued his accomplice, Cataldo Cosentino, up the street and shot him at the doorstep of a funeral parlor. The man died days later in hospital.

Pittston Police Chief Leo Tierney arrived to take the Lovullos' brother-in-law into custody. A throng of residents followed to the police station to give witness in his favor. Whether the boy, a minor, was arrested at all is not clear. The *Wilkes-Barre Record* reported that the deaths might end the recent season of bombings in the city. A year or so later, the elder shooter was injured in a car accident approaching the city. He seems to have remained a free man. Pittston news reports completely redact the younger man and place two smoking guns squarely in the hands of his father. The boy, Tony M., my uncle's friend, ended up at length in Burbank. He was a minor, maybe thirteen, a direct contemporary and friend of my own uncle Sam.

The last of the four bombings nearest the house (there were many more than four altogether on the street) was at the Montedoro Society at 55 Railroad in March 1927. The explosion shattered windows at surrounding houses and blew the second-story porch completely off the building. The remnants of the porch supports, and for a while the second-story street-side door leading to the porch, were visible for years at the structure. The building belonged to Calogero Bufalino. Russell Bufalino had reported the address as his own at the time of his car crash in 1924. By 1928, it was rented to a widower and his four children. Tony Alongi lived with his children above the barroom on the ground floor, which was said to be closed at the time and not a speakeasy at all. Which it was, of course.

Calogero, as the building's owner, had enemies enough but reported for print that he was at a loss to understand who would want to hurt him or destroy his property. Alongi was employed at PA Coal #6 colliery for Santo Volpe, though it's not clear in what capacity, whether labor or management. Alongi and his children were thrown violently from their beds from the force of the blast. The charge was placed beneath a wooden pillar that was said to support a barred door ten feet wide. It tore a two-foot-wide hole in the concrete stoop at the front door and shredded the galvanized tin ceiling above the entranceway.

Charles Consagro was deceased by that time. The family living in his former house, almost directly across the street on the inside angle of the boomerang, took a beating for shattered windows, as did others on the street from the reverberation. Addresses at numbers 53, 52, and 56 Railroad all reported shattered windows.

There were many other bombings on our street and in the general vicinity. On a single July day in 1923, the homes of union stalwart Alexander Campbell and three other men had their porches blown off in actions probably related to an active strike over grievances at Santo Volpe's PA Coal #6 colliery.

CHAPTER 27

THE ODD DUCK

Angelo "Yabo" Bufalino was everything his wealthier and more successful brothers were not, which most of us would think a backhanded compliment. He was poor, but he had either surrendered to that or was content with it. There was a kind of Zen to Yabo. Everything he did was in the right here and now. In retirement in the late 1970s and early '80s, when his clan no longer had demands to put on him, and later when Russell was committed to prison, Yabo was free to follow his own nature. His love of the outdoors never left him. He fished. He hiked. He would disappear on a fishing trip for a few days and come back with tree branches to turn, after curing, into walking sticks or canes. He subscribed to *Chip Chats* magazine. Occasionally, he would carve animals out of wood using a special set of carving knives.

The trajectory of Yabo's life was strongly influenced by the clan system that dictated so many of the aspects of all the lives of the first-generation American children. Their fathers, Salvatore, Nicolo, Rosario, Calogero, and Angelo, were themselves the extension of their own Montedoro clan. Each of them had a certain role to fulfill to keep the family thriving. Salvatore was the brains. Calogero, the money man. Nicolo was the brawn, and he, Rosario, and Salvatore had cooperative roles operating the five family businesses as satellites of Calogero. If any of them had any personal ambition beyond the family, they suppressed it. Their children, to varying degrees by parent, also had roles to play in support of the greater family. The simplest roles were labor in support of a given operation: manning the deli, baking the cookies, taking care of the horses, delivering the goods. Some roles assigned to children were more demanding, such as accepting a marriage partner selected by the parent, sometimes at birth. This was a very common practice in Sicily and was followed in the United States somewhat less in time over succeeding generations.

As if the clan system itself did not present demands enough upon the Bufalino children of Yabo's generation, they also had to deal with the human resource needs of the organization of businessmen that were Calogero Bufalino's associates: Santo Volpe and Steve La Torre.

Santo Volpe, Steve La Torre and Calogero Bufalino, the leaders of the Pittston family, were the nexus of coal region power. By the 1920s, they were the owners of multiple mining contracts and were wealthy men on that account alone without considering the other ventures they pursued individually or as a group, which included bookmaking and gambling of every sort, as well as illegal liquor. They worked in common cause. The problem you had with one of the men was the problem you had with all three.

For each of these men, the old days where they themselves had charged picket lines to keep mines in operation were over. In short, they needed muscle they could trust, not just hire. Ironically, but not surprisingly, none of them wanted to commit their own children to the cause of strikebreaking. Anyone of college material in any of the families was off at college.

Several of Yabo's brothers studied law at length. Charles, born 1905, was the oldest and the presumptive future head of the clan. James had passed tests to enter the Naval Academy in 1928 but chose instead to pursue a medical degree. Charles, already in practice by that time, talked him into law school. Bill Buff wanted to become a priest. Eugene was a Navy man, restaurateur, boxing promoter, and later a union president. But Yabo's future was dictated by his size.

Yabo was big. Gangly in youth, but tall and athletic. There's a story of him jumping off the Water Street Bridge into the deep part of the Susquehanna in Pittston that's not at all hard to believe, given his nature. He was smart enough, and fearless, but not a real academic. Among his siblings in the family, Yabo endured ribbing. They told each other stories about Yabo that highlighted his simplicity. Their favorite Yabo story was "The Dive Without a Name." "We were all at the YMCA pool taking turns naming the dive we were about to perform. Yabo climbed up the high-dive ladder and poised himself and in grand fashion announced, 'The Dive Without a Name.' Then he hit the water in an enormous belly flop."

It was probably on direct account of his size that Yabo was placed in a kind of apprenticeship with my grandfather, his equal in size but more especially the one who could prepare Yabo for the role Calogero intended him to fill. My grandfather, Papa Nick, had been Calogero's direct business partner in a few ventures that required a big man to fill. He ran the Bufalino Hotel and tended bar at the Bufalino Saloon, which was at least once raided by the police, who confiscated a number of knives and firearms from some questionable characters. It was Papa Nick who fired at the men who bombed the Montedoro Society and who was released from police custody when the Rizzo brothers failed to identify him as one of their Black Hand assailants. Papa Nick was tough.

Yabo often spoke well of my grandfather, although many of his cousins among Nicolo's children were less kind about him. Nicolo basically terrorized his children into avoiding involvement in Calogero's dealings or the dealings of the men who were his associates. He did it without apology. All his children became either tradesmen or artisans like my father, who pursued photography. My uncle Sam, a wealthy painting contractor in California, could not say his own father's name without adding "that son of a bitch."

Nicolo took Yabo hunting small game, a role Yabo's own father could not fulfill due to his mining injury. He was also encouraged, as were all the boys, to fight and box. The hunting trips instilled in Yabo a lifelong love of the outdoors.

By the end of the 1920s, the five men of the Bufalino family contributed just two children to the task of keeping order at the mines: Yabo—Salvatore's son—and Russell, who had grown up in service to Calogero's business interests. Russell was slight by comparison. Yabo would be Russell's bodyguard and would reprise that role in his affairs with both Bill Bufalino and Jimmy Hoffa. Yabo would wear Hoffa's money belt in their travels to fix this or that union problem that could be fixed by graft. Here in the 1920s, he was working the PA Coal #6, acting as Russell's bodyguard and running the "electric mule" to raise and lower men and coal cars down the sloped shafts of the mine. He would be called to another role he clearly found distasteful.

On the extremely rare occasion, in the 1980s, when something bubbled up and he had to talk about it to somebody, he would lay it on me. So one day in the kitchen, he was talking about how he had to work to put his brother Charlie through law school, and uttered the somewhat cliché phrase of "You gotta do what you gotta do," using just those words. Then he exclaimed, "I used to work for Joe the Barber!"

For just a second, I thought of Yabo sweeping up hair. Then I realized, *Oh—Joseph Barbara—Apalachin!* I assumed Yabo worked for the man who would one day host the famous Apalachin meeting in bottling or trucking capacity out of his upstate New York Canada Dry business the way Russell had, or as a machinist, the way Yabo himself had for the Bufalino Brothers soda factory in his youth.

I was wrong.

CHAPTER 28

JOE THE BARBER

Joseph Barbara arrived in the coalfields as an ambitious local boy sometime in the 1920s, during Prohibition, the same time that saw John Alaimo return to Pittston from Buffalo. Joseph Barbara has been said to have been Santo Volpe's driver, a position of supreme trust. He clearly had a knack for violence. He had dealings in New York City. Trafficking in guns seems to have been his specialty. Police suspected Barbara and the rest of the Pittston family to be running any number of stills in the region. There were very few jobs someone working the coalfields in the 1920s could do for a man like Joseph Barbara. You could operate a still, build stills, and transport illegal whiskey or other contraband including weapons. Last, on the odd occasion when someone got in the way of any of the above or acted as a competitor, you did "what you had to do."

Joseph Barbara himself was never convicted of anything but was implicated in a number of murders in the coalfields and elsewhere. In August 1931, Barabara was the ringleader of a gang riding in what New York police described as a "bulletproof car," which they tailed and pulled over as part of a manhunt related to a shooting in Little Italy in the previous days that had killed a child. The occupants of the car were heavily armed. One of them reported to police they were driving to commit a murder. Barbara alone was held and the others let out on heavy bond.

Earlier that same year, Barbara had been arrested and released for lack of evidence in the murder of Calogero Calamera on Railroad Street. In 1933, Barbara was believed by police to have murdered Sam Wichner, a rival bootlegger who had stolen shipments of alcohol from Santo Volpe. Following an initial meeting with Barbara and Volpe, Wichner was directed by Joseph Barbara to report to Barbara's house the next evening. Perhaps Wichner was led to believe he would be cooperating with the family in some joint venture. He showed up at Joseph Barbara's house. There, Wichner was believed to have been beaten by Joseph Barbara personally, then tied and left in the back compartment of his own car, which was parked and abandoned on a Scranton street.

Santo Volpe appeared by invitation before the state police for questioning and denied any knowledge of the affair. Joseph Barbara and Angelo Polizzi were held and questioned. Since nobody on the street could identify the men who left the car Wichner was discovered in, the men were released, suffering only the loss of their right to carry a pistol. Although Wichner's wife reported that Sam had been summoned to meet with Joseph Barbara on the evening of his disappearance, there was no witness and no proof that any of the named men were involved in the murder.

The violence attributed to Joseph Barbara continued to mount through the 1930s. People have wrongly assumed that for some period of time that he "ran" the Pittston family, going so far as to report that he murdered the acting boss John Sciandra to assume control. Neither thing ever happened. Sciandra ran the show from around 1933 to the time of his natural death in 1949 and was succeeded by Russell with no questions asked. The Old Guard were "Mustache Petes," as Lucky Luciano would refer to the first-generation gangsters. Nobody unrelated by marriage would ever penetrate their world. And marriage was strictly by invitation.

Joseph Barbara later ended up in trouble in Endicott over the purchase of a large amount of sugar clearly intended to be used in a distilling process. Barbara survived all attempts to convict him and ended up a Canada Dry distributor in Endicott, New York. He would host the Apalachin conference in 1957.

Someone in Barbara's employ, as Yabo was, was in constant danger of being involved in some matter that could get him imprisoned or worse. Yabo did once offer that he had been briefly held in the county jail and then released, but I have no context as to what put him there. I personally doubt that Yabo ever killed anyone, but it's possible, given his work associates. In any case, the 1930s, and the time he spent with Joseph Barbara, broke him. Yabo was briefly institutionalized after suffering a nervous breakdown. It probably saved his life. It certainly altered his destiny for the better, which may have been the point.

After returning from the institution, Yabo could not continue his former role. He could still operate mining equipment, a role he later filled when Santo Volpe reopened PA Coal #6 in 1937. He was still bodyguard material based on his size and demeanor, and he was still fiercely loyal to Bill and the rest of his siblings. If the situation required it, Yabo was still a good brawler, and that role kept him close to Bill and put him in Jimmy Hoffa's sphere.

CHAPTER 29

THE APPRENTICE

By 1928, after his marriage to Carrie Sciandra, Russell Bufalino settled in West Pittston, which is its own borough across the Susquehanna River, a separate political entity, socially and economically distinct from Pittston. Russell began spending more time in the coalfields, acting as a proxy for his uncle Calogero in multiple different endeavors, including sports betting, bootlegging, counterfeiting, and the legitimate coal business. If the triumvirate powers of Santo Volpe, Calogero Bufalino, and Steve La Torre already had it in place that Russell would succeed them in running their combined interests, it was not immediately apparent. It's even possible that Russell's presence in the ranks drove wedges between the Bufalino Brothers and the power elite of the Pittston family.

Nobody wanted to volunteer their own son to participate in running the family businesses, legitimate or otherwise. But Russell was nobody's child, merely Calogero's fully grown nephew and former ward. The thing was, none of the Pittston family would trust anybody from outside their close-knit clan to run their business. The idea that Joseph Barbara would ever hold such a position would have been unthinkable to all three of them. But there was still time to sort that out. Russell was helping to run the store was all, and Montedoresi John Sciandra would be called on to run the store after a series of early 1930s events that made it clear to Santo Volpe and Calogero Bufalino that they needed to step out of the light for a while. Sciandra would run things as the most visible contractor and political fixer until 1949. Whatever Russell's relationship to Santo Volpe and Calogero was, he always held John Sciandra in the highest respect, and it may have been the sixteen years in Sciandra's tutelage that helped bring Russell into his own.

Russell was known from early on for a knack for jewelry, especially diamonds, which remained a big part of his career until the end. According to family sources, one of Russell's own very earliest jewel "heists" was perpetrated against a family member, and it soured relationships between Salvatore and Russell, putting additional pressure on Salvatore's satellite role to Calogero Bufalino.

Salvatore's daughter Pauline Bufalino married Charles Tulumello of Brooklyn, New York, on July 3, 1928. He was a plaster contractor in Brooklyn, and the two lived in Brooklyn together for a short while after their wedding. During that time, my cousin Angelo Tulumello was conceived. Somehow, Charles Tulumello had amassed a stash of jewelry. It was in the form of a treasure to him, and it seems he kept it in his home. Russell knew about it. It went missing. Whatever drove Charles to amass his personal treasure, the scope of which was never clearly stated, he deemed it irreplaceable. The loss of it, and the circumstances of Russell's involvement and family betrayal, played on him, exciting in him an underlying condition. He retreated into a state of schizophrenia from which he never recovered. I personally don't know that such a thing is possible, but that was the family narrative, and it hinged on the theft of the jewelry.

Charles Tulumello spent the rest of his life in an institution. Pauline was forced to return to her father Salvatore's household in Pittston with her infant son. Angelo Tulumello was the last of Salvatore's clan to be raised in Salvatore's household throughout the 1930s. Neither Pauline nor her son Angelo ever forgave Russell but rather held the affair against him all their lives. It was probably the same for Pauline's father Salvatore, who would pass in 1936. In any case, Salvatore harbored bad feelings for Russell over the matter. His relationship with Calogero Bufalino had also been in decline for some time.

Ironically, and possibly to Angelo Tulumello's later satisfaction had he thought about it, Russell's downfall would come out of a jewel heist of a kind, in which Jack Napoli used Russell's good name and credit to secure $25,000 in jewelry from a New York jeweler named Herbert Jacobs in the 1970s. That led to a cascade of ever more negative and threatening interactions between Russell and Napoli that were recorded on an FBI wire, and which eventually took Russell down.

Throughout the 1930s, after Volpe and Calogero stepped aside for Sciandra to take the reins, Russell probably took the place of his uncle in collecting patronage debts, running gambling, and shylocking, and the more day-to-day colliery work. It's probably during that time he assumed the nickname of "the Old Man," acting as he was as Calogero's proxy. It may or may not have been foreordained that Russell would inherit the operations at some later date, but at the time, the work needed doing, and he was there to do it. Like anyone in training, he was going to make mistakes and require the help of his associates and the guidance of superiors.

At a table in the Sixth Street flea market in Wyoming, Pennsylvania, in a little golden four-by-five picture frame, the booth owner had placed a newspaper clipped photo of Russell. I picked it up and showed it to him.

"Did you know him?" I asked.

"He was the boss," he said.

The old man seated in booth center didn't have to tell me he used to be a boxer. It was imprinted onto him so that you could almost tell by the way he sat in the chair. The fight game and sports betting were a big part of life for young men in Pittston in the World War II era. For some, as baseball and other sports had been and continue to be, it offered a means to rise out of poverty. But just for the few.

This boxer was Charlie S. He had trained in Steve La Torre's boxing ring upstairs from La Torre's original pool hall on Main Street in Pittston during the 1940s. He told me the story about how Russell had helped him and his friends out of a problem with a local bookie.

Charlie S. and a few friends pooled their money on a betting slip on which they made picks for an improbable number of games, a whole season's worth of games. By the end of the season, their every pick had come in, and by their own calculation, they should have expected to take in about a thousand dollars to split among themselves. When they approached the bookie who had taken their action, he reported that he had failed to put their slip in on time (presumably in time for the first game of the series), and that nullified their bet. He may have been willing to return their collected contributions, but that was all. Charlie went to Russell and explained the situation.

Illegal bookmaking and gambling of every sort was a huge part of the Pittston family's empire, and by this time, it seems that Russell was somewhat new to the role of overseer. The problem was that either by accident, negligence, or outright theft, this bookie had created a situation that could take money out of their pockets, especially if the story got around that someone had welched on a bet without recourse. People would lose faith in the process, maybe even stop betting. Something had to be done to restore faith in the process.

Charlie reported that Russell told his associates to kill the bookie in question. In Charlie's version of the story, Russell's men interceded on the man's behalf, suggesting instead that he be sent a message in some other way but otherwise be allowed to make good on the bet payoff. Apparently, the bookie was building a home or a cabin on the river north of West Pittston, out in the boonies. They burned it down and sent the message to make good with Charlie S. and friends. And he did.

I don't have so many stories about Russell in that period—certainly very few eyewitness accounts, as you might say. Oddly enough for this story, I think I have a corroborating-yet-opposing version of the same story from within the bookie's own family and perspective, one that also paints a picture of Russell as being someone new enough in his role to require oversight.

"My father was a diminutive man."

Joe S. sat across from me as we sipped beers in his Railroad Street residence sometime around 2020.

"They called him the Little Guy. He was a bookie for Santo Volpe."

One day, for reasons Joe did not know, Russell was said to have made the statement: "The Little Guy has to go."

Well, the Little Guy got wind of the situation. Possibly one of Russell's men told him. Making book was a friendly enough business if you acted in bounds. Possibly someone who knew him tipped him off that he needed to make an appeal.

"The Little Guy made one phone call," Joe continued, "and the word came down that the Little Guy did *not* have to go."

Joe, the Little Guy's son, thought it was great that his father had enough cred in the upper echelon of the organization that he could successfully appeal one of Russell's orders. He may simply have been lucky that Russell was in the prompt-and-fade portion of his training in the use of good judgment, learned oddly enough from people who themselves might have offed the Little Guy but for his good credit with them.

Apart from the problem with his father, Joe S. had no real beef against Russell, and the feeling was mutual. When he said he was getting married and wanted to get an engagement ring, Russell directed him to a jeweler in New York City who personally walked him through stone selection, ring selection, and mounting. As far as I recall, it was on the house. The jeweler, like anybody else to whom Russell referred a party, wanted that party to leave extra happy.

CHAPTER 30

THE FALLING-OUT

By the end of the 1920s, the clan structure and familial business relationships of the first-arrival Bufalino families—at least that part that connected Salvatore and Nicolo, the "Bufalino Brothers," to Calogero—fell apart. The breakup was possibly due to the troublesome nature of the relationship between Salvatore and his (by now) much more wealthy and powerful relation, Calogero. New immigration had all but ceased after World War I. Whatever service Salvatore was providing as a travel broker, hotelier, grocer and advocate for new arrivals was over. The padrone system was being starved out of existence. The Great Depression would be the death knell. Salvatore continued to extend credit to his immigrant charges, even as their ability to work came under increasing threat from work stoppages and decreased demand for anthracite coal. Even the big men were feeling the pinch, and relationships were strained to a breaking point.

The Pittston family of Santo Volpe, Steve La Torre, and Calogero Bufalino also suffered a split among its three principals. Calogero alone remained in league with Santo Volpe after Steve La Torre was shelved to follow his own business pursuits in mining and other businesses thereafter. He would be harassed and threatened for years but never harmed by his former associates. He outlived his antagonists, his former partners, by nearly a quarter century.

The extended Bufalino clan was also splitting up. You can trace the gradual change in relationships of the Bufalino Brothers and Calogero Bufalino in the press. Calogero, Russell's uncle and mentor, had from the first been the silent partner and financier behind several family businesses, most of which existed to support a growing Sicilian community. But slowly over time, the professed familial relationships between the men began to change. A few touchpoints tell the tale.

In the 1913 bombing of the Bufalino Hotel, newspaper reports suggested that the three Bufalino men—Calogero, Nicolo, and Salvatore, as shared owners of the bombed building—were brothers. The article credited all three brothers as having been instrumental in combating the Black Hand menace in 1907, despite the fact that Calogero had been imprisoned for his Black Hand activities during the 1907 trial.

In 1917, Calogero, in a fit of pique over a man he presumed to be a police informant, attempted to shoot an occupant of a store operating in the ground floor of the former Bufalino Hotel, just next door to the Bufalino Saloon. Salvatore was ordered to post bail for Calogero in the sum of a thousand dollars, which the magistrate believed he could afford due to the number of properties he owned as head of the Bufalino Brothers. At the hearing, Salvatore referred to Calogero as being his nephew, quite a demotion from brother. If the violence of the times and of Calogero's associates had not yet convinced Salvatore, a man with a reputation as a respected businessman, to make a final split with Calogero, the 1920s would cause him to rethink.

The rift between Salvatore and Calogero grew deeper. Salvatore continued his own trajectory as a locally respected businessman and advocate for new arrivals. But by the 1920s, the new arrivals had dropped off steeply. Salvatore's income stream was already in maintenance mode by the time he founded the Montedoro Society as a meeting ground and social center for the large Montedoro population of Pittston. It would also serve, via the many political meetings at Bufalino Hall, as a means to channel their votes in a favorable direction politically.

By the time the *Wilkes-Barre Record* published Salvatore's birthday announcement in 1926, Salvatore was already using the letter *T* from his mother Calogena Tulumello's maiden name as a middle surname. He became Salvatore Tulumello Bufalino, probably, to differentiate himself from Calogero. The Tulumello part is there on Salvatore's tombstone in Pittston. From Calogero's perspective, the feeling was mutual, and he would respond in kind.

The Tulumello name may have carried another meaning for Salvatore, one that imparted an air of regality and wisdom to its bearer. According to Salvatore's grandson, a doctor in chemistry, a scholar, and himself a Tulumello, the surname Tulumello derived from Ptolemy Soter, a general of Alexander the Great, whose descendants, ending with Cleopatra, had ruled Egypt. In any case, Montedoro had at least boasted a priest named Tulumello who had been a person of local fame and some fortune, and who was in the family lineage. A relationship to such a person would have imparted an aura of respectability to Salvatore that the Montedoresi would have recognized.

Calogero, equally eager to distance himself from Salvatore, dropped any pretense of relationship with Salvatore. He adopted the initial *D* from the surname of his mother, a Diminuco, to become Calogero Diminuco Bufalino. When he did so is not clear.

In the summer of 1931, Calogero's son, Angelo Charles Bufalino, having just returned from his freshman year of study in the College of Arts and Sciences at Cornell University, passed away from pneumonia. It was a tragic loss for Calogero and his wife. Calogero, a person of significant means and standing as a coal contractor, erected a mausoleum to receive his son's remains and probably captioned it with his son's initials: *A. C. Bufalino*. But that's not how it reads today.

Today, the inscription above the mausoleum reads: *A. Ɑ. Bufalino,* as though someone was directed to drop a line down the right side of the letter *C* to make it into a backward capital *D*. I'm not a linguist or an expert on language or character sets, but that's the best I can make of it, as the outcome of a grudge so deeply felt that it went beyond sense and beyond the grave.

Following the death of my grandfather Nicolo, my grandmother would make regular trips to Calogero's house by streetcar to pay on the mortgage of the family home, whose construction Calogero had financed. My brother made the final payoff trip with my mother and his grandmother when he was about five years old. He described the icy reception they met at Calogero's home some twenty years after the split.

As for the falling-out that eventually exploded the triumvirate rule of Volpe, La Torre, and Calogero Bufalino over the coalfields and beyond, it may have come about as a direct result of the Great Depression, when the ruined fortunes and financial burdens on the individuals made it impossible for them to ante up or otherwise take part in the operations of the group. Steve La Torre lost a substantial amount of money in the stock market crash.

The falling-out may also have resulted from the continued pressure each of the men felt toward the others in relation to their continued refusal to contribute children or other resources to the purpose of strikebreaking. Of course, none of the men wanted their own children involved in thuggery of that kind.

It's sometimes presumed, however, that the final nail in the coffin in the relationship among the three principals of the Pittston family was the financing, conduct, and outcomes of the Campbell and Reilly murders.

James R. Hoffa, president of the
ıational Brotherhood of Teamsters
BT), with his son James P. Hoffa.
*York World-Telegram & The Sun/
John Bottega.*

Hoffa's mug shot, 1939.

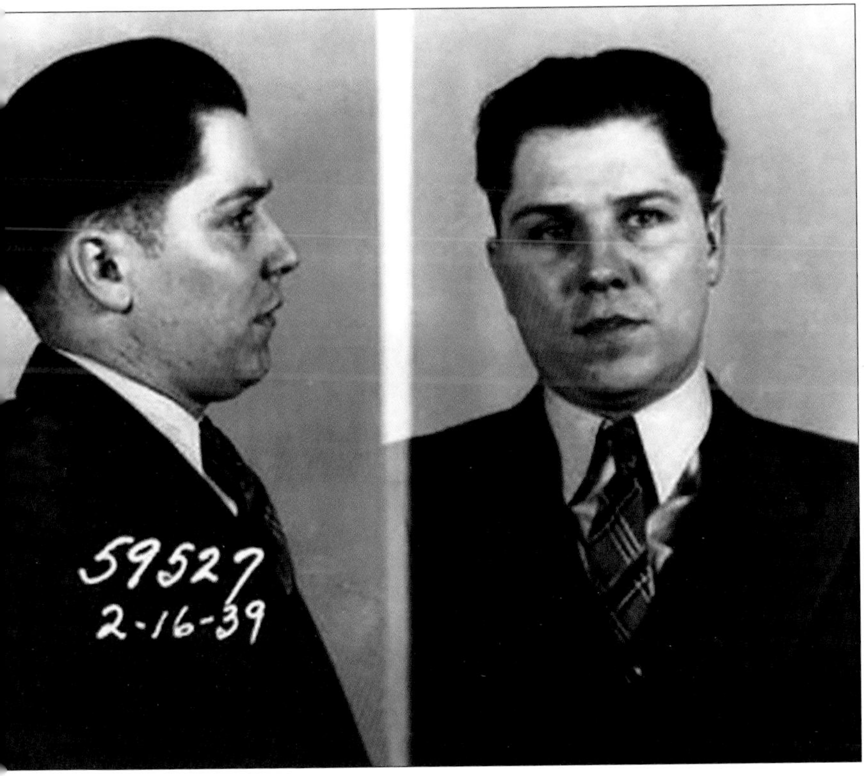

59527
2-16-39

Charles "Lucky" Luciano, born Salvatore Lucania, father of organized crime and boss of what would become the Genovese family in New York. 1931 mug shot.

Meyer Lansky, cofounder of the National Crime Syndicate, 1958. *Library of Congress. New York World-Telegram & Sun Collection.*

Frank Costello, Luciano's successor, testifying before the Kefauver Committee, 1951.

Vito Genovese became family boss after forcing Costello into retirement with a head-grazing bullet. He died in prison in Springfield, Missouri in 1969.

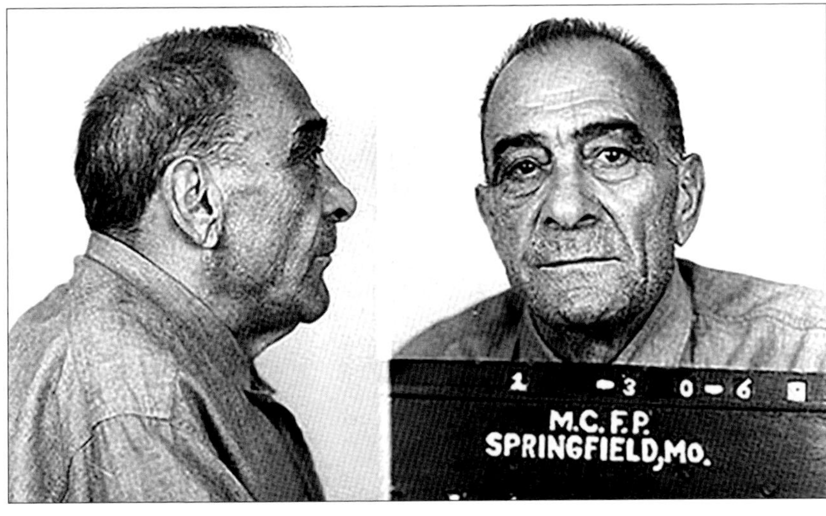

Joe Barbara, aka "Joe the Barber." He hosted the disastrous 1957 Apalachin meeting in upstate New York, which alerted the American public to the Mafia's nationwide existence.

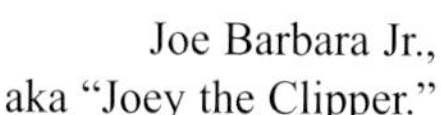

Joe Barbara Jr., aka "Joey the Clipper."

Joe Barbara's house, the site that struck the death knell for the Mafia.

Bill Bufalino, Jimmy Hoffa, and team.
J. B. Collins, Chattanooga News-Free Press.

Bill, Jimmy, and the newsboy.
J. B. Collins, Chattanooga News-Free Press.

Senators of the Senate Rackets Committee and committee counsel Robert F. Kennedy, during a hearing on an investigation into organized crime and jukeboxes, in the Senate Caucus Room, Russell Senate Office Building, Washington, DC, 1959. *Marion S. Trikosko.*

Attorney General Robert Kennedy testifying before a Senate subcommittee hearing on crime, 1963. *Warren K. Leffler.*

ving President John F. Kennedy's
ination, Jack Ruby, Dallas nightclub
, killed Lee Harvey Oswald on live
sion in 1963. Since then, numerous
iracies, accurate or otherwise, have
ated the Mob in JFK's shooting.

Theories abound that Sam Giancana, Santo Trafficante Jr., and Carlos Marcello, the Mob bosses of Chicago, Tampa, and New Orleans, coordinated to eliminate JFK.

The cover of a Teamster match pack features Bill Bufalino shaking hands with Martin Luther King Jr., c. 1965.

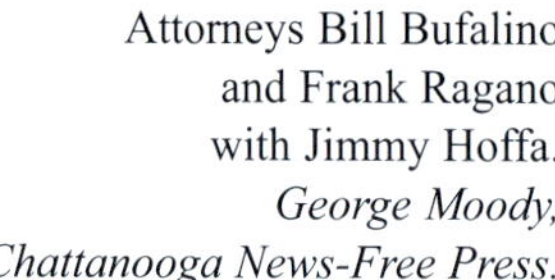

Attorneys Bill Bufalino and Frank Ragano with Jimmy Hoffa. *George Moody, Chattanooga News-Free Press.*

Postcard from boxer Tony Galento.

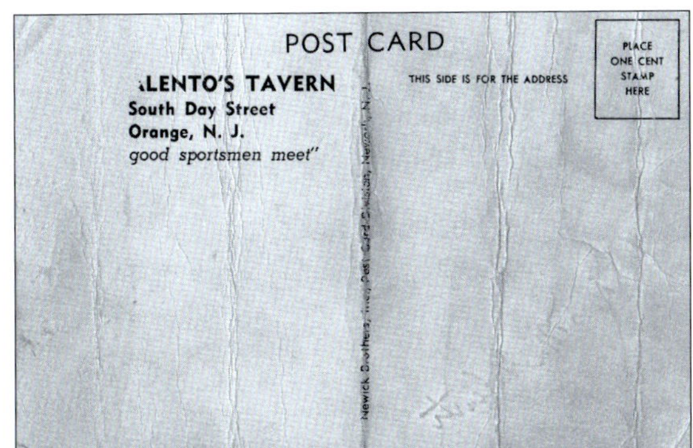

Angelo's musical idol, Nino Martini.
James Abresch.

"I went to see my godfather."
Al Martino meets with
Carrie and Russell, 1970s.
Bufalino Studio.

Rocky Marciano with author's brothers Salvatore (Sam) Bufalir (left), and Nick Bufalino (above) *Bufalino Studio.*

"Hey, Jack!" Angelo Bufalino at his photography studio, Pittston, Pennsylvania, c. 1960, where he stood to get JFK's attention at a motorcade.
Bufalino Studio.

lo and Nino Martini.
ino Studio.

Angelo and his wife Margaret.
Bufalino Studio.

Russell at a family functio
Giuseppina Bufalino (s
and g

Yabo Bufalino, 1984.
Bufalino Studio.

William "Big Billy" D'Elia,
Russell's chosen successor
as head of the Bufalino family.

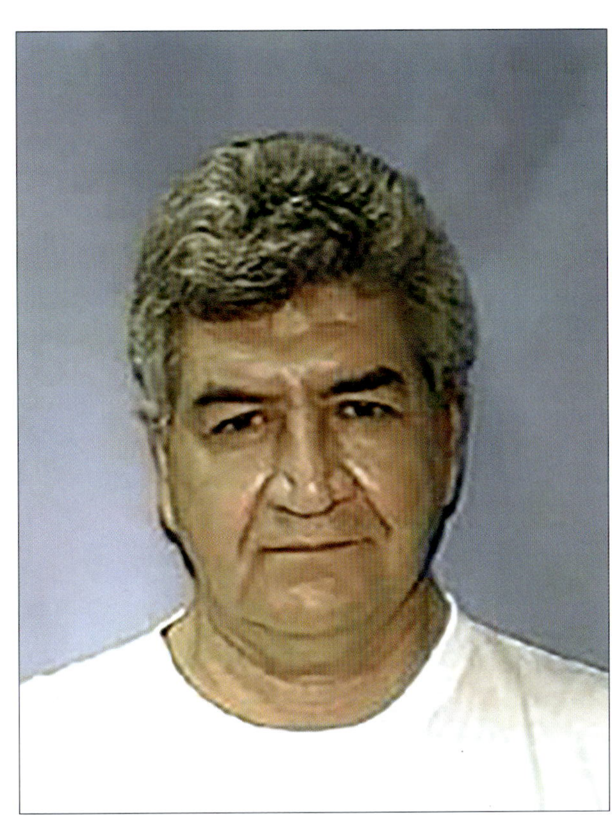

: Sheeran, "The Irishman,"
:onfessed to killing Hoffa.

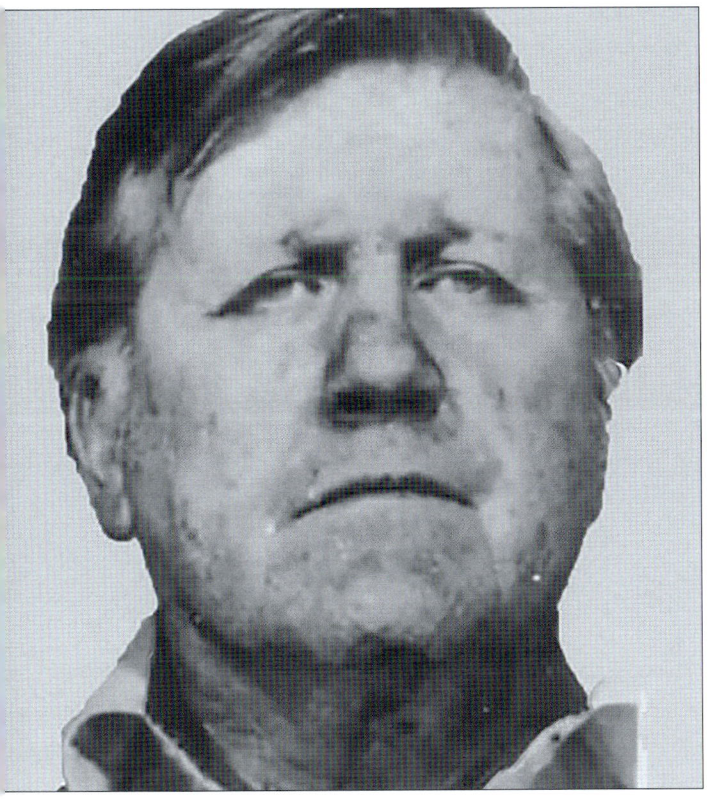

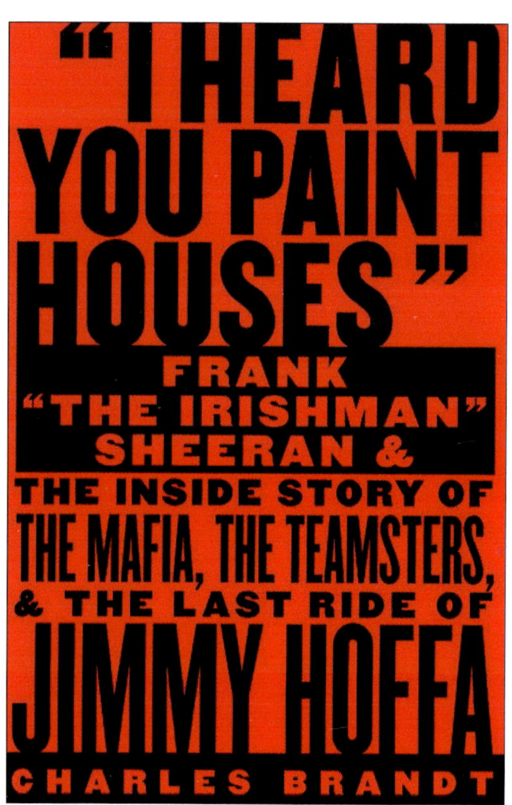

I Heard You Paint Houses by Charles Brandt, the first work to highlight Russell Bufalino's stature in organized crime. Also notable for Frank Sheeran's confession of executing the Hoffa hit. Some, including William D'Elia, have disputed Sheeran's claim.

The Irishman movie poster, Russell Bufalino, Frank Sh and Jimmy Hoffa are de from left to

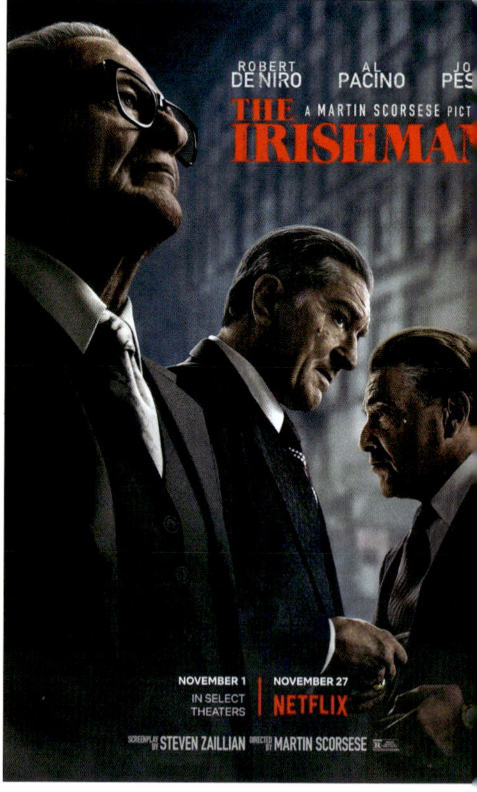

The Quiet Don by Matt Birkbeck, the first full-length biography of Russell Bufalino, but not an inside story from within the family.

fe We Chose by Matt Birkbeck
f "Big Billy" D'Elia's life
Pittston Mob.

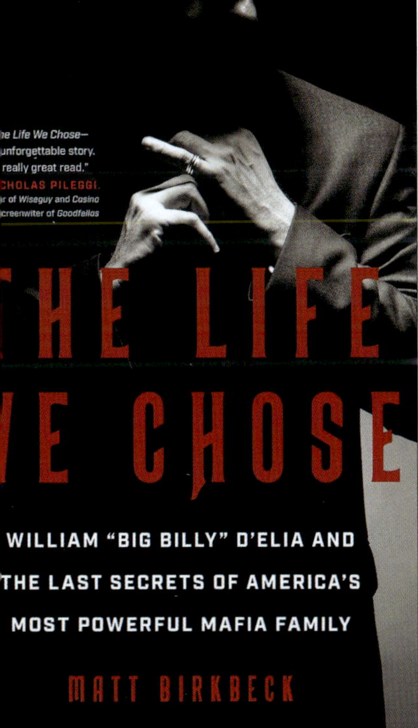

Margaret and Angelo Bufalino, author's mother and father. *Bufalino Studio.*

Charles Bufalino, author and caretaker of the Bufalino estate. *Mo Devlin Photography.*

CHAPTER 31

THE CAMPBELL AND REILLY MURDERS

The big hand came down a second time across my father's mouth.

"What did you see?" asked my grandfather.

"But, Pa, I saw it!" my father repeated.

With the third strike, my father was tasting blood. Light was dawning on Marblehead. He considered his answer carefully.

"Pa, I didn't see nothing."

My father was ten years old. What he hadn't seen were the two cars that sped by him as he bounced a ball against the front of the house. The muzzles of shotguns protruded from the windows of the trailing car. Rigged to fire multiple rounds, the rapid fire of the repeating shotguns sounded like machine guns. He ran behind to see the outcome of the chase: the two dead men in the lead car as it rested against a telephone pole hardly a block up the street. My grandfather's instruction to my father on that day may have been brutal, but it was effective.

The spectacular murder made front-page news and resulted in pleas by Pittston Mayor Gillespie to UMWA officials and the state to help settle the unrest in the coalfields. Nevertheless, my father never for the remainder of his life knew the occupants of the car by name or the issue that brought about their demise. Although the public knew well enough the players behind the event, and the authors of the shooting, they remained silent. Nobody spoke about the Campbell and Reilly murders. It's an all-but-forgotten piece of local history.

The United Mine Workers of America (UMWA) had organized the coalfields of Northeast Pennsylvania by the 1920s, entering into contracts with the contractors in the persons of Santo Volpe, Steve La Torre, and Calogero Bufalino. Among the union rank and file, however, the UMWA was not seen as strong enough to take action when the membership felt it was called for. Worse, the men believed there was collusion between the ownership and the union.

In "wildcat" strikes through the early 1920s, the members of an individual local walked out or away from worksites on their own authority, without union sanction, when, for example, a Volpe crew of rock men were observed to be leaving a mine with coal in their car. These actions by the men put extra pressure on Rinaldo Cappellini, District 1 UMWA president, whose job it was to honor and enforce among his men the terms of the various local contracts. The men became militant. Anarchy bombings became a problem, requiring mine owners to search the lunch pails of miners exiting worksites for sticks of dynamite.

It was in this period that Consagro's house was bombed, across the street from our house, and former Black Hander-turned-detective Lucchino was murdered. The men of Local 1703 turned to an insurgent element within the UMWA to represent them against the weak District 1 UMWA leadership and its suspected collusion with the Volpe/La Torre/Bufalino organization.

Alexander Campbell worked the PA Coal #6 colliery, a Santo Volpe property, and was an activist for the insurgent movement within the UMWA. He had been elected by the rank and file under the terms of the contract to the post of weighman at PA Coal #6 colliery in Pittston. It was a transitional time. In former times, the weighman's job was to estimate, by dead reckoning, the amount of rock-versus-coal that any individual car being weighed contained. This was by way of setting the wage for the crew that extracted the coal. There's a lot of room in there for a weighman sympathetic to the company to shave money off the top for his employer. It was typical of the anthracite mining industry to maintain that no less than 90 percent of what came out of the ground was useless material.

Mechanization of mine workings more than doubled the output of a crew's work. However, the subcontractor or crew contractor received compensation for tonnage of coal, while the mine workers in the union were paid like salaried workers. The rank and file felt they were being cheated on the one hand and rendered unemployed by mechanization on the other under this new system. Conflict was brewing.

The insurgent union members held out for the older weighman system, the old way of determining the miners' wages. Alexander Campbell does seem to have acted in the role of weighman for some time at PA Coal #6. During his tenure, in opposition to Cappellini, he was elected as a member of the International Board of District No. 1 (the parent district of his local 1703 UMWA), of which Cappellini was president. It's unclear if a single event precipitated the action or if he just tired of butting heads with Campbell, but Santo Volpe closed down his works at the #6 in the Christmas season of 1927, placing even my grandfather out of work. PA Coal #6 would not reopen for another ten years.

Volpe's action in closing PA Coal #6 precipitated a grievance against Volpe Coal by Local 1703. In late February 1928, members of Local 1703, led by the progressive president Samuel Bonita, met with Rinaldo Cappellini, the District 1 president, and his personal bodyguard and union organizer, Frank Agati, at the UMWA offices in Wilkes-Barre. Frank Agati was reported to be both a union official and partner with one or more of the major contractors, Volpe and/or La Torre. Clear conflicts of interest like that were common throughout the labor history of Northeastern Pennsylvania at the time and persisted until the last gasp of the deep-mine industry in 1959.

The meeting was heated. Agati was aggressive. He struck Bonita in the face. Both men pulled guns. Bonita won the exchange of fire, and Agati was killed in what most considered an act of self-defense on Bonita's part. Agati's funeral was well-attended. Bonita was arrested and imprisoned for voluntary manslaughter. The union took up a collection for his defense. The stage was set for bitter reprisals against the insurgent forces within the UMWA.

Just two days after the shooting, grievance committee member Sam Grecio was assaulted in front of his wife and shot in the head by two would-be assassins who succeeded in fracturing his skull. He identified the men, who were not tracked down, and warned Campbell to watch out, because he would be next.

On February 28, 1928, returning from a visit to the imprisoned Bonita in Campbell's car, Alexander Campbell and Peter Reilly, Local 1703 secretary, turned off Pittston's Main Street onto Railroad Street toward Campbell's home just two blocks away. They never arrived. As they passed under the Laurel Line railroad trestle, a new Peerless sedan pulled out behind them and raced to pull abreast as three assassins emptied specially modified shotguns into their car, killing the driver and passenger of the lead vehicle.

My ten-year-old father's memory of the scene was especially grisly. Campbell's car came to rest against a telephone pole. The newspaper reported the men inside to be "horribly dead" from multiple ghastly wounds. The driver of the shooter's car may have administered a coup de grâce, according to some witnesses, before speeding off. The murderers' car proceeded up the street to the edge of town, but their progress was soon halted by a slow-moving freight train. The killers made for the woods on foot. They got away but were later identified, and eventually captured. Everyone understood by now that the killers were merely acting as agents of somebody else, and they didn't have to strain their imagination too far to guess who that was.

The *Labor Defender* published an eight-page folder outlining the grievances that led to the murders and the grisly aftermath and reprisal killings. Titled "Smash the Frameup Against the Anthracite Miners," it advocated for the release of Bonita and his associates on the grievance committee, Steve Mendola and Adam Moleski, also charged in the shooting of Agati. People understood the issues. Union problems at PA Coal #6 had been producing a regular stream of dead men since before the race riot of 1906. The Campbell and Reilly murders incited Pittston Mayor Gillespie to request help from the National Guard to restore order to the coalfields. UMWA District 1 president Rinaldo Cappellini was strangely silent. Violence would continue through the 1930s among the insurgency, the UMWA, and the coal operators, but the lost battle over this grievance may have been the insurgency's high-water mark. All that was left was for the brutal economic conditions of the Great Depression, one last bombing or two, and America's eventual participation in World War II to quiet the dissent among the mine workers for fear of the loss of their livelihood.

Stylistically, the Campbell and Reilly murder has never been surpassed locally for its brazenness, its use of specially modified weapons, the sheer shock it imparted on the witnesses, and the fact that it sent Pittston's mayor begging larger authorities to police the coalfields to restore order. It was the last, brutal assertion of total control over the workings at PA Coal #6.

Everybody knew who called for the action against Campbell and Reilly. Anybody familiar with Joseph Barbara and familiar with his later résumé of weapons-transport and the use of armored cars loaded with a gang of shooters would see his stamp all over the

Campbell and Reilly murders. If that's not enough, it would later become clear that the driver of the murder vehicle, Paul Duca, was a gangster who specialized in erecting distilling equipment for the local bootleggers, including Barbara, whose own house sported a working still.

It may have been the over-the-top nature of the reprisals against Campbell and Reilly and others in the UMWA insurgency that broke up the long-standing association among Santo Volpe, Steve La Torre, and Calogero Bufalino as the principals of the Pittston family. Steve La Torre may have failed to ante up his expected share in an expression, perhaps, of dissent. Other rumors suggest that the assassins were never paid their due from a collected till of money that was somehow redirected.

Whatever the reason, by the onset of the 1930s, the Bufalino Brothers and Calogero were on the outs, and the Pittston family had shelved one of its own, leaving Santo Volpe and Calogero Bufalino in leadership positions. But there was one bit of leftover family business to attend to before things fell completely apart.

CHAPTER 32

WEDDINGS IN THE FAMILY

Salvatore Bufalino's firstborn, his son Charles (born 1905), married Santo Volpe's daughter Gaetana on April 23, 1930. Charles had recently graduated from law school, passed the bar exam, and was accepted into the Luzerne County Bar Association. Whether the relationship between Charles and Gaetana developed romantically or by arrangement is not clear. It was not unusual for men in close partnership to commit to each other a child to intermarry and either combine family interests or satisfy family obligations. Salvatore's daughter Mary had refused such an arrangement herself and remained unmarried and committed to her siblings and their families throughout her life.

Santo Volpe's daughter Gaetana's wedding to Charles Bufalino was a lavish and widely celebrated affair. It was full of pre- and post-nuptial testimonial dinners and receptions, stateside and in Montedoro, that were attended by influential political figures and members of the local bar.

On the evening before the wedding a hundred people attended a reception at the Century Club in Pittston that was a kind of testimonial to Charles as an able addition to the Luzerne County Bar Association. The celebration was complete with a toastmaster, entertainment, and an orchestra. Pittston Mayor Ambrose Langan extolled Charles Bufalino's many virtues in an impromptu speech.

On the wedding day, Santo Volpe sponsored simultaneous receptions and festivities in Pittston and in the communal birthplace of Montedoro, Sicily. While the marriage was taking place in Pittston, a Mass was sung in Montedoro. Volpe further put on a feast for some 3,000 Montedoro inhabitants that day and of course celebrated a lavish reception locally.

On their return from a West Coast honeymoon, Charles and Gaetana were again feted at Wilkes-Barre's posh Hotel Sterling. The dinner was said to be hosted by a committee of their Pittston friends as a mark of respect and goodwill. A number of prominent guests addressed the crowd, including Marquis Cesare Grimaldi (fresh from Mussolini's private guard), District Attorney Thomas M. Lewis, John Montana of Buffalo (who was later to testify about his role at Apalachin), and Luzerne County Judge Clarence D. Coughlin.

Santo Volpe had three other daughters marry in the same high-society fashion as Gaetana. The year 1938 saw twin betrothals, announced in the same newspaper article. Stephanie Volpe worked at the West Side Bank, in which her father was a partner, as a bookkeeper. Stephanie married Anthony Agati, presumed by many to be the son of Santo's former business partner and United Mine Workers Union recruiter Frank Agati, whose shooting death precipitated the Campbell and Reilly assassinations. Anthony Agati was just graduating The Wharton School of the University of Pennsylvania with a degree in accounting. Angela Volpe married Ettore Agolino.

A decade later, in 1949, Alfonsina Volpe married a Saraceno from Endicott, New York. Her flower girl was Angela Barbara, likely Joseph Barbara's daughter. A Toni Meli, possibly Angelo Meli's own daughter (Antoinette) and cousin to Bill's wife Marie Antoinette, served as a bridesmaid for Angela Volpe.

CHAPTER 33

THE FIRST BIG CASE

On the evening of January 4, 1931, Calogero Calamera, having just returned from a two-year trip to Montedoro, was making the rounds of friends and acquaintances on Railroad Street. He had lived in Pittston since 1903 and worked as a miner, eventually joining and becoming influential in the United Mine Workers Union. When Alexander Campbell and Peter Reilly were gunned down on Railroad Street in February 1928 and several others were wounded in related actions, Calamera thought it best to leave the country for a while. He returned to his wife in Montedoro and stayed for two years. While there, he had an argument with a traveling companion over the insurgent faction of the United Mine Workers Union. His companion was said to have threatened him.

Calamera returned to the United States at the end of December 1930. He was looking for work opportunities and inquiring among his friends about possible work at one of Santo Volpe's contract mine operations. He dined at the home of Frank Licata and then visited the Bufalino household, probably Salvatore's, to inquire about work. Leaving from there, he walked up Railroad Street toward the township line. He was followed by two men who hailed him as they drew nearer. He recognized one of the men, Gaetano Morello, as someone he had known for years. The men shot him between five and eight times and left him in the street, then continued on their way toward Albert West Park, two blocks away, where police suspected they had a car waiting. They found a .38-caliber handgun with five spent shells at the entrance to the park.

Calogero Calamera staggered to my granduncle Ross's house, groaning, *"Ayuto!"* My cousin James helped him in and called the police, who arrived in numbers to scour the neighborhood. Calamera made it to Pittston Hospital, where he was given a grim prognosis by the attending physician, who told him he had just hours to live. He was urged to identify the men who shot him. He identified Morello as the main shooter but could or did not identify the other party. Calamera then offered that his shooting had been the result of a dispute between himself, Santo Volpe, Volpe's brother Sam, and Calogero Bufalino. His statement was recorded and signed by the authorities present and hospital staff as witnesses.

The local paper said that police initially arrested two men said to have been brothers. It's likely one of the men was Morello, who did have brothers, but ultimately, he alone would stand trial for the murder of Calamera. When Pennsylvania State Trooper Benfante arrested Morello and brought him back to his lodging on Frothingham Street (a block and a half from Albert West Park) the boarding boss informed the trooper in front of Morello that Morello had returned there about 8:30 on the night of the shooting and informed him that Calamera had been murdered.

Morello had an interesting alibi for his whereabouts at the time of the murder. He was, he said, on a bus from Old Forge to Pittston at the time of the shooting. He was returning home from work. His work? He had been tending a still, an alcohol distillery, at the height of Prohibition in the Austin Heights, Old Forge home of Joseph Barbara.

Police decided on a hunch to arrest the likeliest second man they could think of: Joseph Barbara. Barbara's more conspicuous arrests and likely crimes were still ahead of him, but he was already believed by police to be a bootlegger and a known associate of Santo Volpe. Ultimately, police had no evidence linking Barbara to the murder and were forced to release him.

Morello's legal team consisted of attorney Frank L. Pinola and the fledgling attorney Charles Bufalino, who was Salvatore Bufalino's son and, by now, Santo Volpe's son-in-law. District Attorney Thomas M. Lewis had spoken at the banquet sponsored by friends of Charles Bufalino and his new wife at the Hotel Sterling the previous year. Attorney Pinola, for the defense, had been the toastmaster at the same banquet in honor of Bufalino. Possibly to avoid any appearance of conflict of interest, the state's case was prosecuted by Assistant District Attorney D. O. Coughlin, who was nearing the end of his term in the position at the time the trial began with jury selection on March 30, 1931. Benjamin Jones was the judge.

The defense team, Pinola and Bufalino, stated at the outset that they would prove Morello had been on an inbound bus from Old Forge, some five miles closer to Scranton, at the time of the murder. The prosecution had a list of thirty witnesses who would testify. The defense had a near-matching number. It's not likely they all got to speak, given the brevity of the trial.

The witnesses the defense could muster on the "riding the bus defense" included Calogero Bufalino and Joseph Barbara. Calogero Bufalino said he had been walking on Main Street with a group of his associates when they saw Morello depart the bus from Old Forge on the evening of the shooting. Joseph Barbara and a woman said to be his wife (he married two years later in 1933) both testified that Morello had in fact been working at their illegal distillery at Barbara's home that evening.

The prosecution had the witness statement from the murdered man that named Morello as the shooter, which was transcribed at the hospital and signed by the attending physician and staff as witnesses. In addition, to counter the "riding the bus defense," they presented the bus driver on the Old Forge bus line who had been working that evening. He could not place Morello as having been aboard his bus that evening. It's not clear that they presented the state trooper's testimony concerning the boarding boss's statement of Morello's knowledge of the murder.

The trial lasted just two days. The jury deliberated for eight hours. They took the word of Calogero Bufalino and Joseph Barbara over that of the only eyewitness account as expressed in his dying testimony. Morello was acquitted of Calamera's murder. Santo Volpe's new son-in-law, attorney Charles Bufalino, had prevailed in his trial by fire.

CHAPTER 34

SANTO VOLPE STEPS ASIDE

Santo Volpe was at a crossroads in 1933. For almost thirty years, he had been the unquestioned leader and front man of the Pittston family. He probably assumed the role early on when his principal partners, Calogero Bufalino and Steve La Torre, spent a year each in prison for the raid on the Rizzo home following the Black Hand trial of 1907. There was no shoot-'em-up involved in the transition of power. Relationships among the Montedoresi were close, with intermarriages frequent. In that first decade, all three men were working dayside in some capacity related to mining for the Pennsylvania Coal Company. Nights were for freelance business.

For all his fearsome reputation, Santo's name does not appear as a principal actor in any of the many instances of mayhem that earned the Black Hand gang a year in jail or that earned Railroad Street in Pittston its fearsome nickname. He has been incorrectly reported to have been arrested in relation to the Rizzo brothers' home attack and to be present at the Black Hand trial, but that does not seem to be the case. The Salvatore Volpe on trial, who was acquitted, was likely his brother, Sam. Granted, the coal miners had many a justified beef against the Volpe Coal Company. Some miners lost their lives, especially union organizers or activists involved in some dispute with a Volpe property such as the infamous PA Coal #6. In so many cases, however, such as the murder of Paolo Guidice and the precursor shooting of his friend that prompted him to buy a gun for self-defense, the shooter involved was never identified nor was a motive discovered that would lead to Santo.

The increase in union activism in the 1920s, including the insurgent United Mine Workers Union challenge to District 1 leadership, resulted in more direct, personal, and wildly unrestrained responses from the coal operators. The timing of the challenges to the Pittston family's business practices related to their legitimate coal contracts coincided directly with Prohibition. It was the Prohibition years that earned Pittston the name "Little Chicago" for the violence related to traffic in illegal liquor.

Joseph Barbara had arrived in the coalfields as an ambitious and ruthless bootlegger who is said to have become Volpe's own driver. There's no doubt that he became an enforcer, and his hand in silencing corporate enemies is evident in the increasingly spectacular nature and number of the killings of which he was accused but never convicted. Many of the deceased had one unlucky number in common: the number six, as in PA Coal #6.

Joseph Barbara was never tied to the spectacular, movie-style moving-car slaying of Campbell and Reilly, but his hand is all over it. The hit car, the Peerless sedan, was paid for in cash on the day of or before the deed by its driver, Paul Duca, who himself was related to the bootlegging profession as a builder of illegal stills for people like Barbara and Volpe. The heavily modified weapons used in the shooting smacked of Joseph Barbara's expertise in handling and trafficking weapons.

Most of all, although nobody would mention Santo Volpe's name directly, everybody from the man on the street up knew that the stunning daytime murders were directly related to the death of Frank Agati (who was a Pittston family partner and, ironically, a union official) and had everything to do with a union grievance over the closure of PA Coal #6, which was Santo's property. There were precursor shootings to Campbell, organized hits, and they, too, pointed to union matters. If there was any doubt about any of that, the full-page ad taken out by the insurgency within the UMWA pretty much laid it all out for the public, minus, of course, direct name references to any of the three principals in the Pittston family. Even so, the Campbell and Reilly murders of February 1928 were just the start of Santo's early retirement plans.

The murder of Calogero Calamera in 1931 presented a case where the dying man's sworn affidavit named Calogero Bufalino, Sam Volpe, and Santo Volpe as the actors behind his shooting and further identified his assassin. The defense of the shooter required a full-bore family effort to provide alibis and a defense. Calogero Bufalino testified he met the shooter exiting the Old Forge bus at the time of the murder. Joseph Barbara testified the shooter had been working at his house on his illegal still. Santo's new son-in-law Charles Bufalino was the defense attorney in consultation with attorney Frank L. Pinola. They won that case, against damning evidence, but the very next year, Santo ended up associated with a crime in person, and in 1933, his name came up again in relation to a bootlegging murder supposed to have been another Joseph Barbara hit. But first, in 1932, came the John Bazzano murder.

On July 29, 1932, three of the five Volpe brothers, Pittsburgh bootleggers, were killed in an unsanctioned hit at a headquarters they shared with John Bazzano. John Bazzano was a Pittsburgh gangster involved in bootlegging. His headquarters was a coffee shop in downtown Pittsburgh. He had been involved in a partnership with the five Volpe brothers but feared their growing influence and is considered to have ordered their murder. Three gunmen entered his coffee shop at around lunch hour, killing Arthur and James Volpe inside and shooting John Volpe several times in the back on the street out front. This took place in the earliest days of Lucky Luciano's brainchild, The Commission, which had oversight and approval authority over interfamily murders of this kind. The Commission had not been consulted in the matter.

Someone complained to Lucky Luciano. Various reports suggest that the complaint originated either with the surviving two Volpe brothers or with the Pittston family's Santo Volpe. John Bazzano was summoned to the city to account for his actions. On August 6, his body was found stuffed in a burlap sack in Brooklyn. He had been strangled and then stabbed multiple times with an ice pick.

By August 18, police rounded up a party of eighteen men and women they had been following for weeks in relation to the murder. Four were released, including both women. Police suspected that the eighteen had intended to attend a party to celebrate Bazzano's murder, at which the killer would be paid. The fourteen who remained in police custody were prosperous-looking people who claimed to be in the restaurant or grocery business. One of the fourteen, who were held without bail pending a hearing, was Santo Volpe.

According to the Wilkes-Barre *Times Leader*, Santo Volpe originally told police he was a relative of the murdered Volpe brothers, who, incidentally, claimed royal Italian blood. It was only after returning home that he recanted that statement, insisting that he had only met just one of the brothers on a boat inbound from Europe years before. Albert Anastasia was considered a suspect in the Bazzano murder. The case was never solved, but there again was Santo Volpe's name in the newspaper. It would appear again soon.

On February 17, 1933, Scranton police were summoned to an address on Meridian Avenue because of a report of a car that had been parked there all day. Lifting the cover of the rear section of the car, police discovered the body of Sam Wichner, bound with sash cord. He had been beaten severely about the head and was unconscious when he was hogtied with rope around his chest and legs so that he would strangle himself if he awoke and tried to get free. The two men who had been last in his company were questioned and later released. They reported to have seen him last the evening of the murder at about 8:30 p.m., at which time he got in his car and left for Scranton.

Wichner had been a small-time bootlegger who was believed to have hijacked a shipment of whiskey belonging to Santo Volpe. He was summoned to a meeting with Volpe, Angelo Polizzi, and Joseph Barbara. They must have led him to believe they wanted him in on some cooperative venture; otherwise, there's no explaining why he would agree to visit Joseph Barbara the next evening at Barbara's Old Forge home at 9:30 p.m. He was found the next day.

Joseph Barbara and Angelo Polizzi were arrested after police interviewed Wichner's wife and learned about his recent meeting. Volpe was interviewed by the state police at their request, without being placed under arrest. He admitted to knowing Wichner and having seen him months before but denied any knowledge of the meeting or how Wichner died. Unable to secure eyewitness identification as to the man or men who drove Wichner's car to Scranton, authorities released Polizzi and Barbara, though both men lost their gun permits due to having been involved in a murder investigation.

1933 would end with Joseph Barbara married and moving to his new wife's home territory of Endicott, New York. He would be suspected of the murder of Pittston native "Colorado Joe" Morreale the following year in Broom County. With Joseph Barbara, the hits just kept coming. He continued to be affiliated with the Pittston family to some extent. It's been a long time since I read an article that suggested Barbara may have been one of two companions of Calogero Bufalino who deboarded a train in San Francisco only to be immediately arrested on suspicion of suspicion and placed back on an outbound train a few hours later. When Santo Volpe's youngest daughter married in 1949, Charles Bufalino Jr. was the ring bearer, and Angela Barbara of Endicott, Joseph Barbara's daughter, was the flower girl.

In the same year, 1933, Santo Volpe made a conscious decision to step aside as the point man for the Pittston family. It may have been difficult for him to let go of the power, but it may have become apparent that if he remained, he would likely come to be associated with some event or other that might cost him everything. He had a lot to lose: money from legitimate businesses and others, power, and wide political influence. He chose to keep those things and step out of the family limelight. Steve La Torre was already out of the picture due to the mass falling-out of the late 1920s. Calogero Bufalino did not have the proper disposition to court influential politicians the way Santo had. Moreover, had he been asked, he would likely have declined the post. That left Giovanni "John" Sciandra.

John Sciandra was as much on the down-low as Russell in terms of not being a wildly public figure. He was from a Buffalo family but had migrated (probably back) to the coalfields of Northeastern Pennsylvania in 1921, where he worked belowground, eventually contracting and ultimately succumbing to black lung disease. His cousin Carrie became Russell's wife in 1928. He became a mine contractor in his own right in 1935. John kept watch on the family from 1933 until his death in 1949.

Prohibition ended in December 1933. Bootleggers still continued to produce hard liquor because the government-issue hooch came laden with taxes that consumers would just as soon avoid, but the gunslinging heyday was mostly over.

Under John's tenure, labor issues subsided, more likely due to the hardships presented by the Great Depression than any other factor besides the usual fear of reprisal. People needed work more than they needed better working conditions. World War II made mining a patriotic duty since anthracite coal was considered a strategic resource. Still, demand was depressed, and the families of miners in Northeastern Pennsylvania were hurting.

It was in the 1930s that New York clothing manufacturers, businessmen, and/or gangsters, looking for a cheaper labor pool, less-stringent safety standards, and to escape the International Ladies' Garment Workers Union, began to set up shops throughout the area. Albert Anastasia of Murder, Inc., himself had dress factories in Hazleton. Calogero Bufalino and his daughter Dolly (Emanuella) were also factory owners, along with Russell.

Coal mine labor quieted down, but by 1944, with the arrival of Min Matheson, the Pittston family was testing its former union-busting strategies against the International Ladies Garment Workers Union (ILGWU) and adapting to a whole different and—of necessity, since these were women—less-violent way of dealing with labor issues.

A new order was coming into being. Russell was in the last phase of his education under John Sciandra, and before the decade of the 1940s ended, Russell would be talking to Jimmy Hoffa and preparing to come into his own.

CHAPTER 35

DIASPORA

The closing years of the 1930s saw the deaths of two of the Bufalino Brothers: Salvatore Bufalino, who passed at home in 1936 of pneumonia, and my grandfather Nicolo, who passed in 1939 following an operation. "Russell" was listed by first name only among the pallbearers at Nicolo's funeral. Before the great falling-out in the late 1920s, the first five Bufalino families had acted as a closely coordinated clan, sharing each other's business, trials, and triumphs. The first-generation American children in *all* cases remained close with their own siblings and cousins in much the same way as their parents of the first generation had.

It was not until after World War II, when the family members at war returned, gas rationing subsided, and the economy started to pick up that anyone made any significant or life-altering changes in locale. When they did all begin to move, in true clan fashion, they did so together, almost in caravan.

Nicolo's family, my uncles and aunts—Pauline, Caroline, Mary, and Charles—moved west to California in the 1940s following the lead of their eldest brother, Sam Bufalino. The husbands among them were generally union tradesmen and readily found work. Sam worked as a painter before he became a paint contractor. They mostly settled in or near Burbank. My own family joined them all for a time in the 1950s. My father found work at Paramount Studios as a union photographer and later ran someone else's photography business, but he was unsettled in California and rankled under his brother Sam's head-of-the-family status. He moved back to the homestead in Pittston in the mid- to late 1950s to open his own photography studio.

Like my uncle Sam, my father was a member of the beat generation. Gas was cheap, people were mobile, and cross-country road trips were on the menu. We crossed the country at least three times—possibly four—by car to attend weddings and family gatherings at Sam's or Pauline's home. I got to meet all the cousins, including Pauline and Bucky's children, Joe and Nick Micelli.

Pauline would later engineer a marriage, probably with the help of Russell Bufalino, between her son, attorney Nick Micelli, and one of the daughters of Detroit's Bozzi Vitale, the man who brought the Detroit Partnership into the waste management business, first through Tri-County Sanitation and later at Central Sanitation. Nick Micelli, as the operator and attorney for Central Sanitation, would be quizzed by the FBI to determine what role he or the company may have had in Hoffa's disappearance. They were specifically interested in inspecting the incinerator.

As for my granduncle Salvatore's children, a few remained local. Bill's brother Charles, the eldest of Salvatore's children and Santo Volpe's son-in-law, was an attorney who held an elected position in Luzerne County. Within a very short time of his marriage and the start of his law practice, Charles became a partner or outright owner of mine contracts in association with his father-in-law, Santo Volpe. In the depths of the Great Depression, he became moderately wealthy. By 1939, he pursued and won elective office as Luzerne County recorder of deeds. In the early 1930s, his father Salvatore and his uncle Nicolo, cut off from association with Calogero, saw their businesses and fortunes begin to falter. Neither would survive the decade.

Whatever rancor there was between Salvatore and Calogero, it seemed to poison any relationship between Salvatore's relationship with Santo Volpe and, eventually, his own son, Charles. Nevertheless, or perhaps in spite of his father, Charles began to manage the affairs of his siblings. Salvatore, the patriarch, forgotten by all of his former associates and now his son, passed away from pneumonia at home in 1936.

Charles's younger brother James Bufalino had been the family prodigy. He passed U.S. Naval Academy exams and was directed to report to Annapolis in 1928 but chose instead to pursue a degree in medicine. In letters I have seen, Charles cautioned James against association with people "of the wrong sort," arranged for him to have a job as an elevator operator while in school, and encouraged him to abandon the study of medicine for law. James died as the result of injuries sustained in a car accident in 1934 while returning to school.

William Bufalino had secured for himself a scholarship to a university in Rome, Italy, as a result of winning a national radio contest related to essay writing in 1939. He was already enrolled at The Dickinson School of Law by the time of his award. His brother Charles probably had a role in convincing Bill, as he had tried to do with brother James, to stick with the study of law. It may have saved his life. When the United States entered World War II, Bill was drafted into the Judge Advocate General's Corps. He served stateside throughout the war, at Romulus Army Airfield near Detroit, Michigan.

After Bill's honorable discharge from the military, his brother Charles had a special commission for him that would implant Bill into Detroit as a business partner with Frank Meli, the brother of the more notorious Angelo Meli. Bill's acceptance of the proposal became the key turning point in his career and would ultimately cause him to cross paths—and join forces—with Jimmy Hoffa. It's not clear that Charles directed his brother Angelo's (Yabo's) or Eugene's career at all, except perhaps by suggesting they accompany

Bill to Detroit. Yabo had worked at Santo Volpe's PA Coal #6 colliery when it reopened in 1937.

By 1947, Angelo Polizzi, the longtime Santo Volpe associate who had been arrested and held along with Joseph Barbara in connection with the Wichner murder, also headed to Detroit and became affiliated with members of the Detroit Partnership.

Once Bill established himself in Detroit, the remainder of Salvatore's children moved to Detroit with him and worked with him in supporting roles from domestic help, child-rearing, business partnership, and in Teamsters affairs. Altogether, the entourage that assembled in Detroit included William Eugene Bufalino (Bill himself in the lead position), his brothers Eugene Bufalino and Yabo, and two sisters—Adeline (later Koury) and Pauline Tulumello with her young son Angelo. Four of Bill's siblings kept a common residence in the area of Alter Road, Detroit, not far from the suburb of Grosse Pointe. Sister Pauline ran a store for many years nearby and had several times been robbed at gunpoint. Adeline worked with Bill for some unknown length of time in the capacity of a legal secretary. Both women helped with family tasks at home, as did Mary when she visited.

Bill's brother Eugene Bufalino was a veteran of the Navy who had served in the Pacific. For a brief time after his service, he had operated a Miller High Life distributorship out of a former railroad building in Pittston and had also managed a restaurant locally. In Detroit, he would continue in restaurant management but doubled as a fight promoter.

Yabo's career experience had been as a machinist, first at the family bottling works and then as a mining equipment operator. He was not called up for service during the war, possibly due to his age at the time of the draft. He was born in 1912.

The business ventures Bill and family engaged in with the Meli family extended beyond jukeboxes. In the very first stage of their arrival, probably before Bill's marriage, the three brothers went to work together for Angelo Meli in a familiar setting: a bar. They ran the Stork Club (of Detroit) out of a former speakeasy that had been a Purple Gang hangout. It was intended to be a high-class operation and the brothers kept it top-notch. Eugene, handsome and personable, was the front man and the club's manager.

I've seen a photo of Eugene arriving to the club decked out in a stark white suit and hat. His face graces a full-page ad as the cover of *The Cash Box, the Confidential Weekly of the Coin Machine Industry*, volume 8, number 3, week of September 30, 1946. The ad features his image and a quote: "Wurlitzer's Sign of the Musical Note is the greatest crowd puller in our experience."

Yabo, the biggest and toughest of the family, tended bar decked out in a fancy paisley vest. When necessary, he bounced the occasional troublemaker. According to the man I met at Yabo's funeral reception, he sometimes helped a debtor or two find his checkbook.

When the original Stork Club in New York balked at the use of their name, Angelo Meli renamed the place to the Story Club. Whether it was a success or not is not clear. By 1947, the club suffered a fire as the result of a carelessly discarded cigarette. It closed down. Bill was already involved in a second venture with Angelo Meli's nephew, Bill's own brother-in-law. Bill's partnership with Vincent Meli would cause him to lock horns with the Teamsters and have a life-changing encounter with Jimmy Hoffa. Eugene and Yabo pursued different, if related, trajectories.

Eugene spent some time in Detroit as a fight promoter but pursued a career in wine, ultimately becoming vice president, and later president, of a California union local identified by the FBI as the Wine Distillery and Rectifying Workers Union but probably better known as Distillery, Rectifying, Wine, and Allied Workers' International Union of America. The FBI noted that Bill had set up the union. The Bureau generally considered, correctly or not, that the purpose of creating unions was to give people they considered to be gangsters positions that could improve their income and influence and cultivate an air of respectability.

Out of all the siblings, it was Yabo who was the closest to Bill's Teamsters affairs.

Eventually Yabo would train to become a millwright and work a variety of jobs in that field, but he also had many odd jobs. He worked at Cobo Hall in Detroit, probably in a security capacity, and tried his hand selling Christmas trees at a stand he operated in the vicinity of Grosse Pointe. He was also a card-carrying Teamster. Through most of Bill's tenure with Hoffa, Yabo was often at the side of both men. When Hoffa traveled on business, the formidable-looking Yabo wore Hoffa's money belt.

CHAPTER 36

BILL BUFALINO'S SPECIAL COMMISSION

B means to battle for that which is right,
To keep bravely on though rugged the height.
—William E. Bufalino

William E. Bufalino quoted himself on the above in an interview with *The Detroit News*. I have an original typed copy of the poem based on one each of the eight letters in order that spell out his surname. He wrote it at an early age to qualify as an entrant into the G. K. Chesterton Poetry Society. It's not so good as poetry goes, and even Bill never quoted it beyond the first line, but it does express the spirit of combativeness that would characterize Bill throughout his life and career.

Bill was raised by his sister Mary with help from his grandmother Marie Augello Galante. According to Bill, Marie had been the first female teacher in Montedoro. She schooled Bill and his brothers in the classics, recited Dante to them, and taught them to pray in Italian. Bill was capable of better writing than the above, and he proved that when an essay of his won a national contest whose award was a scholarship to study in Italy. The political situation in Italy at the time, and Bill's own enrollment in law school, made collecting on that prize impractical.

Bill started his college career in the late 1930s, studying for the priesthood at a seminary school that is today the University of Scranton. Likely influenced by the recommendation of his brother Charles, as his brother James had been before him, Bill changed his plans sometime in his undergraduate career and decided to pursue a law degree. According to an extensive interview that appeared in the *Detroit Free Press* in February, 1976, which was duplicated in large part for local publication in Pittston's *Sunday Dispatch* in May of the same year, Bill reported that he had simply audited law classes without formally enrolling in the program and later presented himself to the law program dean, who then enrolled him. That enabled him to apply to law school. He completed law school at The Dickinson School of Law in 1942 and ended up in the Army. He was assigned and spent his military career at the Judge Advocate General's Corps at the Romulus Army Airfield outside Detroit.

As Bill's discharge from the military was nearing, his brother Charles had a second career proposal for him. Charles had met with Detroit's Frank Meli, who had been visiting family in Northeast Pennsylvania. Meli was born in San Cataldo, near Montedoro in Sicily, and thus the local connection between Detroit and the Pittston area. Frank Meli's brother was the more famous Angelo Meli. Frank himself had no criminal record at the time. His brother Angelo Meli had been arrested in a murder investigation in the 1920s, was involved in several businesses and activities of interest to the government, and would by 1957 be a candidate for "denaturalization." Otherwise, Angelo Meli had no convictions or prison record at the time. By the 1970s, the government would figure Angelo as one of five "dons" of Detroit and his brother Frank as a lieutenant in the Partnership. Bill's brother Charles proposed that Bill enter into a coin-operated machine business relationship with the Meli family.

According to Bill, he was investigating a military desertion in the city of Detroit when it occurred to him to follow up with Frank Meli as per his brother Charles's direction. He called and made an appointment to meet at Frank's home. At Meli's home, on a Saturday, Bill was introduced to Frank's daughter Marie Antoinette. He dined with the family the next day. By the fourth day after their meeting, Bill proposed marriage to Marie Antoinette Meli. She accepted, and they were married in 1945. To a loan variously reported as $15,000, $20,000, or $30,000 from a local bank in Pittston, Bill added $5,000 of his own money to a till whose contributions came from Angelo Meli and associates, which was estimated to total between $95,000 and $145,000, depending on who was doing the math. Bill and his new brother-in-law Vincent Meli formed the Bilvin (Bill plus Vincent) Distributing Company. They secured a Wurlitzer franchise (remember that brand) and became distributors of jukeboxes.

In the 1940s, Jimmy Hoffa, not yet the International Brotherhood of Teamsters (IBT) president, was leading a group of Detroit area local unions, including the "Jukebox Local" 985, founded in 1945 and headed by Eugene ("Jimmy") James. For reasons unrecorded, possibly intransigence on the part of businessmen that were Bill's associates to negotiate with union labor, Teamsters Local 985 began picketing Bilvin Distributing Company. Bill Bufalino filed a lawsuit against the Teamsters for $100,000. Eugene James, Local 985 president, enlisted Hoffa for guidance, and they all met in court. According to Bill, Judge Chester O'Hara recommended that the parties meet and agree to terms, because he did not want to rule against the union.

The next part of the story was one of Bill's favorite set pieces. I've heard it a number of times. Hoffa reached out to negotiate.

"What do you want?" Hoffa asked.

Bill thought Hoffa was asking if he wanted a beating, so he became confrontational. He answered, "I'll whip you in the alley, on the sidewalk, or in the courtroom."

According to Bill, that earned him Hoffa's respect. That's the family legend of it. They worked out a cash settlement.

Bill supposedly told Hoffa that the Jukebox Local's charter was all wrong and that it would cause trouble in the future. He volunteered to help. Hoffa made Bill the business agent of Local 985 in 1947, and a short time later rechartered the local. Weeks later, Hoffa deposed Eugene James and appointed Bill president, a position to which he was later formally elected. Likely to avoid any appearance of a conflict of interest, Bill forewent his partnership in Bilvin and began a career as a salaried union president, organizer, and consulting attorney to Hoffa's legal team. He would continue in that role beyond his split with Hoffa in 1971.

Bill's relationships with the cofounders of Bilvin would require a lot of explaining over time, especially with regard to Angelo Meli, who contributed, according to McClellan Committee figures, some $46,000 to founding the Bilvin Corporation. The thing was, the names Tocco, Priziola, and Meli were known to law enforcement in Detroit, but sorting out the relationships of Bill's actual partners to their presumptive relatives by the same name and asking Bill to acknowledge or account for this or that arrest for this or that offense on the part of one of his associates twenty years before was getting nobody anywhere. Bill deflected all arguments that suggested he should know the private affairs and financial dealings of his associates retroactive to the 1920s.

Altogether, competition in the coin-operated field was such that currying union favor through graft to prevent strikes seemed like an industry best practice. In 1957, Eugene James appeared and gave testimony in the Hearings Before the Select Committee on Improper Activities in the Labor or Management Field and repeatedly invoked his Fifth Amendment rights against self-incrimination. When asked for details concerning Bill's placement, his own ouster, and his own acceptance of checks from jukebox manufacturers, James repeatedly stonewalled the committee on the advice of counsel.

According to an annotation in the McClellan Committee report, Bill was tried and acquitted of a "jukebox racket" in 1953. His 1957 testimony before Senator John L. McClellan proved to be an exercise in frustration, but just for the committee. Bill did not invoke his Fifth Amendment rights and just went toe-to-toe with the inquisitors as to procedure, rules, and what business it was of his to understand any given associate's police record or financial dealings.

The accusations of racketeering levied against Bill came about from the union's practices in support of Local 985's two major rank-and-file constituencies: a) coin-operated machinery and musical devices (jukebox) repairmen and b) car wash employees. According to testimony, at the time in the Detroit metropolitan area, car washes numbered between 200 and 300. Each of the car washes employed between fifty and sixty people in various capacities. Obviously, car washing in the 1950s was a world apart from the drive-throughs of today. Workers in these establishments fell under Bill's purview as a labor organizer. Bill, coming as he did from the brass-knuckled union politics of the 1920s-era coalfields, had a style that was aggressive, to say the least. Labor organizing for the discreet constituencies within his union required different approaches.

For coin-operated businesses, especially jukeboxes, labor organizing centered on the technicians who serviced jukeboxes. To move its jukeboxes in the Detroit area, the Wurlitzer Company made a business decision, a deal, to authorize only union servicemen to work on their machines. Milton J. Hammergren, retired general sales manager of Wurlitzer, testified before the McClellan Committee that he had contacts in the underworld in New York and

Chicago, including such names as Meyer Lansky, to foster sale or contract leasing of his units.

My recall of testimony concerning the placement of Wurlitzer machines in the Detroit area went like this: step 1: A Local 985 union representative shows up in a bar and scopes out the manufacturer of the jukebox; step 2: If the jukebox is not a Wurlitzer, a single picket is placed outside the bar decrying the establishment's use of scab labor (the single picket just *had* to be Yabo); step 3: Teamsters Union beer truck drivers honor the "picket line" and refuse delivery to the establishment. Of course, the objective was to sell Wurlitzer machines (or arrange for their placement on a lease contract). The sellers of Wurlitzer machines would then split the proceeds from the weekly take with the owner of the business. So Wurlitzer moved machines, the bar got to stay in business, and the union collected dues from somebody, whether the serviceman or Wurlitzer. Everybody was happy. More or less. In the course of the above, Bill was once charged with threatening a competitor who later declined to press charges.

The car wash business was a little less direct. Getting the fifty or sixty employees of 200 to 300 individual car wash operations would take a massive organizing effort. The union took a different track by going straight to the owners, requiring them to pay the entrance fees and local dues for their employees. According to the testimony of Bernard L. Bialkin before the McClellan Committee, he had been approached directly to pay the induction fees and regular dues of the people under his employ. There was none of this organizing folderol; the establishments themselves were basically required to foot the bill for organizing, registering members, and paying their monthly dues to the union, or they would face targeted action in the form of boycott and picketing. Car washers themselves, the presumptive rank and file of the union, complained that they never received cards or had notice concerning union meetings, nor met a steward. One complained of a 40 percent drop in wages after joining the union. The above considered, in 1953, a House subcommittee issued a report stating:

> *[T]here existed a gigantic, wicked conspiracy to, through the use of force, threats of force, and economic pressure, extort and collect millions of dollars not only from unorganized workers but from members of unions who are in good standing, from independent businessmen, and, on occasion, from the Federal Government itself . . . The Teamsters Union, Local 985, through its president William E. Bufalino, is the principal offender and perpetrator of the racketeering, extortion, and gangsterism . . . The union attempted, and to some extent succeeded, in obtaining a monopoly in the "juke-box" business.*

Bill was indicted and brought before a grand jury on charges of extortion. Nothing came of it. He was found innocent. According to Dan Moldea, as reported in *The Hoffa Wars: The Rise and Fall of Jimmy Hoffa,* the judge in the extortion case against Bill was compromised by union contributions to his reelection fund. The case went nowhere.

When it was time to defend Hoffa against federal indictments, Bill was part of the team of attorneys on the job on four separate and successful occasions. When Hoffa was arrested by the FBI in 1957, Robert F. Kennedy vowed to jump off the Capitol dome if he could not convict Hoffa of bribery, conspiracy, and obstruction of justice. I can still see Bill standing at Mary Buff's counter, running his JUICERator machine and dressed in the signature red sweat suit of some Detroit health club as he turned to my father to say, "We sent him a parachute." RFK acknowledged receipt of a parachute from Hoffa's defense team in his book entitled *The Enemy Within.*

In May 1963, Hoffa's luck ran out. He was indicted for jury tampering in Tennessee and charged with attempted bribery of a grand juror in his most recent conspiracy trial in Nashville. Convicted in March 1964, he spent three years in appeals before his sentencing. He reported to Lewisburg Federal Penitentiary in March 1967.

Bill was not, for most of his tenure at Local 985 in Detroit, a practicing courtroom attorney and didn't feel he was getting respect from the attorneys on his team. He had a license to practice law in Pennsylvania, but in order to be accepted to practice in Michigan, he'd either have to retake the bar in Michigan or, in a process called "by motion," he could prove to have worked as a lawyer in three of the five years prior to submitting application for entry into the Michigan Bar. He decided during Hoffa's internment, between 1967 and 1971, to set up an office and a practice in Pittston, at his family's homestead, hardly two hours' drive from Lewisburg.

It was in those years that I and my family had more frequent and regular contact with Bill, his son William Bufalino II (we called him "Billy Boy"), and Bill's brother Yabo (Angelo). Bill remodeled the first floor of his father's half of the house, the old general store in Pittston, hung up a shingle, and went to regular work to fulfill the three-year-out-of-five requirement to satisfy the "by motion" criteria to apply for entry to the Michigan Bar Association.

Eventually, he was accepted to the Michigan Bar in 1972. He continued to hold a union position in the Teamsters and drew additional pay as a special counsel. He then began work to fulfill his lifelong dream of moving into a private practice in Detroit with his son William Bufalino II in 1975–76.

CHAPTER 37

THE APALACHIN DEBACLE

On a day in early November 1957, New York State Trooper Sergeant Edgar D. Croswell was at the Vestal Motel investigating nothing more exciting than a bounced check when Joseph (Joe the Barber) Barbara's son Joseph Barbara Jr. (a.k.a. "Joey the Clipper") rolled up in an expensive car and arranged to book a number of rooms. Looking around the lot, Croswell could see a number of expensive vehicles already parked on-site.

Sergeant Croswell knew Joey and his father, Joseph Barbara Sr., owned a Canada Dry distributorship and sold alcoholic beverages in and around Endicott. Joseph Barbara was long-associated with the underworld and was suspected in several murders but had never been convicted of anything. The year before, Carmine Galante, with his lengthy police record in New York City, had been identified in a routine traffic stop near Barbara's home. His suspicions aroused, Croswell alerted headquarters to the room rentals and suspicious out-of-town rich cars and set a course for Barbara's estate.

Arriving at the home on November 14, Croswell started recording license numbers, and when several of the cars were registered to known criminals, he alerted headquarters. The New York State Police set a trap by setting up a roadblock some distance from the house. Alerted to the activity, general panic ensued among the visitors to Barbara's estate. Some jumped in their cars; others started running into the woods. About fifty escaped in that way. The first car that Sergeant Croswell of the New York State Police stopped as it exited the Apalachin meeting at Joesph Barbara's estate contained Vito Genovese. At the wheel was his driver, Russell Bufalino. They were among the sixty apprehended along with other notables, including Carlo Gambino, Joe Profaci, and Joe Bonanno.

The attendees were questioned as to the purpose of the meeting. They generally responded that they were visiting the home of a sick friend (Barbara had recently suffered a heart attack) and to attend a barbeque. Several of the attendees were convicted of "conspiring to obstruct justice" by lying about the nature of the meeting, but the convictions were later overturned on appeal.

The real "net" and score for law enforcement that came out of the meeting was that the bust highlighted the existence of what FBI Director J. Edgar Hoover had refused to recognize in the past: the fact that an organized body of individuals running rackets countrywide did in fact exist. Reeling in the aftermath of the bust, Hoover had to grudgingly accept that organized crime existed, but curiously, he refused to use the word by which everybody else called it: Mafia. What better way to preserve his own legacy and keep his job than to continue to refute the very clear existence of the organization while simply casting it in a new name of his own choosing: "La Cosa Nostra" (This Thing of Ours), based on a conversation between two individuals on a wiretap discussing some individual venture. (Technically, the "La" is a misnomer, and simply "Cosa Nostra" is the accurate title.)

For Russell Bufalino, the outcome of the Apalachin meeting was particularly severe. It triggered a decades-long effort by the United States government to deport Russell to Italy based on a questionable orphan's court registry in Luzerne County and the FBI's list of known transgressions captured in his "Top Hoodlum" profile. When, in January 1958, Agent J. M. Hastetter of the Bureau of Immigration and Naturalization Service asked Pittston police to provide

Russell's arrest records, he found that Russell's local police records had totally vanished and had taken with them the entire Pittston Police Department's records for the years 1934 through 1938. That must have been a wild time, beginning as it does with the massive reorganization that must have taken place at the end of Prohibition in December 1933.

Two aspects of Russell's affiliations and presumed power have confused many, myself included. The first is the question of his association with Joseph Barbara and the second is the scope of his power and reach. As a family member, I am prone to underestimating Russell's influence. The idea that he should be the penultimate authority, someone "above The Commission," as his successor William D'Elia has said, escapes me still, but I accept it. As for his relationships to the northern tier of New York, I'm very dubious. In *The Quiet Don*, Matt Birkbeck reported Russell to have come out of the Magaddino organization in Buffalo, citing his arrests in that area as evidence. His appearance in Northeastern Pennsylvania along with Joseph Barbara has fueled speculation that they had both been dispatched to the region to run the show for Buffalo. No such thing.

Joesph Barbara never "ran the show" in the coalfields of Northeastern Pennsylvania. Moreover, he did not come down from the Magaddino organization as much as he was later incorporated into it. He was a local resource in the coalfields at first. Russell may have been on his payroll in the 1950s as a mechanic, but that was on paper. In the coalfields of the late 1920s and 1930s, Joseph Barbara was a driver, enforcer, and bootlegger. The work he did, he did for the Pittston family, the oldest guard of Sicilians whom Lucky Luciano's generation would have derided as "Mustache Petes." He was active in their organization until, it seems, his marriage and relocation to Endicott in 1933.

Many assume, and you can still read, that Joseph Barbara killed John Sciandra and took over the organization from him. Nobody bothered to tell Sciandra. He died of natural causes—black lung, a common ailment of coal miners—in 1949. Russell was first Calogero Bufalino's, and then John Sciandra's protégé and successor. His lifetime territory was Pittston and the surrounding region in the Wyoming Valley of Northeastern Pennsylvania. His reach? Burbank, California, and beyond. People underestimate the money, power, and influence of the hard coal region at the turn of the twentieth century and make their assumptions of Russell's influence based on the Rust Belt status the region acquired as the anthracite deep-mine industry collapsed in 1959. The thing is, Northeastern Pennsylvania was Genovese-affiliated from the start but not in the way of a subservient organization and more in the way of a partnership.

The historic connections between the Northeastern Pennsylvania Pittston family and the Genovese family went all the way back to the Lupo-Morello gang in the early 1900s. The Lupo-Morello syndicate founded the organization that Luciano would make his own when he established The Commission. The family would eventually take its name from Luciano's underboss Vito Genovese to become the Genovese crime family, after he wrangled it from Frank "The Prime Minister" Costello in 1957.

Sam Lucchino's testimony in 1910 put Lupo and Morello away for a long stretch on a counterfeiting rap, and Sam was possibly murdered in retribution for his troubles. In fact, Lucchino's brother-in-law Steve La Torre and other locals had trafficked in money counterfeited by the Lupo-Morello gang. When Don Vito Genovese returned from Sicily in 1945 following the death of a witness that might have put him on death row, it was Santo Volpe who was said to have surrendered his seat at the table to Genovese.

Some have suggested that the purpose of the November meeting at Barbara's estate was to settle disputes arising over an isolated incident, the October 1957 murder of Albert Anastasia. Others suspect that Anastasia's murder was part of a larger scheme to prevent

Frank Costello from petitioning The Commission to restore him to power in the Genovese family. From the perspective of Frank DiMatteo and Michael Benson, authors of *The Cigar: Carmine Galante, Mafia Terror*, the whole purpose of the Apalachin meeting in Vito Genovese's mind was to "abolish Luciano's Five Family system and proclaim himself king of the underworld." It would make sense, considering Genovese sent his button man (and future family boss) Vincent "Chin" Gigante to murder Costello, who escaped with only a scratched cranium and a sudden penchant for retirement.

I have struggled to understand how a person as powerful as Russell could be presumed to have been relegated to a role like making lodging arrangements for associates from around the world in the vicinity of Barbara's estate. Booking travel and hotel arrangements like a concierge? A boss like Russell? Somehow that never squared for me with author Charles Brandt's characterization of Russell being "one of the most powerful Mob bosses of his day, if not of all time."

The only way it makes sense to me is in light of DiMatteo and Benson's theory. Russell helped call the meeting on orders from Vito Genovese himself, through a half-century of partnership with the organization Genovese—the man who would be king—now ran.

CHAPTER 38

MARY BUFF

Somebody owed Bill's sister, Mary Buff, big-time. In the period following the Apalachin meeting, the government wanted to deport Russell Bufalino. It set about conducting investigations to discover his country of birth. The FBI had checked Russell's birth records in Luzerne County and discovered that the orphan's register had been tampered with. Jammed in between two records was an entry that was an attempted forgery, first penciled and then inked, in ink too modern to match the 1903 records. Further research led them to a birth record in Montedoro, Sicily. Then they set about discovering who had tampered with the record. The person suspected of tampering would have to have behind-the-counter access to Luzerne County records. It would have to be someone connected to the Luzerne County Courthouse.

Mary herself worked for almost twenty years in the courthouse as a clerk in the Orphans Court, probably thanks to John Sciandra's influence over the politics of the 1930s and 1940s. Two of her brothers, Bill and Charles, were also closely involved in Luzerne County politics and frequented the courthouse. Brother Bill had been working with a law partner for a time out of the Bennett Building on public square in Wilkes-Barre, the Luzerne county seat. Mary's brother Charles was a practicing attorney who had served a term as recorder of deeds for Luzerne County. At least two other parties were considered likely candidates for the tampering besides Mary and her brothers. Multiple handwriting samples were collected.

At a deportation hearing in Philadelphia, Mary just confessed to having tampered with the record. She said she had simply been acting "as a matter of routine" to correct what had been an error of omission. She may have done it just as she said. It would also be just like Mary to take the heat and protect one of her brothers, as a family obligation. She might have underestimated the outcome of her actions in either case. Mary was released from her staff position in the courthouse just a few months short of concluding a full twenty-year term of service that would have entitled her to retire with a pension.

Mary was born in 1908 and was just fifty-two years old in 1960. She retired. She had help from her brother Bill and others in the family. Bill paid the property taxes to keep her in the home. The rent from her upstairs tenants was her income along with Social Security benefits. She simply lived next door and kept house day in and out, and that's how I came to be her charge during periods of illness or in the summer days when my parents were at work at the photography business downtown. For all of us left at the house, she was Aunt Mary. The family explained her removal from the courthouse position as something that just happened due to a change of administration.

In the mid-to-late 1970s, Mary's solitary life in Pittston changed suddenly when all her siblings from Detroit, minus Eugene, showed up for prolonged stays as her houseguests and eventually became her upstairs tenants. Bill was in declining health. Detroit was falling apart. The Alter Road neighborhood they lived in was experiencing 1970s-style social upheaval. Pauline had been robbed one too many times at her store. They all came back to Pittston during the years I was away at college. One by one, they passed, leaving just Yabo.

For all the time I knew her, Mary lived in a kind of poverty, but she rarely complained about it. She had just enough of what she needed to get by. She accompanied Yabo on vacation trips to Florida. She involved herself in the lives of the people in the building. Her upstairs tenant's daughter Debbie was the apple of her eye. Her nieces and nephews would visit on occasion, and there was always me. She gave us our first sip of wine, cooked pizza for us, taught us card games, tutored us in conversational Italian, and shared the treasures of the household, including her Italian-language version of *Sicilian Ways and Days* by the English Woman, Louise Hamilton Caico. We marveled at the ornate dining room table, a reminder of the family's prominence, and the upright Eastlake piano in her living room. We helped her clean and paint the house when necessary. We did the chores she needed help with.

As for family history, Mary was the primary source. There was clearly a lot she wouldn't say, but what I knew about Russell growing up among her family in Pittston, about her father's injury and Russell's father's death in the mine, about Bill especially, and Yabo, all started with Mary and proved true through research. Her house eventually became mine through tax sale, with the remaining artifacts from Bill's tenure at the Teamsters and a wealth of material still waiting to be curated.

Like Yabo, Mary was fiercely proud of her whole family, including her father and all of her siblings. Mary's relationship with Bill was somewhat complicated, partly by her circumstances, partly by the way he would occasionally snag an artifact or two to take back to Detroit—a brass doorknob here, a lamp there. It irked her. Sometimes, like a spited parent might, she shared the details of her frustration with me as I grew old enough to understand. But still, regardless of how valid or deep-seated her resentment, whenever Bill came to town, Mary was clearly in her glory, and she reveled in his accomplishments.

Whenever Bill made the press throughout the 1960s, Mary would get a clipping. Mary bragged about how he had defeated the Grosse Pointe points system and his accomplishments in court. She shared the *Teamster* magazines that her sister Adeline, Bill's legal secretary, would forward to her when they contained an article about or editorial written by Bill. As I look at the 1971 copy of *Teamster* magazine sent her by her sister, I see the cover is annotated with "Bill's picture—page 11 and page 15."

Whoever Mary was acting to protect in her testimony before the deportation hearings, and whatever resentment she may have had on that account, she never seemed to hold anything against Russell himself. On the contrary, the one discouraging word she ever expressed to me about Russell was the single 1960s-era complaint: "He never visits."

CHAPTER 39

THE GODFATHER COMES INTO HIS OWN: THE RISE OF RUSSELL BUFALINO

Russell was about forty-seven years old in 1949–50 when he finally came into his own as the head of the organization that would shortly take his name. He didn't arrive by killing his predecessor or plotting anyone's downfall. He came more in the way of a middle-aged prince assuming control of an organization, the depth of whose power and influence has never been fully measured. The heavy lifting of establishing the family had been accomplished through brutal power plays that left a trail of bodies stretching back to 1903, establishing not just the reputation of the family but of Pittston as Little Chicago during the Prohibition years.

Russell arrived at the helm of the Pittston family for two reasons: 1) the Pittston family would in no way surrender control of their organization to someone who was not quite literally trusted family, and 2) ironically, the founding members of the family would not want or allow any of their children (with certain exceptions) to live the kind of life they had lived to build the organization. Russell's advantage was his disadvantage. He was nobody's child, an orphan, Calogero's nephew and ward and later his proxy, a smart and talented pauper who became a prince. There was none of this "making his bones" business about it. There were people to do that. People like Joseph Barbara.

Russell earned his keep as a mechanic and driver at a time when souping up cars to beat government agents across the county line was a highly marketable skill. He would later develop a knack for dealing in jewelry, especially diamonds, and enough mastery over the art of shylocking that he owned a part of every cash-strapped business in Northeastern Pennsylvania, something in no short supply following the collapse of the deep-mining industry in 1959.

When Santo Volpe and Calogero Bufalino moved behind the scenes in the 1930s, having "shelved" Steve La Torre, they gave the reins over to their cousin, John Sciandra, and Russell moved into the second phase of his apprenticeship. It's possible that Sciandra, Russell's wife Carrie's cousin, may have gentled Russell's disposition a bit in the ensuing sixteen or so years until Sciandra's own passing in 1949. Russell revered Sciandra, to all accounts.

The bloodletting that had made the Pittston family locally ascendant had become a little less necessary with the end of Prohibition and the end of the major United Mine Workers' conflicts in the middle 1930s, but there was no question in any quarter who was in charge and what outcomes troublemakers would face. That lesson was learned time and again until we in high school in the 1970s knew to keep our mouths shut and trust nobody.

By the time of John Sciandra's passing in 1949, the question of Russell's ascendancy was a no-brainer. There was just nobody else with Russell's depth of experience or his apparent sagacity. All the old guard leadership except Steve La Torre would be deceased by 1960. Steve La Torre outlived Santo Volpe by over a quarter century, passing in 1984, and even latecomer children like myself and my classmates could see him on the street or at the frequent high-stakes card games at his son Joe's place, La Torre's Rec (a downtown pool hall).

Russell inherited control over gambling of all kinds—from boxing to the horses at Pocono Downs to the betting slips my friends used to hand out in high school, courtesy of the teacher on staff in the Italian leather shoes and smart jacket-and-tie combos—and who was "the bank" to whom every bookie in town laid off their excess action. Russell owned dress factories and probably had a piece of every business on Main Street in a dozen different communities. He was entrepreneurial in his own ways, acquiring the closed-circuit broadcast rights to the second (Muhammad Ali) Clay-Liston fight and who knows what all else countrywide, but his lifelong specialty was dealing with union and striking workers, most notably the United Mine Workers of America, the International Ladies' Garment Workers Union (ILGWU), and the Teamsters.

Russell would earn his title of "The Quiet Don" on his own in the face of multiple severe personal and business challenges that could not be solved by any of the brutal methods that were the first pick of his predecessors. The losses would keep coming as body blows from 1957 through the 1960s. In November 1957, Apalachin put Russell on the map and started over a decade's worth of deportation hearings and rulings that had him at one point packed and ready, literally within hours of boarding a plane to Italy.

In 1958, Santo Volpe, the former revered head of the family, passed. If he had been an adviser of any kind to Russell, that was over. In the same year, the International Ladies' Garment Workers Union went on a national strike, impacting the numerous factories that Russell and his Apalachin associates owned in town.

In January 1959, there was a double-fisted blow to the Pittston family's economic interests. First, in early January 1959, Fulgencio Batista fled Cuba as it fell to forces under Fidel Castro, destroying the stake ownership Russell and others had enjoyed in a major Havana casino and racetrack. Persistent local rumors suggest that Russell himself fled before Castro's advancing troops, leaving a cache of money buried on the island. Next, in the same month, the anthracite deep-mining industry suffered a last knockout blow when the Susquehanna River poured in through the shallow roof of a mine covered by the ice-choked river and flooded the deep works of the entire Wyoming Valley of Pennsylvania. It knocked out whatever remained of the region's founding industry and sparked investigations into the ownership of the Knox Mine Company (which had been founded by John Sciandra).

In 1960, Calogero Bufalino, Russell's uncle and mentor, passed. Russell was on his own at last, and the decade of the 1960s would start the collapse of the last sustaining industry of the region: the dress factories. As an owner and partner in dress factories, mines, and other multiple local businesses impacted by the flagging local economy, Russell had no end of problems to solve.

Through it all, he became known as "The Quiet Don" for an unflappable demeanor that only failed him but once and at just the wrong time. Anything he learned in life about negotiating deals and securing the peace, he learned by growing up inside an organization made up of some of the most violent and dangerous men of their day, including, if not especially, his own uncle Calogero Bufalino, in whose household he matured.

In his person, Russell portrayed a gruff, brusque, tough-guy demeanor, probably assumed from his youth, when the slight, visually disadvantaged young man had to find a way to command the respect of the very gruffest and toughest anthracite miners who themselves were in awe of the Pittston family's leadership and associates. Get to know him and you could find him plinking on a piano, as he did on Mary's upright Eastlake (even with the missing digit or two). He could speak the language of boxers, miners, entertainers, and opera stars. Above all, he understood and spoke the language of business. As for the most dangerous people in the underworld, they sought and accepted his advice, sometimes using him to fill in as needed when gaps arose in their organization.

When Joe Colombo, at length, approved the script for *The Godfather,* Russell Bufalino became involved in the production. Marlon Brando records his initial meeting with Russell in his autobiography. He said Russell sent two envoys to his trailer asking to meet him. Brando records Russell's name as "Joe Bufalino" but reports that he was complaining about the way the government was treating him—that made it Russell, all right. At least Brando correctly reports that Russell walked in "regally." Russell would have much to do with the production, including coaching Brando on appropriate demeanor and behavior required to accurately portray a don.

The Godfather we see on-screen may be an amalgam of the entire Pittston family leadership, or it may rest in the person of either Santo Volpe or John Sciandra. Russell was frequently on the other end of the phone with the actor when not physically delivering him to the set. Who knows, but the raspy voice Brando assumed may have arisen from Russell's boyhood interaction with Sam Lucchino, since Brando himself once said in an interview that he chose the raspy voice to suggest that the character of Don Corleone had once been shot in the neck. William D'Elia, in *The Life We Chose,* reports Russell's belief that Brando thought he was above Russell and that Russell therefore considered Brando a punk.

The Godfather movie was released in March 1972, and in June of that year, much of the Wyoming Valley of Pennsylvania was wiped out by the floods resulting from Hurricane Agnes. Russell's Kingston, Pennsylvania, residence, like most of Kingston, was underwater. Russell and his wife Carrie briefly stayed with her relations in the family home of Russell's predecessor, John Sciandra.

One evening on return from New York, Russell sank into a chair in the living room as John's teenage granddaughter came into the room to ask him what it was like working with her favorite actor. "He's a degenerate!" Russell groused. "He lives on an island with a woman who's not his wife . . . They've got a bunch of kids . . ." He didn't bother to tell her about the Mighty Moon King's apology to Russell for mooning his men, who were among the 500-odd crew of extras on the set of the wedding scene after shooting had stopped. Brando at least had enough respect for Russell to set the record straight that the mooning was not an act of disrespect aimed at *him*.

My brothers knew Russell better than I did. My nearest-in-age brother had eleven years on me and came of age in the early 1960s. They had a childhood's worth of interactions with Russell that included meeting both Rocky Graziano *and* Rocky Marciano and countless trips to New York City's Metropolitan Opera House and Delmonico's courtesy of Russell and his contacts. By the time I arrived, like an omen, on the fifty-third anniversary of Russell's father's death in a mine in 1904, the Apalachin meeting of November 1957 was hardly two months away. I would have less interaction with Russell than my brothers had, and he would visit the house less frequently throughout the 1960s due to the relentless surveillance and constant pressure he was under.

Russell had well-earned a reputation as a man of mystery. The intimate details of his life were never up for grabs. When I shared with someone very close to Russell that he had siblings who testified at his deportation hearings, the party told me I must be wrong. In his speech and manner, he was undeniably tough enough to satisfy the hard-bitten coal miner and capable of holding his own on the streets of New York among the most notorious gangsters of his day. If he had a superpower, it was silence. If he had a weakness, it was a surprisingly good nature.

Despite a necessary gruffness among men, Russell was well liked and considered to be fair to a fault. Charles Brandt, author of Frank Sheeran's *I Heard You Paint Houses* narrative, once said he couldn't find anyone to say anything bad about him. There's an often-repeated story about how Russell found a former neighbor, an older man, patching shingles on his roof. He called to the man to come down and sent a few of his men over to finish the job for him. His generosity was not the result of some prison-house reformation but a part of his character and was something he displayed when he didn't have to, even when he was under duress.

Bill Longworth was a local reporter and news anchor at WBRE-TV in Wilkes-Barre, Pennsylvania, when I worked there in the production department in the 1980s. When Russell was brought before a grand jury in New York on a charge of conspiracy to commit murder, Bill and his videographer were chosen to make the trip to New York and get what they could for broadcast.

Bill was a real talent, baby-faced, likable, and had the right journalistic chops to take the main anchor seat on demand, a thing he was frequently asked to do. He was locally famous. During a break in testimony, he found Russell and his men seated on benches outside the courtroom. He asked to be allowed to speak to Russell. Russell was facing ten years in prison if convicted, and he was already almost eighty years of age, so it's easy to imagine he was a little preoccupied.

"Mr. Bufalino, I'm Bill Longworth, and I work at WBRE-TV."

Russell was gracious. "I know who you are. Carrie and I watch you every night on the news."

Bill did what they sent him to do, which was to ask Russell if he would grant him an interview after the hearing.

"Absolutely not," Russell replied, with a half-laugh.

Bill would have chosen that moment to disarm Russell with his signature eye-rolling, head back with a silent, open-mouthed guffaw. Now that they had that behind them and had shared a private joke, he could ask for a consolation prize. "Would you do me a favor, then?" he asked.

"What is it?" was Russell's wary response.

When the day's hearings concluded, a crowd of people that included Russell and his entourage headed out of the courtroom and toward the stairs to the lobby where Bill Longworth and his photographer stood amid a throng of local and national reporters, each identifiable by whatever logos they could strap onto cameras, jackets, or—especially, if only by that time—the branded plastic cubes they placed around their microphones.

Russell and his group made their way down the stairs as Bill did what he could to get Russell's attention. Russell spied the NBC peacock on Bill's microphone cube, and he moved his group toward Bill. When he got near enough, Bill retracted the mic long enough to say words to this effect: "Mr. Bufalino, do you have anything to say about today's hearing?"

He then thrust the mic back out toward Russell, who appeared to fill the camera lens as he growled into the microphone, "I have no comment."

Favor delivered.

While his cameraman packed up his gear to change location, Bill stepped outside to scope a place to do a stand-up. He saw Russell and his men preparing to enter their car. Russell looked up the steps, caught Bill's eye, and winked.

That's a small thing, I know, but it shows Russell to be generous. From at least the time he came into his own, for whatever reason—an embarrassment of riches, "Big Man" syndrome, a new-age noblesse oblige, or as a means to garner support—Russell would do what he could for you if the request was reasonable. Moreover, anyone to whom he referred you would exceed his expectations just to please Russell. I never got to meet either of the Rockys or visit the Metropolitan Opera House like my brothers, but I may just have gone them one better.

The FBI was relentless about tracking Russell, especially after the Kennedy assassination and more so after Hoffa's disappearance.

William "Big Billy" D'Elia suggested that the whole post-Hoffa Jack Napoli affair, which finally put Russell away, was an FBI setup from the moment Napoli invoked Russell's name to walk out of a jewelry store with twenty-five thousand of dollars' worth of jewelry for which he had no plan to pay. In the 1960s, Russell wouldn't speak on a phone landline out of fear it was tapped, choosing instead long car rides to meet parties in person. One random FBI wiretap I ran across made me laugh. It was kind of a eureka moment from my childhood.

On September 3, 1964, according to a transcript, Russell Bufalino telephoned Charlie at Mogull's Camera and Film Exchange on Forty-Eighth Street in New York City. Russell identified himself as "Russ from Pennsylvania" and inquired concerning print copies of movies made in 1935 starring, as the agent recorded, "some person with an Italian-sounding name." One of the films, titled *Music for Madame,* featured actress Joan Fontaine. Bufalino indicated that he had a considerable collection of old films. The discovery made me laugh since it finally made sense of an episode from my family I never did understand. It's a snapshot of "one of the most powerful and influential organized crime figures in history, if not the most powerful" doing some phone research for my father.

Nino Martini was an opera tenor who performed at the Metropolitan Opera. He starred as a dashing lead in several movies during the 1930s, including *Music for Madame, The Gay Desperado, One Night with You,* and *Here's to Romance.* Dean Martin's first stage name was "Dino Martino," in honor, I suppose, of his musical idol. My father had reams of reel-to-reel recordings of his favorite athletic tenor, who thought nothing of singing one particular throat-busting aria five times in succession in encore performances following a show. My father had met Nino Martini at the Irem Temple in Wilkes-Barre during World War II, he said, when an Army uniform and his last name served as a convincing backstage pass. One of the highlights of his life was spending half an hour conversing with the tenor backstage in the mother tongue.

One day in the 1960s, after a quarter of a century had passed since meeting his idol, my father decided to look up Nino Martini. To our family's surprise, Nino answered the phone himself from Verona, Italy, and claimed to remember my father! This led to a few years of correspondence and a few solo trips for my father to Italy to visit in person.

Finally, in 1971, Nino invited my father, my mother, and myself to three nights of opera at the ancient Roman amphitheater, the Arena di Verona. And off we three went on a monthlong assault on Italy from Milan in the north to Montedoro, Sicily, and all points between, including Vinci, with a four-day stay carved out for the Verona visit with Nino and his wife Nancy. The monthlong trip was over-the-top, a grueling assault on the Old World with hardly a three-day stay at any one spot from Milan to Sicily and back to Rome. I'll spare you the gory details, but I'll never forget sharing the hallway of a train car with a herd of sheep in Sicily.

In Verona, Nino Martini and his wife Nancy were exceptionally graceful hosts. I could never understand what about a middle-class photographer put him in Nino's company, but there was never a suggestion or a hint that Nino saw it that way at all. He put us up in a fine *pensione,* nothing huge or ostentatious, just dripping with old class.

We met every night at the old Roman amphitheater, the Arena di Verona, to see, on successive nights, *Cenerentolla* (*Cinderella*), *La bohème,* and, I believe, *The Barber of Seville.* I swear I saw Orson Welles in the lobby of our hotel one day while I was waiting for my parents to come down. I had seen him on *The Mike Douglas Show* on one of my sick days at Mary Buff's. Portly, well-dressed, and bearded, he harumphed around his cigar and snapped a newspaper over his face to escape my slack-jawed stare. *Yeah, that's Orson Welles, all right,* I thought. *What am I doing here?*

One afternoon, I was a passenger in Nino's car with my father. We were driving around the Veronese hills, following Nancy and my mother in Nancy's car, when another driver cut Nancy off. Nino, alarmed, glanced at my father and said, "You see dot? I keel him!" and pressed the accelerator to chase the offender down the road. I'm certain that if Nino had rounded a corner too tightly and my father been thrown out the window and tumbled down a steep embankment to land impaled on the spikes of an iron fence, he'd have thought it was the best day of his life.

Nino Martini was a perfect gentleman and his wife the most gracious hostess. At thirteen years of age, I did not understand how my family with all of our middle-class faults belonged in their company. Finding Russell researching Nino's movies for my father gave me the hint that maybe he had a hand in hooking the old man and Nino up, providing me with memories of Italy and Montedoro I would never have had otherwise.

And all my brothers got was to meet the two Rockys.

CHAPTER 40

BILL'S GREAT EXPECTATIONS: THE 1960S

Bill Bufalino's personal and political fortunes began changing for the better at the very onset of the 1960s. The findings and recommendations of the U.S. Senate's Select Committee on Improper Activities in the Labor or Management Field hearings precipitated a federal court ruling that a) placed the Teamsters Union in receivership and b) specified the creation of a court-appointed board of monitors to "clean up" the way the union operated. In 1957, Teamsters president Dave Beck, his reputation damaged by the committee's grilling, chose not to continue as president or seek reelection. Hoffa was elected to the presidency at the Miami Beach convention that same year.

Between 1958 and 1960, the court-specified board of monitors wrangled over changes to the union bylaws. When Daniel B. Maher, the union's one allowed representative on the board of monitors, announced his retirement (with some opposition from the court), Hoffa proposed Bill Bufalino take over Maher's position. There was heated debate for months over the appointment between March and May 1960. Bill was ultimately accepted, and Hoffa had his own handpicked man in place to ensure that suggested reforms went his way.

In roughly the same time frame, Bill Bufalino decided to upgrade his lifestyle. He wanted to buy a plot of land and build a home in the affluent Detroit, Michigan, suburb of Grosse Pointe. The realtor's agency he contacted was a member of a realtor's association that acted in league with a property owner's association. Their coordinated aim was to ensure that Grosse Pointe property values would not be negatively affected by a sale to a person of the wrong type. The realtor engaged a standard Grosse Pointe evaluation process. A private detective was hired to question people with knowledge of the applicant and add their observations and findings to determine the party's desirability. This produced a score on "the point system." It was a system so nakedly racist that it could not possibly have survived the civil rights movement of the 1960s. All it needed was a soft breeze to drop it like a dead leaf. What it got instead was Hurricane Bill.

The point system worked on a scale of 100 points like a standard school test. Most applicants could get by with a score of fifty, but some applicants had to do better, because the system was *weighted*. Not a Protestant? You had to score higher. Polish? You had to score five points higher. Southern European, including multiple countries and Italy? Fifteen points higher. Jewish? Thirty-five! Some ethnicities were not considered at all. Other questions judged a person based on accent (pronounced, medium, slight, none) and "swarthiness." Bill's complexion was noted as "medium swarthy" and his Italian-ness cost him on the weighted scale.

Of course, it did not help that Bill was often in the public eye, subject to investigation along with Hoffa in conflicts and disputes related to Teamsters organizing methods and other activities. His neighbors were hesitant to talk about Bill to the detective. His invitation to testify before the McClellan Committee hearing did not help at all. He was denied his purchase request.

Bill subsequently filed suit, naming as parties to the suit everybody involved in the denial from the property owner to the individual realtor to the realtor's association to the homeowner's association for damages amounting to a million dollars. It was a slander and libel suit based on observations made and shared among the parties in the suit. Bill does not seem to have won the case or received a settlement, but the point system was effectively shut down as a direct result of his action. In a short period of time, Bill Buff was living in Grosse Pointe, the refuge of old money in Detroit, and he had a new line item for his résumé. He wasn't just an attorney, labor leader, and union organizer anymore. Now he was a civil rights leader, too, and his associates outside the Teamsters had plans for him.

The FBI beat me to the conclusion by fifty years, but in my defense, I was just five when they got the word from an informant. I had watched Bill's star rise in the *Teamsters* publications during Hoffa's imprisonment. I knew about his role on the board of monitors. But in the 2000s, when I stumbled across the pack of matches that sported an image of Bill Bufalino shaking hands with Martin Luther King Jr., that was the icing on the cake. I could tell that Bill was being groomed to take over the Teamsters, and the FBI had wind of the plan.

According to an FBI memo released under the President John F. Kennedy Assassination Records Collection Act of 1992, an informant told the FBI as early as January 26, 1963, that Bill was being groomed to take over the Teamsters presidency. The informant was adamant about his assertion based on hearing talk among people who were in a "position to know." On March 3 of the same year, he reiterated his "watch-and-see" claim by adding that Bill was "clean," meaning he had no criminal record and was a lawyer. At that time, he said, every effort was being made to insulate Bill from anyone who was active in any kind of racket. The source reported that Sicilians in other cities would be trying to consolidate and extend their influence over local unions to take advantage of any opportunity to take over, such as an opportunity resulting from a Hoffa imprisonment.

Of course, the prediction never materialized. Hoffa may have gotten wind of the plan himself, or he may have lost trust in Bill along the way, or he may simply have been looking for a more pliant person to be his second-in-command given the coup against him led by a trusted ally in December 1963.

Hoffa had been pragmatic about his relationships with organized crime, and he had no illusions about the potential outcomes of their involvement in union affairs. When Frank Wortman targeted Teamsters Local 688 president Harold J. Gibbons in 1952, he told Gibbons he'd kill him if he didn't place one of Wortman's people on staff. Gibbons went to Hoffa, who told him he had two choices: He could add a mobster to his staff and then watch as he took over, or he could "buy a pistol, and the first son of a bitch comes in the door, you shoot him in the head." Gibbons took the advice and became Hoffa's executive officer and Teamsters vice president on Hoffa's ascent to the presidency in 1957. They worked together well for years.

Gibbons and Hoffa fell out over the Kennedy assassination. Gibbons flew the Teamster headquarters flags at half-staff on the occasion of JFK's assassination. That upset Hoffa, who was happy about the assassination. He could now say that his chief antagonist, Bobby Kennedy, was "just a lawyer." He dressed Gibbons down for making him look like a hypocrite. Gibbons, who was secretly hoping Hoffa would be imprisoned, led a failed coup against Hoffa and resigned his position, along with four other of Hoffa's assistants. Hoffa appointed Frank Fitzsimmons to the seat Gibbons vacated, that of executive assistant.

Following the Gibbons affair, Hoffa most likely would have been cautious about anyone with ambition getting near enough the seat of power to take advantage of an opportunity to seize control of the union he considered to be his very own. Knowingly or not, Hoffa closed the door on Bill's ambitions during the 1966 Teamsters election by running Frank Fitzsimmons as vice president.

CHAPTER 41

THE GODFATHER

Bill Bufalino had one major challenge to the perceived "cleanness" that put him in the running to succeed Hoffa, and it was his relationship with Russell Bufalino. Russell had been the subject of the FBI Top Hoodlum Program investigation in the early 1950s, he had testified (by taking the Fifth) before the McClellan Committee, and he was, throughout the 1960s, at the top of the government's list for deportation.

Like literally *all* the first-generation American children of the combined Bufalino households of Salvatore, Nicolo, and Rosario, Bill had grown up scrapping with his brothers and cousins outside the Bufalino Brothers Store to entertain the old men and establish an internal pecking order. In their own way, each one strove to be at the top of the heap and chose specialties and professions in which they could excel.

My father was a well-respected photographer who worked for a time at a Hollywood studio as a staff photographer; his brother Sam was a painting contractor in Burbank who would come to own an apartment complex a block square. Bill's brother Jimmy had been the family genius but died young. Charles, Bill's older brother, married into coal contracts and was an elected official. For all Bill's success with the Teamsters, Bill was not Hoffa-level yet, and the steady stream of newspaper articles featuring Bill arguing this or that Teamsters matter that ended up at Mary's door were a call for her approval. Bill's ambition for recognition was general, however.

Like a few in the family, Bill wanted to take his career as far as it could go. So when the FBI tailed him to a bookstore in 1976, Bill bellied up to the counter with a stack of books he called research to the Black cashier. He was preparing to write a book. "You know, I marched in Alabama with Martin Luther King." He expressed surprise that the man did not know him. "You don't know who I am? I am the attorney who is representing the people upstairs . . . Haven't you seen me on television?"

The other unifying aspect of everyone's childhood was their general worship of Russell. He was such a regular at the homestead and family businesses, such an in-town presence for most of their childhoods, that, cousin notwithstanding, he was the hero of all the young men except perhaps Yabo, who worked cheek-to-jowl with Russell and Joseph Barbara. There's hardly one of the first-generation American Buffs that did not at one time or another seek out Russell's counsel or direct help in getting grounded in some endeavor. All of them maintained good relations with Russell, so far as it was possible in their individual situation, for all of their lives. The coup that Bill scored that put him on top of everyone in the family was his *extra-close* relationship with Russell. The magic hat trick Bill had to achieve, then, was to balance his non-association with racketeers with his own deep desire to be known as someone important in his own right by borrowing some of what he perceived as Russell's shine.

It started well enough for Bill following the McClellan Committee hearings, when he sued *Time* magazine in 1962 for preparing and publishing a genealogy that linked him with Russell. According to an FBI memo, *Time* had cast Russell and Bill as direct family. Bill reached a settlement with *Time* in a libel suit for a total of $25,000 paid over the course of two years. He pressed *Newsweek* on the same account, and then attempted to sue Bobby Kennedy for presenting the same chart, eight-feet long, in the televised hearings. In doing so, he successfully put to bed any notion of any relationship with Russell. But then, out of either an excess of hubris or with the bulletproof feeling that they all had that Hoover would not pursue the matter vigorously, Bill couldn't help himself but to share the counterargument.

In an FBI memo, Bill is recorded as indicating over the years he had been very close to Russell Bufalino and considered him to be a very close friend. But somehow that wasn't strong enough for Bill, not strong enough to convey his own true stature. So he clarified:

> "[The government says that] *in the underworld, you either have to be born in it or you have to get in by marriage," William Bufalino says proudly. "I married a Detroit girl . . . If you want to charge me with something regarding Russell Bufalino, charge me with the fact that I selected him as my number one friend . . . Because my daughter . . . is the godchild of Russell Bufalino and his wife. In other words, we selected them to be the godparents of my daughter. This is a closer relationship than a brother.*

The American ear may not have been finely tuned enough to the nuance in Bill's statement and probably completely missed his meaning, although he spoke quite plainly at the end. The godfather relationship in Sicily in Bill's father's time was nothing like either the popularized understanding that comes from the movie *The Godfather* or the common Western meaning where to be someone's godparent imparts a responsibility on the part of the chosen godparent to raise or mentor a child if the child's own parent dies.

Louise Hamilton Caico describes learning about the godfather relationship from her guide, Alessandro Augello, in *Sicilian Ways and Days*. She reports that the godfather relationship places no direct responsibility between godfather and child. The real relationship of "Cumpari San Giovanni" existed between the men. If I ask someone to become my child's godfather, I am suggesting that he and I enter into a relationship, regardless of family ties, that makes us closer than brothers. Bill might as well have said, "I am Russell Bufalino's 'inside man' in the Teamsters." If you consider the extent to which Teamsters pension fund money on loan built Las Vegas, his statement and professed relationship with Russell might have been considered explosive.

In the above, Bill had blamelessly told everybody the plain truth. Nobody understood what he meant or ever followed it up. That kind of loose talk went right up and down Russell's spine but probably did not sink Bill's chances at being Hoffa's successor. Russell was extremely cagey about letting any personal information slip, especially the kind that suggested that he might have been in a position to influence the operations of a major labor union powerful enough to shut down the country.

You may see a clip of Russell Bufalino online at a trial being deliberately evasive about his relationships and the timeline of those relationships with Frank Sheeran and Jimmy Hoffa. At great length, he answers that the place of his first meeting with Hoffa was in "Detroit," and the occasion, "another wedding."

According to Dan Moldea, Hoffa was well-acquainted with Angelo Meli by the mid-1930s. In 1936, Hoffa married Josephine Poszywak in Detroit. Bill married Marie Antoinette Meli in Detroit in 1945. Chances are good Russell met Hoffa on one or the other of those two occasions. Whichever it was, Angelo Meli might have been there as well.

CHAPTER 42

DEAR JIM

I can't put my hands on the document I am about to reference, and I can only recall the thrust of it. That may not be important in light of the very obvious and public falling-out and split between Bill and Hoffa. Altogether, the artifact I discovered had more importance to me than to the public's general understanding of Teamsters politics in the 1960s. It was brand-new information to me and was the second of three reveals that began in the wake of my mother's death that led me to write.

Working in the soda factory, the first-floor cellar of my house, a month or two after my mother's passing, I opened what looked like a box of just stuff from Mary's half of the building. I had purchased Salvatore's half of the building in a tax sale in 1997, and in the interim, I had moved most of the remaining family belongings from the ground floor of her building, which Bill had used as his office, to my half for safekeeping. I was renting out the other half of the house.

And in my hands was a legal pad with cursive writing: *Dear Jim*. Maybe it said *Jimmy*, I'm not sure. I don't recall it being more than seven pages long. I read it. I did not realize that Hoffa was the intended recipient until I got to the main thrust of the letter, which is all I frankly remember about it. Then I had no doubt.

So, why should this letter be in my hands? First, it had probably risen from Bill's own downstairs office. Second, it was common enough for Mary, Bill's sister, to have copies of a great many things associated with Bill, from newspaper clippings to *Teamsters* magazines. She had even shared with me a finished copy of the letter Bill wrote on behalf of Russell, addressed to the authorities in Italy, that attempted to convince the receiving party not to accept Russell as a deportee from the United States. And why should *she* have these things?

Mary's sister Adeline acted as Bill's legal secretary in Detroit for some time. Like the other members of her family who had followed Bill to Detroit, Pauline and Yabo, Adeline was an active part of Bill's extended family life. Since Bill wanted Mary's approval, he may have directed her to forward these things. Or maybe what I had in my hands was a draft of the eventual eleven-pages he delivered for Hoffa's eyes only, something he worked on himself in his local office.

I'll summarize the content in extreme brief and paraphrase:

Dear Jimmy,

You know the love and respect I have for you and the battles we have fought and won together [some of which were listed].

I would very much appreciate it if you could please stop calling me a cocksucker in front of the federal marshals.

Your friend: Bill

At the time I found the letter, I had not known about the falling-out of the two men. I still only knew the accepted lore of the family, which was long on heroism of Salvatore and Bill, Salvatore's leadership in the community, and our family fighting the Mob. Bill was a labor leader; Russ was the black sheep and distant relative. That's all I needed to know.

I put the letter aside while I arranged for the removal of many non-artifacts and just cellar junk. Those were bad days. I contacted a government agency in relation to difficulties I was having with a jurist in a distant county. The receiving agent was aghast at what I shared and said I should expect a callback. To sweeten their interest, I told them I had the letter from Bill in my cellar. It disappeared. I may simply be a terrible curator—it's hard to say. Lots of traffic in the soda factory in those days.

I never got a call back. I'm glad I learned that lesson before the next and final discovery, which I would keep close to my vest for fifteen years.

CHAPTER 43

EMERGING FROM HOFFA'S SHADOW

Bill's slander and libel lawsuit against the Grosse Pointe screening system and its agents did not result in a cash settlement for Bill, but it started a cascade of events that would spark a state investigation and ultimately lead to fair housing legislation. The legislation was based on an administrative rule put forth by other liberal actors in the state Democratic Party, Rule 9. That rule prohibited discrimination in housing sales. While others have claimed credit for the subsequent actions that led to the rule, they have failed to give credit where it was due, even when they cite the seminal lawsuit that started the whole affair. The *Detroit Free Press* expressed their own view on February 7, 1963, claiming in an article that Bill Bufalino was "the Father of Rule 9."

Bill was not shy to embrace the title. In his usual manner, he energetically inserted himself into the 1960s hot-button civil rights issues. In doing so, he created an identity all his own, and crafted a public image morally distinct from Hoffa's and his own previous brass-knuckled persona. His special niche was at the meeting place of civil rights and the labor fight. His growing reputation as a fair housing leader fueled Bill's rise in the popular press and began to offset his former perceived image as a take-no-prisoners labor organizer whose tactics sometimes discomfited business owners and excited the authorities.

By 1968, Bill was speaking to college students at Notre Dame on the relationship between labor unions and students by invitation of the university's Student Management Club. In 1969, the Italian-language newspaper *La Voce del Popolo* of Detroit dedicated a half of its October 17 bifold English page to print Bill's entire remarks as principal speaker of a Columbus Day banquet held at Cobo Hall, Detroit. In 1971, Bill and seven other Detroiters received an award for their contributions to Detroit's Conference of Ethnic Communities.

Bill would be the first to point out that civil rights was not just a black-and-white issue. Joe Colombo established the Italian-American Civil Rights League in New York City to make the same argument and advocate for social change resulting from Mafia stereotyping. Bill was coming into his own, apart from Hoffa. The Teamsters matchbook emblazoned with the photo of Bill Bufalino shaking hands with Martin Luther King Jr. may have been over-the-top, but it was pure Bill.

Bill continued to press on civil rights issues for all ethnic groups into the 1970s. By 1976, Bill cast himself more in the role of a civil libertarian at large, intent on defending the "little guy" by anyone's definition from big government oppression.

It was in that mindset that he made history in the defense of Stephen Andretta, a person of government interest in the Hoffa disappearance. Andretta was hauled in before a one-man grand jury, which was allowed under Michigan law. He was denied counsel. Bill stationed himself outside in the hall. When Andretta was asked a question, any question, he asked to exercise his right to speak to counsel, and so he traveled out into the hall to speak with Bill.

Andretta did that 1,203 times. Bill had the one-man grand jury pulling his hair out by turning what should have been a two-day session into an eleven-day ordeal.

While some felt he was making an ass of himself by blustering around the courthouse, making motions, others credited Bill with inventing an effective counterstrategy to combat the one-man grand jury.

CHAPTER 44

THE SPLIT

The 1960s were not Jimmy Hoffa's decade. Convicted in two trials involving jury tampering, attempted bribery, conspiracy, and mail and wire fraud in 1964, he spent three years in appeals before his sentencing and eventual imprisonment at Lewisburg Federal Penitentiary in Pennsylvania.

In 1966, the Teamsters reelected Hoffa president to a second five-year term, but given the possibility of conviction and imprisonment, Hoffa ran Frank Fitzsimmons as vice president—just in case. Fitzsimmons was a longtime loyalist. Hoffa expected Fitzsimmons to follow directives about running the union in case he himself should be incarcerated. That was why Bill came from Detroit to visit Hoffa on what Bill himself reported as a weekly basis during Hoffa's imprisonment in Lewisburg.

As you might expect, Frank Fitzsimmons was not quick to follow Hoffa's directives in every respect. He was making changes to Jimmy's union that would decentralize the power Hoffa himself had enjoyed. Hoffa's frustration with Fitzsimmons increased. At the same time, Hoffa cannot have helped noticing that Bill's star within the Teamsters was on the rise. Bill was pressing ahead on the themes of civil rights within the union. I recall that Bill came to have a regular slot, like a franchise, in the regular monthly *Teamsters* publication, in which he frequently discussed civil rights issues as they related to labor. Other old Hoffa allies like Anthony "Tony Pro" Provenzano were becoming openly hostile. Hoffa grew increasingly disturbed by what he considered betrayals and injustices. It got to the point that eventually, by the time of his release, Hoffa would be talking about himself in the third person.

I became more acquainted with Bill during the Hoffa years as he visited Lewisburg weekly. He would often show up at Mary's for a short stay of two or three days in the company of either or both Yabo and his son, William Bufalino II, who the men called "Billy Boy." His local legal affairs sometimes saw him retreat to his office downstairs from Mary in the old general store, where Hoffa's original oak desk was the centerpiece of his inner sanctum. Somehow I missed the memo about Bill's falling-out with Hoffa. It was probably a subject unfit for a young boy's ears.

Hoffa's falling-out with his onetime close ally and handpicked monitor Bill Buff was well-publicized and often spoken about by Bill Buff himself. If the nature of their split was not clear enough, that was all right; it was a private matter between friends. I have read that Bill Buff delivered to Hoffa an eleven-page handwritten letter for Hoffa's eyes only. It was in the form of a Dear John letter, and the split was final.

Bill shared details of his grievances against Hoffa with *The Detroit News* in 1976. Hoffa was clearly hating prison time in Lewisburg and accusing Bill of both getting him into prison and doing nothing to get him out. Hoffa was probably reliving some paranoia resulting from the coup against him led by Harold Gibbons following Kennedy's assassination. Hoffa had run out of trust in Fitzsimmons, and was now running out of faith in Bill.

Bill, for his part, was still actively cultivating his very public role as a civil rights leader, and his activities on Hoffa's part were getting in the way. On one occasion, Hoffa dispatched him to the

Atlanta airport to meet with an individual concerning a Teamster's wife, Viola Gregg Liuzzo, who had been murdered on the civil rights march in Selma, Alabama. At first, Bill thought the men carrying the black umbrellas that surrounded the party he was meeting were the FBI, but the man said not to worry—they were his people. Bill realized he was talking to the KKK. Hoffa figured they could help him in the South. Bill couldn't get over what he perceived as a betrayal of his interests. He thought it was a pretty bad way to be used by his former boss.

On another occasion, while in prison, Hoffa directed Bill to West Virginia to broker the silence of a juror who had indicated she might be amenable to accepting a bribe. Bill was appalled and smelled a trap that could cost him, if not his reputation, then possibly his freedom.

And then there were the phone calls Bill received at all hours at home from Hoffa's now-released prison associates, whom Hoffa had promised jobs or just money. Bill reckoned that Hoffa's interest in helping these people was to build up a cache of good deeds to put before a parole board.

Bottom line: Bill had probably run out of use for Hoffa, and Hoffa had definitely run out of use for Bill. Bill figured that if he stayed too close to Hoffa, he'd end up being thrown under the bus by his former boss, so he made the split. Publicly, Bill would speak openly about how Hoffa used people, was hotheaded and capricious, and was generally unsuited to continuing in his role, while Frank Fitzsimmons, on the other hand, was the paragon of wisdom and just the right man to move the Teamsters forward. Bill was solidly in Fitzsimmons's camp.

Bill contrasted Hoffa and Fitzsimmons in the *Detroit Free Press* in 1976:

"Frank Fitzsimmons is an entirely different personality. His mind works with exacting precision. He too (like Hoffa) has an analytical mind, but he is not impetuous. He moves slower but he has more calculated moves." The comparison reminds him, Bufalino says, of a Sicilian saying taught to him as a child by his grandmother, Maria Augello Galante of Montedoro, Sicily: "He who goes slowly and carefully will arrive in one piece."

CHAPTER 45

YABO IN DETROIT

Yabo had followed Bill to Detroit along with his brother Eugene, his sisters Adeline and Pauline Tulumello, and Pauline's young son Angelo. Eugene worked a number of jobs with Yabo for the Meli family, including restaurateur and club manager, and he even spent some time as a fight promoter before leaving for California to get into the wine trade, eventually becoming the president of a distiller's union set up by his brother Bill. In Detroit, the four siblings kept to a common house on Alter Road and continued as a clan. They helped Bill by keeping house and providing material support along with working their day jobs. Adeline worked for some time in the capacity of Bill's legal secretary. Pauline put her son Angelo Tulumello through college, running a store in the vicinity.

Yabo continued on his former trajectory as a tradesman, becoming a journeyman millwright and moonlighting. He could always handle a brawl, so bartending at the Story Club with his brothers for Angelo Meli was a natural assignment in his early days. Union organizing required people to man picket lines, and Yabo was right there for Bill whenever he was needed, such as when a given bar needed a single picketer to protest the establishment's use of nonunion (non-Wurlitzer) repairmen or when a car wash or other establishment failed to succumb to pressure to unionize. A Teamster himself, he also traveled with Bill and Hoffa whenever muscle was needed. He always was there to attend his younger brother. On one occasion,

Bill experienced a nasal hemorrhage and Yabo bundled him into his car and drove fifty-two miles in under thirty-odd minutes through six red lights to get him care.

At some point, Yabo took a job as a millwright, which set him traveling back to Pennsylvania for work, though it's not clear he was dedicated to that role long-term. He held a number of odd jobs, often at the same time. He sold Christmas trees at a street corner stand near Grosse Pointe that he fought in court to set up. He worked security at the arena in Cobo Hall in downtown Detroit. He watched Sugar Ray Robinson KO Chuck Taylor of Pittsburgh at the Olympia Arena on Grand View Avenue in a bout that lasted ninety seconds and was finished before some fans had found their seats. When he wasn't traveling on Teamsters business or helping organize on Bill's behalf, Yabo enjoyed the role of acting as a favorite uncle for Billy Boy and Bill's growing family.

Yabo had always been an outdoorsman, ever since my grandfather taught him to hunt as a youth. Camping and fishing were almost his first nature, and he would often take off alone for days at a time to hunt, fish, or otherwise just "commune." The wild was what set Yabo apart from his siblings. It was the arena he mastered. He once organized an elk hunting trip in Michigan. According to Yabo, licenses for elk cost a hundred dollars at the time. It's not clear how the party divided the territory they would hunt or whether they made any organized effort to drive their quarry toward some kill zone or not. What is clear is that Yabo was posted alone in some area separate from the rest when three or four big, wide-antlered bucks wandered right into his area. He raised his rifle and waited. He never took the shot. Buck fever. It was enough for him to know he could have had it. Ever a lover of the outdoors, Yabo purchased several lots on Bois Blanc Island, Michigan, as a retreat for himself.

Yabo does not seem to have been anyone's "soldier" per se, despite having connections through his family to the Detroit

Partnership. But he knew everybody in that arena, right up to Angelo Meli. When he was on his free time, his pursuits included gambling and frequenting clubs and fights with his associates, many of whom had underworld ties. If Northeastern Pennsylvania, with its gambling parlors, turf wars, and murderous characters, had not already taught him, Yabo learned in Detroit a very important life lesson about being happy with what you have.

The FBI followed Yabo and Bill in Detroit as well as Eugene when he left for Burbank, California. The Bureau basically followed everyone in Russell's sphere. The phones at my father's photography studio in Pittston, Pennsylvania were tapped, though that may have been on another account altogether. In Yabo's case, an FBI informant attached himself to Yabo around 1963 and traveled with him to meet Angelo Meli at his farm in the country. The informant took notes of everything that transpired or was said to send up the line to the Bureau. Some of the transcript ended up in an FBI report released under the John F. Kennedy Assassination Records Collection Act of 1992 identified as record number 124-10342-10185. Many paragraphs of the above-referenced document pertain to Angelo (Yabo) and are descriptive of himself and life events that shaped his character. A few paragraphs describe the peculiar facets of Yabo's character and the identity of the man at his funeral reception. He also relates a story of a life lesson Yabo took to heart concerning the death of a friend.

Yabo picked up the informant on a Sunday in June 1963. They were destined for Angelo Meli's summer home on the St. Clair River. On the way, Yabo stopped at his brother Bill's house, the new place in Grosse Pointe. Bill was visiting someone in St. Clair Shores and was not at home. The informant recorded that Yabo "took photographs of some flowers in the Bufalino gardens" before they left. That was Yabo. The natural world lit his fire, and when he wasn't hiking or hunting or fishing in it, he was looking for ways to capture it to enjoy later.

Arriving at Meli's summer home/farm, the informant noted the presence of a lot of women and children on the grounds and described the men playing cards with Meli: the owner of a local hot rod shop and his friend, the owner of a stamping shop, who was traveling from Burbank, California. A third member of the party the informant described as "Dominic (LNU) [last name unknown], a little, short guy who looks 'like a mole' and who was raised around the Franklin Settlement with the informant." Without a doubt, this was the man from Yabo's funeral reception who laid out Yabo's life in Detroit for me, claiming Yabo was "like a father" to him.

One evening in 1963, Yabo told the informant the story of his friend Roy Calabrese, whose body was found garroted in the trunk of his car in February 1962. Roy Calabrese had been a runner in a betting parlor specializing in the numbers racket. Eventually he became a bookie in that racket. It is supposed by some that Roy was scamming his employer by reporting the day's winning number to an accomplice who would then back-engineer a ticket with the numbers provided by Roy. Papa John Priziola noticed, and Roy endured a beating over the scam. Some assume that Roy continued the practice and it cost him his life. Others attribute his death to the belief that he had turned informant. Yabo's belief about the matter put him in the camp with those who considered Roy to be an informant.

Yabo's version of the story, which he related to the informant, cast Roy's downfall as a cautionary tale about wanting too much, a sin with which Yabo would never thereafter be associated. Yabo told the informant his opinion that Roy had been trying to muscle in on a large craps game on St. Jean Avenue that was run by Joe "Whip" Triglia. When Triglia failed to succumb to Roy's power play, Roy dropped a dime on the game one evening just before leaving. Conspicuously, the police raid occurred minutes after Roy left the game. Of course, nobody could prove that Roy had turned informant, but they may have had enough of him anyway and decided to just play it safe by killing him.

Yabo took the episode to heart and always stayed in his lane. His humility and loyalty paid dividends in any case. Angelo Meli owned a co-op in Florida and extended the use of it to Yabo for vacations, seeing as how they were in the family way through Bill. Yabo and his sisters, including Mary, made liberal use of that accommodation yearly during the deep northern winters.

By 1976, agents assigned to Bill Bufalino noted that his health was visibly in decline. He was just fulfilling his lifelong dream of setting up a law practice in partnership with his son, William Bufalino II. By 1982, he would retire from the practice. Alter Road was becoming a bad neighborhood during street violence in the 1970s.

The clan dissolved.

Yabo and his two sisters returned in turns to Pittston to stay with Mary next door to us. Pauline passed away in Pittston in 1974. Mary herself passed in 1981. Adeline returned to Detroit and passed in 1983. Sometime shortly after Mary passed, Yabo returned to Pittston for good. He would be my on-and-off neighbor through the 1980s.

CHAPTER 46

JFK: THE BUFALINO CONNECTION

I remember it in slow motion, like you would remember a near-death experience or a slow slide in a car on black ice toward a collision. That's the mystery of it to me, because my life was nowhere in the balance of events. I may have contracted a state of hypervigilance in sympathy with my father's own PTSD. I don't know.

I was six years old, watching television in the living room, my stomach on the floor and my face in my hands. At a sound, my father, sitting reclined in his La-Z-Boy lounger to my right shouted, "Oh, my God!" and somehow propelled himself into the air from a prone position like a cat struck by ball lightning. He had been especially tweaked in the days before.

In the moment, he seemed capable of defying gravity. In his mind, like mini explosions, came a series of scenes that marked the milestones of his childhood: The assassinations of Lucchino, Campbell, Calamera landed in order behind his eyes like the windowed displays of a slot machine registering all cherries.

Before his backside returned to the chair, like a sibyl, he shouted out, "He's the patsy!" It was as though he and the events unfolding on the screen in front of us became connected in some way that spanned the distance of half a country and time. As I returned my eyes to the television set, Lee Harvey Oswald was just realizing he'd been shot.

From that moment on, at least until the release of the Zapruder film in the 1970s, the Kennedy assassination became my father's central obsession. He had been a Kennedy man literally since before I was two years of age, during the McClellan Committee hearings, despite the grilling Russell and Bill took from JFK, RFK, and the Committee. It didn't bother Russell, and it didn't bother my father. JFK was just doing his job.

Russell supported JFK in his 1960 run at the presidency for the same reason others in Russell's line of work would have done. They would have been satisfied with either Nixon or Kennedy, but they favored JFK and helped him, especially, as some would say, in Chicago. So when the Kennedy campaign made a swing through Pittston, my father waited for the motorcade to go by his North Main Street studio and shouted, in his best and loudest sergeant-in-the-Army voice, "Hey, Jack!" When JFK turned to the voice, my father was gesturing frantically to the big sign above his photography business that read *Bufalino Studio* in letters two feet tall. JFK laughed. My father talked about it for years.

After Kennedy assumed the presidency, my father followed the news as LBJ became the subject of Senate investigations related to his financial dealings with Bobby Baker in the 1950s. I was still reading *Fun with Dick and Jane* as my father's personal library overflowed with topical political themes like *The Bobby Baker Affair* and RFK's *The Enemy Within*. After the assassination, his library grew to include books like *The Witnesses* and *The Death of a President*. So that was how I learned to read. "See Dick run. Run, Dick, run. The gun in the sniper's nest was first identified as a Mauser."

Safe to say, my father was dialed in to all things Russell, Kennedy, and Hoffa. The three men themselves were his personal heroes, and the events of their lives or their passings fairly occupied his mind in the 1960s. The assassination of JFK, and my father's own suspicions about Oswald's role, kept him unsettled throughout the remainder of 1963. When the February 21, 1964, edition of *Life* magazine arrived featuring a photo of Oswald on the cover with rifle and a pamphlet tucked under his chin, he spent just a minute studying the photo before he reached for the telephone.

My father was a classically-trained professional photographer, and a good one. He studied at the Antonelli School of Photography in Philadelphia on the GI Bill after World War II. Some of my father's coursework involved modernist and artistic techniques, employed by the likes of William Mortensen, who used the lens and negatives as a stepping-off point into surrealist imagery. By scraping away emulsion or adding density to a negative with pencils, Angelo Bufalino could do just about anything with a negative to produce a realistic photo. When he saw that the shadow under Oswald's nose in the magazine cover disagreed with the shadow on the ground behind him as to the time of day, he had another cat-struck-by-lightning moment. He contacted Jim Garrison, the New Orleans Parish District Attorney, who had assumed the role of Oswald's posthumous representative and would eventually write *On the Trail of the Assassins*.

My father's cavernous photographic studio below the old Lithuanian Club at 89 North Main Street in downtown Pittston had a heavy, two-story tall, triple-layered, staggered black crepe cyclorama curtain that acted as a backdrop for large wedding parties and as a baffle or blackout curtain to protect his darkroom lair from any light leakage. In the aftermath of his own personal revelation about the *Life* magazine cover featuring Lee Harvey Oswald, he would use darkroom hours to further his theory about Oswald. It was from there that he contacted Garrison. Occasionally, a return call would be fruitful enough that it would send my father looking for someone else in the studio to hear what he was hearing by picking up the party line in my mother's office.

At those times, he would emerge from the fug of his darkroom into the studio half-light-blind and stiff-armed, fighting his way through layers of heavy black curtain like Karloff's mummy shrugging off a two-thousand-year sleep, furiously struggling with the grotesquely tangled fifty-or-more-foot extension cord of his phone as he, cigarette and handset in hand, turned this way and that like a marlin on a line to free himself from the tangling cord, all the while gesticulating wildly with his free hand for somebody, anybody to please and quickly pick up the party line extension. He wanted a witness to the conversation.

It was on one of those occasions that I, at age six, picked up the receiver in time to hear Lee Harvey Oswald's mother plaintively ask, "Mr. Bufalinah, do you have any information that might vindicate my son?"

My father cannot, of course, have been the only one to notice the discrepancy and question the validity of the photo on the *Life* cover. But not everyone who noticed would have been brazen enough to seek out and call Oswald's representative or go on record with a statement. My father was brazen as hell. The FBI knows that well, and any mass disclosure is going to feature my father's name, repeatedly, for a number of reasons, including the much better one below.

I think we Buffs—at least my father's household—might have gotten through the whole Kennedy business without any serious notice by the FBI if my father could have avoided making those repeated calls to the White House. Of course, he would have a drink or two to buoy him up beforehand. It's only every third or fourth day you call the President of the United States, after all.

It always started the same way, with directory assistance. I'd be lurking in the hallway, top of the street-side stairs with Consagro's ghost, trying to stay out of eyeshot, listening with dread: *Okay . . . Directory assistance . . . Maybe he's calling California . . . Nope . . . Pennsylvania Avenue . . . Okay . . . For gosh sakes, write the number down! Every time you ask for an operator, you spend seventy-five-cents!*

And then he was on the phone with the White House switchboard: "Hello, I would like to speak to Lyndon Baines Johnson, please." He threw the "Baines" in like your parents do, to let him know, *You're in big trouble now, mister*. There would be a pause and a question on the other end of the phone, to which he would reply, "A citizen."

This is another instance where my father was not alone in his suspicions that LBJ had a role in the assassination. The belief had rooted itself in the public psyche. According to Michael Benson, author of *Gangsters vs. Nazis*, Jack Ruby himself told Gerald Ford and Chief Justice Earl Warren (of the Warren Commission) that he had killed Oswald out of a sense of patriotism. What's more, Ruby told Warren the plot to kill the president was hatched out of the right-wing John Birch Society and that it had been hatched by (then president) "Johnson and the others."

Barbara Garson wrote a play about the Kennedy assassination, a satire, of course, in which she transposed the events of the assassination onto Shakespeare's *Macbeth*. She called it *MacBird*. But that's where my father left the rest of humanity behind. Not one to sit by quietly, he just picked up that phone and had at it.

The FBI was surprisingly unamused by the White House calls and appeared at the house one afternoon to question my father on a number of topics, including his repeatedly being awarded the contract to provide photography for the Pittston Area High School Yearbook. I was puttering around the kitchen table, grabbing a soda from the refrigerator as Agent Jones had a dossier unfolded on the table.

When the agent asked how my father was able to secure the Pittston Area high school yearbook contract year after year, my father answered, with a characteristic finger pointing at the agent's face, "Because I'm the best goddamn photographer in Pennsylvania, fella."

Well, he *was* good. Maybe even *that* good, at portraiture at least. The only non-cockeyed photo of Russell I know of was taken in my father's studio. But this was Pittston, after all, and it probably didn't hurt at all to have a list of acquaintances that included Russell and his close associates. Pittston politics, even school board politics, was kind of that way.

Sometime in the 2000s, a computer model was produced—at great expense, I hope—to prove after fifty years that the photo on the cover of *Life* magazine featuring Oswald was *not* faked, that there was no nefarious plot, that the light of the sun could in fact have itself lied about the noontime shadow under Oswald's nose and the 3:00 p.m. shadow on the ground.

I don't know enough about the study, but I've had three careers: one in television and the others working graphic arts and programming computers. I know that light is capricious, and computer imagery starts with the desired output and works backward to produce the effect.

Maybe there was *not* a vast, global conspiracy to kill JFK after all. But if there was, then the thumb still stuck in the bloodshot, pulpy eye of the beast is very likely Angelo Joseph Bufalino's, and that is, at least, something.

CHAPTER 47

HOFFA'S DISAPPEARANCE

On July 30, 1975, the Wednesday of a week that was to end on Friday, August 1, with a wedding at Bill Bufalino's Grosse Pointe home, Jimmy Hoffa went missing. The FBI reports that Hoffa arrived at the Machus Red Fox restaurant around 2:00 p.m. and left between 2:45 and 2:50 p.m. He is believed to have traveled to the Machus Red Fox to meet with Anthony "Tony Jack" Giacalone and New Jersey's Anthony "Tony Pro" Provenzano, both of whom later denied there was any such arrangement.

The FBI notes suggest that Hoffa did not appear to have been abducted but noted also a lack of eyewitnesses to his departure. There are differing versions of what car he got into and with whom. Some suppose the Sheeran version is correct. Others insist Sheeran's story is a fabrication. I have nothing to offer about that. What's certain is that Jimmy Hoffa left Machus Red Fox restaurant with someone and rode off into a few different myths—none of them good. His car was found in the restaurant's lot the next morning.

The FBI became involved when Hoffa Jr. reported Hoffa's disappearance as a kidnapping/extortion matter. They crafted the Hoffex (a portmanteau of *Hoffa extortion*) memo on that basis. The memo contained a suspect list with names and profile information of Hoffa associates and potential enemies and a rundown of their relationship to Hoffa and their recent activities. Among the notes in the memo were an accounting of the clientele of Machus Red Fox on the day of Hoffa's disappearance and notes of discussions with five patrons who had interacted with Hoffa on that day between his arrival at 2:00 p.m. and his 2:45 to 2:50 departure. Named among the local Detroit suspects were Chuckie O'Brien, Anthony "Tony Jack" Giacalone, Vito "Billy Jack" Giacalone, Raffaele "Jimmy Q" Quasarano, Paul Vitale, and Rolland McMaster. The named suspects from outside of Detroit included Anthony "Tony Pro" Provenzano of New Jersey and his close associates including Stephen and Thomas Andretta, Salvatore "Sally Bugs" Briguglio, Gabriel "Gabe" Briguglio, and Frank "The Irishman" Sheeran.

Bill Bufalino had famously broken ties with Hoffa in 1971. He seemed to keep his union post, however, and collected fees as a special counsel for the Teamsters, working for various locals. In 1975 and 1976, he and his son William Bufalino II were setting up a joint legal practice in Detroit. Both Bills, father and son, became involved in the defense of several of the men listed as suspects in the Hoffex memo. They were doing it pro bono, without payment.

On December 4, 1975, Thomas and Stephen Andretta, Salvatore and Gabriel Briguglio, Rolland McMaster, and Frank Sheeran answered subpoenas to appear before a grand jury. Bill Bufalino was present in their defense. When Dan Moldea asked Bill why he was representing the men, and why for free, Bill responded, "If someday they have some money, they can pay me. If Hoffa were here right now, he'd say: 'Continue defending these people. they weren't the ones who did it.'" Pressed to clarify, Bill added, "Tell the FBI to look into the CIA. And tell the CIA to look into the FBI. Then you'll have the answer." Then he added his own belief that Hoffa's murder was related to those of Sam Giancana and "Handsome Johnny" Roselli.

Bill Buff was crazy smart. He was hooked in to so much private information about both the Teamsters and the Pittston family through his cousin/godfather Russell Bufalino that he sometimes—as when he told the FBI that he and Russell were closer than brothers—couldn't help but let something slip. It drove Russell crazy, of course. But in referencing Roselli and Giancana, Bill was making reference to a public suspicion that was, at the time, under Senate investigation.

Circulating on the conspiracy mill since the 1960s had been multiple interweaving theories: a) the CIA had enlisted the Mafia (through Sam Giancana and Santo Trafficante) to murder Fidel Castro; b) the CIA had been behind the Kennedy assassination, owing to its own embarrassment over the Bay of Pigs disaster and Kennedy's professed desire to disband the agency; c) that the Cuban government was behind the Kennedy assassination in retaliation for the CIA's plan to kill Castro *and* the Bay of Pigs disaster; and d) the Mafia set its sights on killing JFK over its loss of revenues related to Kennedy's failure to provide air support at the Bay of Pigs disaster. The Bay of Pigs so stuck to JFK's legend that Richard Nixon is said to have referred to the JFK assassination in coded fashion, calling it "That Bay of Pigs thing".

Altogether, the round-robin accusations and lack of clarity were too much for the Senate, who dubbed 1975 the "Year of Intelligence." The United States Senate Select Committee to Study Governmental Operations with Respect to Intelligence Activities, later known as the Church Committee, was in 1975 investigating, among other things, MKUltra, COINTELPRO, and other acts of intelligence agencies, including the CIA and National Security Agency (NSA). Bill was specifically referencing the committee's interest in presumptive CIA assassination plots against heads of state. He was suggesting that, to conceal its own involvement in such matters, the CIA and/or the FBI enacted a policy of silencing witnesses.

Unfortunately for Russell Bufalino and Jimmy Hoffa under that theory, they both had been in-the-know about the Castro plot. William "Big Billy" D'Elia's account references Russell's own concern about the fate of both Sam Giancana and Johnny Roselli in relation to the CIA's Castro plan. Russell's concern over Hoffa's ever-looser lips was based on a belief that, if Jimmy started to spout off about his and Russell's involvement in the Castro affair, that Russell himself (and Hoffa) might share the fates of Giancana and Roselli. At least, that's just one thread of the tangled web intended to provide Russell a motive for the Hoffa killing.

Johnny Roselli had already testified before the Church Committee twice, mostly concerning his knowledge of the CIA's plot to kill Fidel Castro. Roselli had apparently been approached by an ex-FBI agent in Las Vegas to help him enlist Sam Giancana and Santo Trafficante into the plot. There *were* attempts to kill Castro that came about as a result of the deal, but they all failed and the campaign ended by the time of the abortive invasion of Cuba and the debacle at the Bay of Pigs.

Roselli was summoned a third time into a private session in April 1976, where he was asked to testify about the JFK assassination. Roselli told the committee in private that he had a suspicion, unsubstantiated by facts, that Castro agents had been involved in the Kennedy assassination. Roselli's business partner later explained that Roselli had CIA clearance to talk to the committee and be as forthcoming as he liked because it was all going to come out anyway.

Roselli apparently did *not* clear his testimony with the underworld, however. When the committee sought to speak with Roselli a fourth time, three months later, it was found that he had gone missing. He was later found in Dumfoundling Bay, Florida. His body, piecemeal, had been packed into a fifty-five-gallon oil drum that had been poked full of holes, sealed, and weighted down with chains. This was not the modus operandi of the CIA, it was said, nor the Cuban contingent in Florida—this smacked more of a Mob hit. But you never know.

Sam Giancana, for his part, never made it to a first session with the Church Committee. Deposed as the head of the Chicago Outfit by Paul "The Waiter" Ricca and Anthony "Tony" Accardo, he had returned at the request of the committee from Mexico and was staying under police protection at his home in Oak Park, Illinois. On June 19, 1975, someone Giancana probably knew—some say it was Anthony "Tony the Ant" Spilotro—traversed neighborhood backyards in the dark, climbed fences, and crawled through a cellar window to shoot Giancana seven times in the head and neck with a .22-caliber gun from behind as he prepared a dinner of sausage and peppers. He had been shot one of the seven times in the mouth, suggesting that the motive for his killing was related to "talking."

So here is Bill Bufalino in late 1975, implicating the CIA in Hoffa's disappearance, presumably over Hoffa's knowledge concerning the Castro plot, and maybe, just maybe, the somewhat-related topic of the Kennedy assassination. Was he being honest, or was he just using the public conspiracy mill and the government's immediate concern that it had lost control of its intelligence agencies to cast blame afield and protect his clients?

As usual, Bill, always on the attack, did something completely outrageous. I can see the look on his son's face as Bill directed him to take the action. When "Billy Boy" was fresh out of law school and visiting with Bill in Pittston, I would often catch his white-faced and pop-eyed reaction to some outrageous thing Bill said or action he intended to take. It was that kind of quick stare that said, *What the hell did he just say? And what am I in for now?*

Now, in the "Year of Intelligence," Bill was being crazy smart again. Bill Jr. went to the Wayne County Clerk's Office in Detroit and filed two names under which he would be doing business in the future: The first was the "Bufalino Intelligence Agency" (Assumed Name Number 312391). The second was the "Bufalino Bureau of Investigation" (Assumed Name Number 312392).

For the purposes of my narrative, I'm more interested in the disposition of Hoffa's body after the Cubans, the CIA, and La Cosa

Nostra collectively had finished with him. I'm relying on the FBI's first gut belief, the public testimony of William D'Elia, Russell's chosen successor, on the only part of Sheeran's narrative that William D'Elia has not debunked and on the words reported to have come out of Russell's mouth as related by a guard at Leavenworth. The FBI followed leads to confirm the theory, but their work was cut short due to a turn of events that made further investigation impossible. Their working theory, and everyone else's listed above, was that Jimmy Hoffa's body was cremated.

The FBI followed the cremation theory to a well-known funeral home in Detroit whose clients were sometimes people of interest to the Bureau. Upon discovering the facility had no crematory on-site, the FBI turned to the incinerator at a waste hauling site associated with Bozzi Vitale: Central Sanitation.

Central Sanitation was the second of two waste hauling ventures pioneered by Bozzi Vitale. The first, Tri-County Sanitation, had been sold off following a bizarre imbroglio caused by one of Bozzi's sons-in-law, Joseph Barbara Jr. At the time of the FBI's investigation, owing to Barbara's imprisonment at the time, Central Sanitation was being run by another of Bozzi's sons-in-law, my own first cousin, Nick Micelli.

Joseph Barbara Jr. was, of course, Joseph Barbara's son, the man who was a onetime bodyguard for Santo Volpe in the Pennsylvania coalfields and, much later, host of the Apalachin conference. They called the elder Barbara "Joe the Barber." Junior they called "Joey the Clipper." Joseph Barbara Jr. joined a long list of Bufalino family associates from Northeastern Pennsylvania to New York State to the Detroit Partnership.

Nick Micelli was my own Aunt Pauline Bufalino Micelli's son. Her husband, like other male relatives through marriage, was a union man in Burbank, California. Nick studied law. Pauline wanted him to be somebody. She took him to Detroit and made the connection to Bozzi through channels unknown that might have included Russell himself or relatives already established in Detroit. Nick Micelli ended up marrying into the Partnership by way of Bozzi Vitale. It's worth wondering if Russell Bufalino intentionally spurred the introductions to stitch family operations in the United States together coast-to-coast through associations with the Teamsters and via the Detroit Partnership.

The FBI suspected that Bozzi Vitale's predecessor plant, Tri-County Sanitation, had been used for disposal of bodies by one means or another, whether incineration, shredding, or via some other process. That belief, and their own cremation theory, led them to Central Sanitation. Nick Micelli, as the plant attorney, toured the FBI through Central Sanitation. He explained that there *had* been a body or two in the past, a drunk or homeless person who crawled into what he thought was a container full of boxes that turned out to be a compactor. Still, Nick said, it was more of a compactor than a crushing machine, and those who fell victim to it were more asphyxiated than actually crushed.

As for the incinerator, it's just that and not a crematory. He showed them around the incinerator. The agents looked but decided it was worth another look. They set a date. Central Sanitation burned down in the interim.

Dan Moldea investigated the Hoffa case for many years and is quoted in a previous chapter. Scott Burnstein has been more active in research in the last twenty years. On the 50th anniversary of Hoffa's disappearance, Burnstein hosted a symposium in Detroit featuring Nove Tocco and former Federal Prosecutor Richard Convertino. I won't spoil their narrative by revealing their findings, but their combined belief is that Central Sanitation's incinerator was used, at the end of a grisly intermediate process, to dispose of Hoffa's remains. I should note that the intermediate process they propose solves a problematic aspect of cremation in an incinerator, which falls some

800 degrees short of producing the temperatures of a proper crematory. James Hoffa, Jr. publicly voiced his agreement with Burnstein's theories in the same July-August 2025 timeframe.

It's also worth noting that a recent book by David W. Tubman cites the remembrance of his parents, who were driving in an area of Detroit serviced by Central Sanitation on the day Hoffa disappeared. Driving past a property later suspected of being the murder scene, Tubman's father, who was familiar with the Central Sanitation route schedule, noted that the truck was off its normal route. Moreover, they claimed to have seen someone being wrestled into the back of the truck. This one part of the Tubman story strengthens my own belief that Central Sanitation, and my family members, were involved in his disappearance. All roads seem to lead to Central Sanitation.

There's a lot of misinformation about the workings of organized crime, and of course that is intentional. Occasionally someone will come along and say, "The Detroit Partnership would never let anybody come in and kill Hoffa without their permission." To that comment, I'll just present a list of Northeastern Pennsylvania people and operatives who existed within the Detroit area, or had influence in Detroit. The list ties Northeast Pennsylvania to Buffalo, Endicott, and Burbank, all through Detroit. It's a partial list, of course, and it starts with the troupe of Salvatore's children who followed Bill to Detroit, most of whom, minus Eugene, were present in Detroit at the time of Hoffa's disappearance:

- Bill (William Eugene) Bufalino, former Teamsters Local president
- Yabo Bufalino, Bill's brother and sometime bodyguard to Hoffa
- Eugene Bufalino, restaurateur/fight promoter while in Detroit (in California by 1975)

- Adeline Bufalino, Bill's sister and sometime legal secretary
- Nick Micelli, Bill's first cousin once removed, attorney for Central Sanitation connecting Burbank to Russell and Detroit through Bozzi Vitale
- Joseph Barbara Jr., associated though his father and possibly Stefano Magaddino, connecting Buffalo to Russell to Detroit
- Russell Bufalino himself, as a wedding guest
- Frank Sheeran, "The Irishman," who confessed to killing Hoffa
- Angelo Polizzi, Santo Volpe's business partner, who was arrested in conjunction with Joseph Barbara over the Wichner murder—deceased as of 1957
- Countless other unknown parties related to Russell through business

If the Five Families of New York, together with the Chicago, Detroit, Las Vegas, and other bastions of Cosa Nostra, comprised a National Syndicate, the above Pittston-to-Endicott-to-Buffalo-to Detroit-to-Burbank connections suggest that Russell's Pittston family was well-integrated with it, and speaks to Russell's relative importance and "reach."

CHAPTER 48

LA VIDA YABO: THE 1980S

All Paths of Glory Lead to the Grave!—Never Forget!

I never forgot. I still have the note I found under my windshield wiper forty years ago. It could only have one author: the redoubtable Yabo, my Socrates, the last of my own chosen surrogate fathers. The last I would need.

Yabo had little money and few possessions. Sometime in the 1980s, he sold the oak desk out of Bill's downstairs office, which had been Hoffa's own desk before he ascended to the Teamsters International presidency. He lived on Social Security and Black Lung benefits. But he went out, bet on the horse races at Pocono Downs, and had dinner with friends at a popular diner. He augmented his income, as many did in Luzerne County in the 1970s, by selling name-brand clothing out of the back of his beat-up orange Econoline van. It was probably stuff fresh off the trucks in New York in the era of the mass New York truck hijackings that were shared among loyalists as a way to help them make ends meet.

I believe that if Yabo was left to his own devices in life, he would have been some kind of artist. At least, he looked the part. When he went out on the town, he looked like Salvador Dali on a tear. Black shoes shined just right, black pants and white shirt, and black tie, all capped with a big black woolen overcoat (custom made for William E. Bufalino), and atop his head, a black French woolen beret worn pulled back, accentuating his receding hairline. That's how he would look dancing on the air at the locally broadcast dances for seniors, where he met Geraldine, whom he would take as his first wife at age seventy.

Mostly, Yabo was an enigma, just like Russell. He had no stories about his life except for a carefully curated few: a narrow escape from a bog when hunting, which he had rendered into a painting by a local artist; the car accident in 1963 in Detroit that nearly scalped him; a hunting trip in Michigan. Very rarely, he would divulge some aspect of his former life in the coalfields. I didn't pry. I was probably not the best audience for any talk about the 1930s because I had no frame of reference. I was glad he was there, because he was still formidable, and my mother was alone when I was at work. I looked in on him. I visited him when he moved in with Geraldine and again when he came back to the house when the marriage failed. My own father passed in 1983. It meant a lot to have Yabo around after that. He was my last contact with the Buffs of my father's generation.

One summer morning in the 1980s, Yabo's kitchen door was open, and his back was to me. He was dressed house-casual in a pair of pants, his big torso poking out of a wife beater T-shirt as he cooked his lunch on the small gas stove. Sausage and peppers. Trite, I know. I hailed him as usual, and he waved me in. It was one of those rare days he was going to lay something on me, and judging by his state of agitation, this was going to be a good one.

Russell was in prison at the time. Not the first imprisonment in Connecticut for extortion, not the easy one where he brought Thanksgiving dinner in for everybody. By this time, he was in Leavenworth. He had been arrested quickly upon his 1981 release from his first prison stint on changes that he conspired while in prison to kill Jack Napoli. He was sentenced to a second term by November 1981.

Not unlike other heads of families throughout the 1980s and 1990s, who fell to prosecution under the Racketeer Influenced and

Corrupt Organizations Act (RICO), Russell continued to exercise authority from behind bars by sending orders through attorneys and associates to maintain and steer family operations. William D'Elia was a frequent visitor to Russell for personal reasons and to receive guidance as necessary. On this particular day, Russell's directives were issued to William Bufalino's son, William Bufalino II, Yabo's nephew. He had orders to pass them on to Yabo.

Yabo must have just finished speaking with "Billy Boy" when I breezed in. He was hopping mad. He explained what his nephew had laid out for him. The authorities were looking for an Angelo Bufalino, who, they supposed, was running affairs in Russell's absence. Not my father and not Yabo, the Angelo in question was Russell's own former right hand, who had been pushed to the side in favor of "Big Billy" D'Elia. Very few people knew at the time that D'Elia was Russell's handpicked successor. The Angelo the authorities wanted remained loyal and was still a valuable asset to Russell. Russell did not want to throw him under the bus.

Russell's direction to Billy Boy was: "Tell Yabo to turn himself in as the Angelo they're looking for."

"Billy Boy" took that in and didn't speak for a second, thinking the words he later used to eulogize Yabo: *Yabo was my favorite uncle, a guy who was in my house every day as a kid. I was so young, I couldn't wrap my lips around his name, so I called him Uncle Wow.* He may also have noted that the ploy would not work, unless the authorities were stupid or complicit in the deception.

Then he answered Russell, "You don't know what you're asking me to do."

"I know what I'm *telling* you to do," Russell responded. "Now, go do it."

"Billy Boy" did as he was directed. On an open phone line, just in case Yabo didn't have the nerve to follow Billy's next instruction, he then told Yabo to in no way comply with the demand. All of this was in defiance of Russell, of course, but more so out of real love and concern for his uncle. That is just one of the reasons "Billy Boy" tops my list of favorite Buffs outside my own siblings.

Yabo was beside himself. "Can you believe that son of a bitch?"

That was the day he talked out loud about the resentment he felt toward members of his family, starting in the 1920s when he helped finance his brother's education by working at some iffy assignments. Yabo did all kinds of jobs to help out. He worked for a while as Russell's bodyguard at PA Coal #6 colliery. He moonlighted as a truck driver for hooch. He was once briefly arrested and held in the county until sprung.

"You do what you gotta do," he said, trying his best to explain the extremes of his life at the time of the Great Depression. "I used to work for Joe the Barber!" Joseph Barbara. Working for him meant anything from truck driving to running a still to serious gotta-do stuff, the kind of stuff Yabo didn't really have an engine to do. The kind of work that maybe sent him over the edge for a while.

That's when Yabo finally decided to make a final break with Russell. It was a gutsy move for someone in his seventies. He never spoke about it, or Russell, again.

CHAPTER 49

BARELY A PARAGRAPH

> *You do not need to leave your room. Remain sitting at your table and listen. Do not even listen, simply wait, be quiet, still and solitary. The world will freely offer itself to you to be unmasked, it has no choice, it will roll in ecstasy at your feet.*
>
> —Franz Kafka

Yabo started a memoir while he was living at the nursing home. Its discovery was the last of the three reveals that began in the wake of my mother's death. I found it when I was looking for something at the house in Pittston. I had purchased Salvatore's half of the homestead at tax sale in 1997. I was in the downstairs cellar, the first floor of the old general store at 47 Railroad that Bill converted into a law office, and I stumbled onto the box containing everything Yabo had with him at the nursing home. Yabo's treasured personal belongings all fit into a shallow box of manageable size, except for the few custom-made woolen overcoats and the clothing that remained in closets at home.

In the box was a book I bought for him when he entered the nursing home. It was a Depression-era coal region memoir by author Patrick M. Canfield titled *Growing Up with Bootleggers, Gamblers, and Pigeons.* I thought the subject matter would be of interest to him. He apparently liked the book very much. Also in the box were sparse personal effects, some clothes, a robe, some knickknacks (Yabo was fond of gadgets like the digital timepiece fobs of the 1980s), some pens and pencils, and a yellow legal pad I recalled seeing at one of my visits.

The legal pad memoir had maybe twelve to fifteen stories altogether. There were a few old standards in the mix—stories from the oral traditions of the family, a few personal tidbits about his work as a journeyman millwright. I learned about an elk hunt he participated in and his brush with buck fever. It was hardly great literature, but it was good reading, and it clued me in to a number of things I had not known before, including the existence of the Bufalino Hotel. And then there was the one far-left-field story, barely a paragraph long, that knocked me off my pins.

Before I cracked open Yabo's memoir, I only knew what they told me about the family. I could wonder how two coal miners saved up enough money to build a big house and start five businesses, but I took it for granted that my grandfather and granduncle had done so. I had a sense of pride about that, which led me to want to preserve some of their legacy and in part was responsible for me buying the other half of the house at tax sale.

I had read Sheeran and Brandt's *I Heard You Paint Houses* as well as Thomas Hunt and Michael A. Tona's well-researched "Men of Montedoro" article for *Informer Journal.* I had casually read a few other things over the years, starting in college with Steven Brill's *The Teamsters.* But it was all casual reading, and I had not invested much into my own research of the family. That was going to change.

Altogether, the important things I knew before finding Yabo's memoir in 2011 were the following few things: I knew that Frank Sheeran suggested Hoffa was cremated. I had the information from the Pittston mortician about the memorial vases. I had seen

Bill's draft letter to Hoffa outlining his grievances over the way the imprisoned Hoffa was treating him, which I called out in the "Dear Jim" chapter. Public as their falling-out was, it was news to me at the time. I also knew from talking to Yabo that he had only stopped taking orders from Russell Bufalino during Russell's Leavenworth imprisonment. This time, I was the cat about to be struck by ball lightning as my eyes fell on the title of one of Yabo's memoir pages called "Memorial Vases."

> *Memorial Vases*
>
> *I made two memorial vases at* [redacted] *Alter Road in Detroit. They now adorn[redacted] funeral parlor.. His mother stayed a night or two on Alter Road, Detroit. Mrs.* [redacted]*, born about 1900, was a friend of your mother* [Author's note: Angelo Tulumello's mother, Pauline, Yabo's sister.] *Your mother accommodated her. Good people. I gave them to her to adorn her funeral parlor.. They are there now, May 20, 1992. To reinforce the concrete mold, I had to insert twisted wire hangers and smashed tin cans.*

And that's all. It's a complete *nothing* of a story on its face. If I had read it without having had the discussion with the mortician, I would have dismissed it. But here, Yabo was solving a little mystery. Yabo is the man who made the memorial vases, not Bill, and he made exactly two vases, probably in his lifetime, out of molds that were so imperfect he had to bind them together with wire and brace them with crushed tin cans.

First question: *Why?*
Second question: *When, exactly?*
Third question: *Did Yabo make the memorial vases with the express purpose of giving them to someone, or just to make them?*

Fourth question: *Is there any significance to the fact that the vases ended up in a family-associated mortuary in Pittston, Pennsylvania?*

Fifth question: *What prompted Yabo to assemble the molds and concrete to make the vases?*

Sixth question: *Was this something someone directed Yabo to do?*

Seventh question: *What about this story made it important to relate to its intended recipient, Yabo's nephew Angelo?*

Eighth question: *Was Yabo sharing this item hoping the reader would understand its true meaning? Is it a confession, or did Yabo have a suspicion that he might have had a closing role in the Hoffa affair?*

It's worth noting that Yabo's intended recipient of this one remembrance was his nephew Angelo Tulumello. Tulumello was a doctor of chemistry and the family scholar. He had very little use for Russell or the family at large apart from Yabo, my mother and myself. He and his mother blamed Russell for his own father's lapse following the theft of his fortune. Did Yabo count on him to take special meaning from the story? To glean something from it? To do something with it?

I know how crazy that sounds. But the shadow of a doubt haunted me for a long time until I had to learn as much as I could about the family and the town, about Russell and Bill and Yabo, to prove that I was wrong so I could stop being bugged about it. I failed. If Yabo had a black cloud hanging over him—and he did—I had become the inheritor of the cloud.

Assume for a second that Hoffa was cremated—a popular belief and the FBI's first hunch. Now he's ashes. Nick Micelli, my first cousin and the attorney for Central Sanitation, may have had a hand in rendering—perhaps delivering—the ashes as the FBI suspected. Bill, Yabo, and Russell (and Frank Sheeran and Nick Micelli and others) were all in Detroit for a wedding to be held on the Friday of the week Hoffa went missing. Russell had been giving orders to Yabo his whole life. He knew Yabo was a craftsman with an artistic flair.

If Russell wanted to either memorialize or simply transport Hoffa's remains to a location with a family association, what better way to do it? Who's to say he didn't have a bag of concrete mix, maybe already opened, delivered to Yabo with the molds? If Yabo failed, no harm, no foul. And if he succeeded, Hoffa's mortal remains may have been hiding in plain sight since 1975 in Pittston, Pennsylvania.

As a memorial? As a trophy? If it sounds crazy, out on a limb, I completely understand.

But there it is.

CHAPTER 50

AND PITTSTON BURNED

As I write this chapter on December 23, 2024, the Ann Lee Frocks building on Pittston's Main Street, hardly a block away, is burning. It was owned and operated by Angelo Sciandra in the 1950s, an associate of Russell's who was also at Apalachin. It had been one of the last remaining properties to host a dress factory in Pittston. A Pittston landmark and a survivor of the 1970s fire boom, it was like a monument to the industry.

The International Ladies' Garment Workers Union (ILGWU) announced a general strike over anti-corruption and industrial wage-disparity in 1958. They took Pittston's forty-plus union shops out on strike against an ownership class unlike most others, several of whom were present at Apalachin in November 1957. Russell may have owned five of the Pittston shops outright and probably had a financial interest in many of the others. It may have been or not, but I think of Ann Lee Frocks as being the place Min Matheson, the local ILGWU giant of an organizer, famously answered a taunt about her husband's absence on the picket line by wagging a finger in Russ Bufalino's face, shouting, "I don't need to bring Bill up here, Russ, because I'm twice the man you'll ever be!"

Min Matheson is justifiably famous for heroically organizing thirty-six or more shops in an impossible district. The battle cost her a murdered brother and the loss of her father to heartbreak. She's less well-known for attending a meeting with Russell, Sciandra, and other important local shop owners in New York City, against her own better judgment and without consulting ILGWU headquarters. In the agreement that probably resulted from the meeting, some shops were allowed to operate despite the strike.

The local dress business started in the 1930s. Demand for anthracite coal in industrial use had slowed but not stopped altogether. Times were bad due to the Depression, and to make it worse, they were changing too. The diesel engines that powered the next-generation trains and ships needed oil, not coal, and oil was increasingly heating homes. Miners and crews in Northeastern Pennsylvania were underemployed, and families were struggling.

At the same time in New York City, the International Ladies' Garment Workers Union was making life difficult for sweatshop owners in the Garment District who profited from women doing piecework in conditions that were often unsafe. Dress manufacturers looked for a place they could continue their labor practices and maintain their profits unmolested. They looked for workers able to work as seamstresses and who were hungry enough to do the work without complaint. They looked to Depression-era Northeastern Pennsylvania. They came to Pittston and the surrounds in numbers, bringing contract work with them. Russell and his associates all either owned or partnered in factories. Albert Anastasia, the "Lord High Executioner" head of Murder, Inc., owned a factory in Hazleton, well south of Pittston but still in Luzerne County.

Russell had literally grown up surrounded by union conflicts in the mines, and the Big Three operators of Northeastern Pennsylvania knew how to game that system. First, they infiltrated the workforce with anti-union members from the earliest days. That was easy enough to do when the workers you imported owed you a stake of their wages. Then, through the anti-union actors and by whatever other means, they elected their own associates into union position after union position. The outcome would be that the company had the bull by both the horns and the tail. Northeast Pennsylvania had, until the very end of its deep-mining industry at the Knox Mine, mine owners acting in official union capacities. In this way, the company *was* the union, and the miners under the UMWA in Pittston felt they were paying dues on the one hand to be under-compensated on the other, all with the approval of the UMWA. It added to their sense of outrage and powerlessness, and it spurred violence.

The system of clear conflict of interest above was so rote and taken for granted as practice in Northeastern Pennsylvania that Bill would try to incorporate it into his post-Teamsters work with his son together in their shared law practice. In the days following Hoffa's disappearance in 1976, an FBI agent tracking Bill made notes to the effect that under a plan put forward by Bill Sr., which was reported in the *Detroit Free Press* on February 16, 1976, Bill would act as a negotiator for rank-and-file union members of certain enterprise while his son Bill Jr. would take the part of the management of the same enterprise. The agent recording was aghast at the clear conflict of interest implied in the proposal, but for all I know, it may have gone down just that way.

Union penetration into dress factories of Northeastern Pennsylvania was confined to six shops by 1944, when Min Matheson and her brother were dispatched to the region to help organize. The women's union required the owner class, including Russell, his relatives, and his friends, to take a slightly different approach, possibly because they couldn't get at the individual women as directly or easily as they had the male miners in the early part of the century.

One of their strategies was to create and foster membership in a union-in-opposition to the ILGWU. Bill may have organized the union for Russell. It has been referred to as the Northeastern Pennsylvania Needleworkers Association or the Anthracite Needle Workers Association of Luzerne County. I lost the reference to this claim, but past research has suggested their motto was something like *Join Us or You'll Be Sorry.*

Men and women worked the dress factories in various capacities, from cutters to assemblers. A contract came to the factory with the bolts of cloth and dress template patterns attached. A good cutter could take a template expected to turn out X number of dresses and produce several more dresses than expected as overruns, which for the manufacturer became dresses to sell at a high profit.

In the 1960s in Pittston, there was scarcely a vacant apartment or garage or available space that was not somehow attached to the industry turning out dresses, jeans, belts—you name it—for nationwide distribution through companies like Leslie Fay. We rented our twenty-by-fifty-foot soda factory downstairs to a company called La Bella Fashions. They packed the space with women and machines.

The dress business was huge in Northeastern Pennsylvania by the 1950s. It buoyed the local economy, put women to work outside the home, and made up for the decreased demand for anthracite coal. In 1959, following the Knox Mine disaster that flooded the deep-mine workings of the northern coalfields, the mines were shuttered for good, and the dress factories were all that remained to prop up the local economy.

When the dress companies started experiencing trouble competing with manufacturers outside the United States, the last bulwark of the local Pittston economy began to collapse. Owners didn't just close factories and other businesses in which they had interest. They began burning them down to collect the insurance as well. Nearly every week in the Pittston of the early 1970s, when my friends and I were in high school, there would be a fire somewhere on or near Main Street in some dress factory or other business belonging to Russell or his associates.

When they burned a dress factory, in order to maximize their profits in the venture, they would save the working machines to either use or resell. Equipment that did not work they left to the flames. In place of the good machines they removed from a factory, they would install machines from a previously torched factory. And the dresses on-site? They removed them to sell later.

In one instance, a remembrance contained in *Sewn in Coal Country: An Oral History of the Ladies' Garment Industry in Northeastern Pennsylvania, 1945–1995*, compiled and edited by Robert P. Wolensky, Tony D'Angelo reports a story that was common knowledge among my classmates. They took the dresses from a property they intended to burn and placed them for safekeeping on the second story of the building that housed the Yatesville Police Station, just outside of town.

Talk about safekeeping. What place could be safer than that? They could get around investigators who noted the serial number mismatches on the pre-burned machines. They could handle insurance adjusters. They did this repeatedly throughout the 1970s. When the Pittston fire chief was questioned by reporters about the literal epidemic of fires that befell the city throughout the early 1970s, he simply shrugged his shoulders and blamed it all on "a run of bad luck." My classmates and I rolled our eyes and shut our mouths.

In Pittston, we understood the culture of corruption all too well. Our families had nearly a century of seeing what happened to people who talked. We just watched it work. The more outrageous a behavior, the less we had to say about it, at least officially. But we did find a way to express it after all.

When Hurricane Agnes produced the flood of 1972 that leveled Wilkes-Barre and the communities on the west side of the Susquehanna River and south, Pittston got by with very little water damage due to its just slightly higher elevation.

Of course, Pittston had been previously scourged by the fires, so the whole area was more or less in shambles. We had a way of talking about that.

"Wilkes-Barre flooded," we would say. "And Pittston burned."

EPILOGUE

MEMORIES AND LEGACIES

Of course, I did ask the mortician who showed me the memorial vases, at a chance meeting at a coffee shop, when exactly—what year—he received the vases from Bill Bufalino. Was it in the seventies, perhaps? He didn't remember. He was young, he said. That Bill Buff gave them to his mother was all he recalled.

Now, with Yabo's first-person testimony, I have to assume that either the exactly two memorial vases *he certainly made* joined a company of other vases made, perhaps by Bill, or not. By now, it should be abundantly clear to the reader that I think James "Jimmy" Hoffa was cremated and that his mortal remains were encased in concrete in the form of a few memorial vases hidden in plain sight in a Pittston funeral parlor long associated with our family.

So, why exactly did I keep that to myself? Why did I not contact the authorities? If you knew my hometown, you might understand.

Hemingway called Paris "a movable feast." Had he been around to visit Pittston in the 1980s, he might have described it as "a floating craps game." The old-timers were still around—the aging, retired coal miners and not a few henchmen. The old men still gathered to play cards at the Montedoro Society and the few other societies that remained among the multiple ethnicities that made up the town. Gambling of every kind—sports, horses, and even casino-style operations—existed throughout the Wyoming Valley. Some were exclusive, by invitation only.

On the north side of Main Street at 44–52 North Main sat the American Theater building. It was the larger of two theaters in operation in the city, the other being the 1914 700-seat Roman Theatre. Both theaters were appointed well enough in the pre-movie era style that they could host traveling Broadway shows that took a circuit leading them straight through Scranton, Pittston, Wilkes-Barre, and beyond. It was said to have shuttered in the late 1960s.

One winter day in the mid-1970s, I was walking by and was ushered inside by a friend who was standing outside below the marquee. A relative of his was inside doing some work on the building. He led me up a flight of stairs to the cavernous Green Room, where I entered a permanent installation casino of inlaid felt tables supporting every kind of gaming. The deep-silled and wide double-hung windows were neatly papered halfway up with construction paper. Stacked three feet tall, six feet wide, and three or four deep on each sill from the base to the top of the paper, hidden from street view, were deck upon deck of boxed playing cards. The American Theater was maybe a block and a half from the Pittston police headquarters at city hall on Broad Street.

In the Pittston of the 1970s, you could walk into La Torre's Rec (pool hall), right behind Babe's Pizza on Main, and walk smack into a high-stakes card game run by Steve La Torre himself, the last of the old-time Black Handers. The buildings on Main were deep, maybe eighty to a hundred feet.

La Torre's was full of pool tables from the glory days, but about four of them up front toward the counter were in playable condition and lit to any degree. They served the clientele of young wannabe hustlers and other school-skippers that found a warm spot to hang, with pinball and pool and cigarettes for sale at the counter for a nickel apiece. Regular among the adults were Steve La Torre; his son Joe; Joe's children, Toke LaPorte and Joe Sweeney; the guy in the black overcoat with the shotgun concealed behind it (who was really just on duty for the games); and Billy the Bird (a World War II pilot who was a little unstrung). It may not sound like it, but La Torre's was like a haven and boys' club.

We'd walk the bare planks of the pine floor between the tables, and when the far back of the room was clouded in cigar smoke, we knew to avoid the fire escape. Steve La Torre and the gang were exchanging thousands at the table back there. On the wall was a gigantic scoreboard in open view that tracked out-of-town sporting events in their season. Pictures of it graced the newspaper. Settled bets, like the one that made Joe La Torre deliver a lobster dinner in person, were popular story fare. Gambling was still the culture of the old mining town, mines or no. Downstairs in the cellar, a boxing ring that used to grace the upstairs of the original La Torre's Pool Hall, when the fight game was big locally, sat packed in storage.

When I started college in 1975, I worked at a pizza shop whose owner doubled as a bookmaker. Long story. On Friday nights, he'd take me to local gambling venues, including the Mayfair Supper Club and the dance-hall-sized permanent installation on the main street of Old Forge, barely four miles away. There, pistol-packing was the rule of the day, and the crowd at the tables was thick and the action intense. That's where I first saw Dan Flood's own congressional aide, with sweat pouring off his brow, a pair of dice in his right hand and a stack of bills in his left, having a go at craps. I was so young and naïve that the men would rub my head for luck.

All around me, all through college and lasting well into the 1980s, people were on the phone at the pizza shop asking for the line on the Giants game ("Babe, it's for you!"), passing betting slips, and losing homes and fortunes at tables and racetracks up and down the valley. It was a parade of state police, local police, lawyers, judges, prison guards, gangsters, politicians, and regular people. Not all of the police and staties, of course. Just enough to make you understand that the world had its own way of working that you'd never see on television.

In recent times, Luzerne County is famous for the Kids for Cash scandal of 2008, a kickback scheme between a real estate developer and two Luzerne County judges. The judges, it was said, received kickbacks in the form of a finder's fee for imposing harsh sentences on youths that resulted in their tenancy in the developer's newly constructed juvenile detention centers.

Scranton, just north of Pittston, lost a mayor in this century to charges of conspiracy, bribery, and extortion. The former head of the Pennsylvania Crime Commission, Frederick T. Martens, is quoted as saying, "It's like shooting fish in a barrel in Pennsylvania. You just turn over a rock. You are guaranteed to find something."

That's Luzerne County. Lackawanna, Montgomery—just pick a county, it's all the same in my home state. The Keystone State has been flush with money and corruption since the Walking Purchase of 1737. But hey, it's home.

In the fifteen years I've had to mull and worry over saying something to anyone about my suspicion, I played out two scenarios and decided there would be just one outcome of each. I could go to my local underworld representative, or I could visit the local authorities in one of a number of forms.

I could only imagine one outcome: "What? You found *Hoffa*? Hold on, I'll be right there as soon as I get this silencer screwed on."

I became convinced that the only safe way to go was public and to as large an audience as I could find. Of course, now the only chance I'm taking is to make myself a laughingstock, which is why I add the consolation prize of some private family details and a timeline of the growth of Russell's family. Those will bear out.

In any case, I'm the wrong party to take the story to the grave. I'm the only one left who's enough in-the-know to provide the context and show how it all might plausibly fit together. I feel a moral obligation to share it. I'm not scared anymore.

And after all, as Bill Buff would say: "B means to battle for that which is right . . ."

APPENDIX A

PITTSTON CRIME FAMILY TREE

Bosses

1903–1908: Stefano "Steve" La Torre / Calogero Bufalino
1908–1933: Santo Volpe
1933–1949: Giovanni "John" Sciandra
1949–1994: Rosario Alfredo "Russell" Bufalino
1994–2008: William "Big Billy" D'Elia

APPENDIX B

BUFALINO FAMILY TREE

Nicolo Bufalino and Giuseppina Castellino Bufalino

- Calogena (Caroline), b. in Montedoro
  - Vincent Costanza
  - Josephine Costanza
  - Mary Costanza
  - Nick Costanza
  - Angelo Costanza
  - Ralph Costanza
- Mary Bufalino, b. 1909
- Salvatore (Sam) Bufalino, b. 1912
  - Nicholas Bufalino
  - Josephine Bufalino
- Charles Bufalino
  - Nicholas Bufalino
  - Josephine Bufalino
- Pauline Bufalino Micelli
  - Nicholas Micelli
  - Joseph Micelli
- Angelo Bufalino, b. 1918
  - Nicholas Bufalino
  - Salvatore Bufalino
  - Josephine Bufalino
  - Charles Bufalino

- Julia Bufalino Conway, b. 1921
  - Charles Conway
  - Lester Conway

Salvatore and Luigina (Galante) Bufalino
- Charles Bufalino, b. 1905
- Pauline Tulumello, b. 1907
- Mary Bufalino, b. 1908
- James Bufalino
- Adeline Bufalino Koury, b. 1915
- Angelo Bufalino (Yabo), b. 1913
- William Eugene (Bill) Bufalino, b. 1919
- Eugene Bufalino, b. 1917

Rosario and Vincenza (Baiera) Bufalino
- Charles Bufalino
- Angelo Bufalino
- Sam Bufalino
- James Bufalino
- Caroline Bufalino Forlizzi

Calogero (Charles) and Emmanuella Volpe Bufalino
- Angelo Charles Bufalino, b. 1912
- Emmanuella (Dolly) Falcone, b. 1928
- Josephine Bufalino, b. 1918
- Mrs. Angelo Capitano

Angelo and Maria Cristina Buccoleri Bufalino
- Giuseppa Bufalino Cordaro, b. 1897
- Calogero (Charles) Bufalino, b. 1898
- Cristina Teresina Bufalino Cannella, b. 1900
- Rosario Alfredo (Russell) Bufalino, b. 1903

APPENDIX C

GENOVESE CRIME FAMILY TREE

Bosses

1890s–1909: Giuseppe "The Clutch Hand" Morello
1909–1916: Nicolò "Nick Morello" Terranova
1916–1920: Vincenzo "The Tiger of Harlem" Terranova
1920–1922: Giuseppe "The Clutch Hand" Morello
1922–1931: Giuseppe "Joe the Boss" Masseria
1931–1946: Charles "Lucky" Luciano
1946–1957: Frank "The Prime Minister" Costello
1957–1969: Vito "Don Vitone" Genovese
1969–1981: Philip "Benny Squint" Lombardo
1981–2005: Vincent "Chin" Gigante
2006–present: Liborio "Barney" Bellomo

APPENDIX D

THE BUFALINO, SHEERAN, AND D'ELIA ACCOUNTS

Russell Bufalino

The stories of Frank Sheeran, William "Big Billy" D'Elia, and Russell Bufalino are in complete accord in one respect: They all agree that Jimmy Hoffa's body was cremated. This idea was one that the FBI embraced for a time but was forced to abandon when the supposed incinerator was itself incinerated in a fire. Russell Bufalino is not on record discussing the particulars of the murder, but according to the testimony of retired Leavenworth prison guard Kenneth LaMaster, as shared with the *Gangland Wire* podcast, Russell copped to having Jimmy Hoffa cremated. It is not surprising that Frank Sheeran, as a close confidant of Russell's, and Billy D'Elia, his chosen successor, share their belief in the cremation story. It is only in the particulars of the disappearance and murder that Frank Sheeran and Billy D'Elia's narratives differ.

Frank Sheeran

Frank Sheeran claimed to have shot Hoffa in a home left vacant by arrangement with a connected realtor. The home in question was much later searched, and blood was discovered that did not conclusively match with Jimmy Hoffa's. In Frank's account, Russell put himself and Frank in the position to make the hit to keep them both safe, meaning it was a kind of loyalty test by the parties who authorized the murder. Russell is supposed to have told Frank, "They get bosses, too." According to Sheeran, he left the house immediately after the shooting and was not an eyewitness to the cleanup or disposal of Hoffa's body but came to understand that Hoffa was cremated.

William D'Elia

"Big Billy" D'Elia does not believe that Frank Sheeran killed Jimmy Hoffa, based on his own travels with Russell and meetings he witnessed on the subject of the murder. He did mention the Johnny Roselli murder as being on Russell's mind and expresses Russell's own concern about being dragged into the Church Committee hearings to testify about the attempts on Castro's life. So, D'Elia is in agreement that self-preservation was in Russell's forethoughts but intimated that Russell was much more of a regretful author of Hoffa's murder than Frank has represented him to be in his own narrative. As to the disposition of Hoffa's body, Billy can be heard to say "Hoffa was cooked" in radio and TV interviews.

APPENDIX E

WHO SAID WHAT ABOUT HOFFA

Russell Bufalino

"We cremated . . . him." According to some sources, at least.

Given their mutual relationships with Russell, Frank Sheeran and Billy D'Elia's one shared belief regarding Hoffa's cremation probably sources to Russell.

Frank Sheeran

Frank's story, originally written in collaboration with author Charles Brandt in his book *I Heard You Paint Houses*, has been faithfully retold in the movie *The Irishman*. According to Frank, Russell Bufalino felt forced to accept the sanction for the hit despite his own regard for Hoffa and felt forced to enlist Frank to do the shooting as a kind of loyalty test to satisfy his superiors. He did it that way, he said, to keep them both safe.

Frank reported that, on the way to Bill's daughter's Detroit wedding, he parted company with Russell and the women for a few hours, jumped a commuter plane, landed at a field where a car waited, and drove to Machus Red Fox to convince Jimmy to get into the car to drive to the meeting. They arrived at a home that was up for sale and vacant, a meeting place arranged by a complicit realtor.

Sheeran claims he shot Hoffa and left, returning to Russell and their wives to resume their car trip.

He expressed a belief that Hoffa had been cremated in the aftermath of the shooting.

William D'Elia

Bill D'Elia agreed that Jimmy Hoffa was cremated but otherwise did not corroborate Frank's story. Billy D'Elia, Frank Sheeran, and Russell Bufalino expressed the belief that Hoffa was cremated, which is not surprising, given their close relationship.

The FBI

One of the FBI's first theories regarding Jimmy Hoffa's disappearance was that he had been killed and his body cremated. They pursued this theory to the Bagnasco Funeral Home, whose clients had at times been people of interest to the FBI. Finding no incinerator on the premises, they next pursued their theory to Central Sanitation, which was considered by the FBI to be Mob-controlled. There, the author's cousin, Nick Micelli, gave them a tour around the facility and the incinerator. The FBI wanted another look at a later time, but Central Sanitation ironically burned in the interim, depriving the FBI of any closure on their theory.

Michael Franzese

"He's in a very wet place," said Michael Franzese, the reformed Colombo family capo once referred to as the "Yuppie Don."

Mr. Franzese has high confidence in a theory he has been entrusted with but that he has not yet brought forward. If my interpretation of the facts that led to my conclusion is proven wrong, then mine will be just a grotesquely poetic outcome we all might wish to be true. At least, in my humble opinion, it's the best to date.

Gianni Russo

Gianni Russo, who played the ill-fated Carlo Rizzi in *The Godfather* and wrote *Hollywood Godfather* and *Mafia Secrets,* claimed Jimmy Hoffa was crushed in a car.

Richard Kuklinski

Richard "The Iceman" Kuklinski confessed to author Philip Carlo in his book *The Ice Man* that he was paid $40,000 to kill Hoffa by stabbing him in the head with a hunting knife after picking him up at a restaurant in suburban Detroit. He then drove the body to a New Jersey junkyard where he placed it in an oil drum and set it on fire, returning later to dig up the drum and place the body in a car that was sold for scrap metal and compacted.

The story seems a little fantastic and contains way too much driving and far too much handling.

Donald Frankos

Donald "Tony the Greek" Frankos told *Playboy* magazine that Hoffa was buried under Giants Stadium. The FBI discarded this theory based on a belief that Tony the Greek couldn't have been where he said he was. They didn't bother to follow it up.

Frankos has further stated Tony Provenzano ordered Hoffa's hit, and it was carried out by Jimmy Coonan and John Sullivan with the aid of Charles "Chuckie" O'Brien, who was along to gain Hoffa's trust. His body was said to have been "ground up in little pieces, shipped to Florida, and thrown into a swamp."

Joe Franco

Joe Franco, a former Hoffa associate, asserted that two "federal Marshals or agents" showed Hoffa their credentials and ushered him into a car bound for the airport. There they boarded a plane and threw him out over the Great Lakes.

Johnny Roselli and Sam Giancana were scheduled to appear before the Church Committee investigating assassination and other practices employed by the CIA, FBI, and NSA in 1976. Their gangland-style deaths sparked rumors that federal authorities were eliminating witnesses who could offer detail regarding their use of the Mafia in failed attempts to assassinate Fidel Castro.

Curiously, around the same time, Argentina's military dictatorship disappeared between 10,000 and 30,000 left-wing dissidents during the Dirty War. Some of the *desaparecidos* were said to have been dropped into the ocean.

Marvin Elkind

Marvin Elkind, the Renaissance Man, claimed no knowledge of who killed Hoffa, but reported that union carpenters rushed the construction of wooden forms at the Renaissance Center project.

The forms complete, tons of cement were poured, and into the mix went Hoffa's body.

No rebar or reinforcing structure on a project like that? Just a straight pour? This theory was probed further by Detroit news media on the fiftieth anniversary of Hoffa's disappearance. A second witness to the event provided a convincing account in televised interviews. You never know.

Tony Zerilli

Detroit Partnership acting boss Tony Zerilli asserted Hoffa was buried in a makeshift grave beneath a concrete slab of a barn in Oakland Township, Michigan.

Billy D'Elia's famous quote, "Hoffa's not on the farm," was likely rendered to dismiss this theory.

Frank Coppola (via Dan Moldea)

Hoffa associate Frank Coppola said that Hoffa was buried in a steel drum beneath an elevated highway near a Jersey City landfill. The FBI received permits to dig the site but has not released any findings since 2021.

David W. Tubman

In a recently published book, *Jimmy Hoffa Is Missing: The Gap: A Long-Held Family Secret— Until Now!*, David W. Tubman recounts the eyewitness testimony of his parents, who related details of an apparent abduction involving a Central Sanitation truck that was present at a location off its normal pickup route. Mr. Tubman further expresses his theory about the aftermath of that abduction.

The testimony of Tubman's parents is important in that it validates the FBI's theory that Central Sanitation may have had a role in the Hoffa disappearance. This does nothing to harm—but rather strengthens—my belief in Central Sanitation's involvement in the Hoffa murder.

James P. Hoffa

James Hoffa Junior subscribes to a theory put forth at a 2025 symposium presented by Scott Burnstein, Nove Tocco, and former Federal Prosecutor Richard Convertino. Central Sanitation looms large in that theory as well.

Charles Bufalino

The author's conclusions are revealed in this very book—hope you didn't just skip to this section.

APPENDIX F

NEWSPAPER CLIPPINGS

CORRALLED BAD GANG.

State Police Get Twenty-five Members of Iron Hand.

Under County Detective Mackin's Direction Desperate Men Who Terrorized Pittston Suburbs Are Caught in Drag Net—Story of Their Persecution of Three Brothers.

A blow which was delivered yesterday to an organization of Italians styling themselves the "Iron Hand" and similar in its intents and purposes to the "Black Hand" and "Mafia" societies which have wrought terror among the foreigners of this country for years, is believed to be the heaviest ever delivered to such an organization, for in one round-up twenty-five of the members of the society were rounded up and were safely lodged behind prison bars.

This coup d'etat was perpetrated by the district attorney's office, the whole thing being carefully planned by the new county detective, Edward Mackin, and as carefully executed by himself, assistant county detective Jones, Chief Loftus of Pittston and Captain Page of the State Constabulary, the latter with thirty-five men under his command.

SCARED FIFTEEN FAMILIES FROM HOMES.

The affair occurred at Pittston and its suburbs and that town was in a fever of excitement all day long, the Italian residents particularly, being highly elated over the capture of a gang which has terrorized them for months. The operations of the gang have been so bold and their crimes so flagrant that within the last two months fifteen Italian families have moved from the vicinity, life there having become unbearable for them.

The gang carried its operations too far, however, came in contact with three resolute men and are now in a fair way of spending years in prison, for the district attorney declares that he has sufficient evidence to convict on several different charges and will push the prosecution to the utmost, being determined to rid the county of this class of cutthroats and robbers.

RESOLUTE RITZ BROTHERS.

The men who proved the Waterloo of the gang are Joseph, Charles and Salvatore Ritz, three brothers who resided in Browntown until it became unsafe for them longer to reside there.

The persecutions of these men started way back in the early part of 1906. One night a letter was slipped under the door, this being a favorite method that the society had of notifying its victims of persecutions to follow. The brothers were resolute men, however, had worked hard for their money, had invested it in real estate and did not propose to give up of their hard earned money to any body of men. They paid no heed to the letter.

Then a second letter made its appearance. It came through the mails and demanded that $500 be turned over to the society. It was signed the "Iron Hand." One of the brothers then took the two letters to Chief Loftus at Pittston, who promised to investigate the matter.

A third letter was received, also through the mail. This letter demanded that $500 be taken and deposited at a spot near the No. 4 breaker at 11 o'clock on a certain specified night. The three brothers, together with an uncle, visited the designated spot, taking the money along with them. They also took their guns. They deposited the money and then lay in wait all through the long night hours, but nobody appeared. They took the money back home.

THREATENING LETTERS.

Then in rapid succession three more letters were received; all through the mail and all reiterating the demand for money. Then a new ending from the society went to the brothers [illegible] times and asked that the letters be given back to them, stating that they were sent only as a joke. [illegible] the brothers gave them the four letters [illegible] to produce the other two, [illegible] threatened [illegible] danger if he did not return the other two letters.

Then, late in June the strong arm attached to the "Iron Hand" was first exhibited, and after the family had returned [illegible] home and proceeded to amuse themselves [illegible].

Still the brothers did not give up. A few days later a couple of the gang stopped one of the brothers on the street in Pittston and demanded money. The brother was alone and he gave them $5. Still later another brother was approached and he gave the solicitors $5. From time to time they gave up various small sums and secured peace for a time, the members of the society becoming so friendly that they called the brothers to a meeting in the woods near the place and after having the brothers spend some money for their entertainment, they told them that they could now live in peace.

The members were not satisfied yet, however, and soon apparently regretted their promise, for they once again began to demand money and make threats. The brothers decided that they would give up no more. They armed themselves heavily and awaited further trouble—and it came.

DYNAMITED HOUSE.

On Christmas eve the family went to bed. The wife of one of the brothers heard some one moving about the house. She stepped to the window and saw some men surrounding the house, while a couple of them were stooping down near the porch. She awakened her husband and he, too, saw the men. He watched and saw them strike a match and then rushed down stairs and to the door, believing that they were trying to dynamite the house, and he thought of escaping. When he opened the door, however, he was covered by the guns of two men standing outside and commanded to stay in the house. He could do nothing else and so stood there until the men ignited the dynamite and the explosion occurred. This explosion tore off one end of the house, and containing the kitchen, and ruined all the kitchen furniture and utensils. It caused a monetary loss of about $300, but fortunately no one was injured.

Then the demands for money were repeated, but the brothers were determined that none should be given. So matters continued for a month, the brothers in danger of their lives and the neighbors watching the progress of the affair, but not daring to offer aid.

FIRED SHOTS INTO HOUSE.

Once again in the dead of night the gang appeared. Charles Ritz was home, as were the rest of the brothers. All were in bed, but the wife of Charles was down stairs. A stranger came to the door and demanded to see Charles. His wife stated that he was in bed and could not see the stranger. The man insisted and she finally went upstairs and told Charles, awakening him from his sleep to do so.

Charles came down stairs and greeted the man. He was invited outside for a private conversation, the matter being urged as one of importance, but he declined the invitation. The stranger insisted and Charles finally stepped through the doorway. As he did so he saw one man standing on each side of the doorway with leveled guns in their hands, while in front of the house and about it were other men.

He jumped back into the house in surprise and slammed the door shut. As he did so several guns were discharged through the door and the discharged whistled about him as he fled up the stairway. The wife had been watching the affair and had awakened Salvatore. Charles ran for his gun and got it. He went back down stairs and saw the whole crowd fleeing up the road. He fired ten shots at them, while Salvatore fired twice from an upper window. Two men dropped and lay there for some hours, but were afterwards carried away.

The following day two of the men arrested yesterday came to the house, told Charles that he had killed one man and the other man was nearly dead and that $500 would be required to keep the matter quiet.

CONFERRED WITH DISTRICT ATTORNEY.

The brothers then thought the matter was becoming too serious for them to fight alone and two of them came to the district attorney and made a complete statement of the facts, leaving one brother at home to guard the house. Mr. Mackin then investigated the matter and found that the statements, so far as they could be confirmed, were true. The brothers then vacated their houses and moved to Pittston. Affairs were becoming too strenuous, even for them.

The names of nearly a score of the members of the society were placed in the hands of the county detective. The Ritz brothers volunteered to assist any force that might be sent to their aid, in identifying other members whose names were unknown to them, but whom they had met in one way or another.

COUNTY DETECTIVE PLANS ARRESTS.

Mr. Mackin accordingly called upon Capt. Page for aid, and the latter responded by placing thirty-five men at his disposal. Arrangements were also made to have the men wanted detained at their working places and not allowed to leave them after once entering. Arrangements were also made to prevent any word from reaching them inside the mines, where most of them were at work. Men were also stationed at the stations to prevent the suspects from leaving them.

At 8 o'clock yesterday morning Capt. Page with his thirty-five men entered Pittston, congregating at the city hall. Here one squad was placed in general supervision of Mr. Mackin, another in charge of Mr. Jones, another in charge of Chief Loftus, and another in direct charge of Capt. Page.

For the troopers themselves Lieut. Lumb was second in command, while Sergt. Grubseld was in charge of the picket squad, Sergt. Boyd of the mounted squad and Sergt. Walsh of the searching squad.

These squads were again subdivided, some going to various mines where the men were at work, while others searched the homes. Here they found four of the men wanted, but they found other things that were more startling. No resistance was offered at any place, but the means of resistance were there, for the searching party gathered a wagon box full of arms of all kinds—guns, revolvers, rifles, magazine guns, dirks and other ugly looking weapons. In some houses where there was scarcely furniture enough to keep the rooms from looking bare, several hundred dollars' worth of first class weapons of various kinds were found. These were confiscated and taken for evidence.

POLICE AT SHAFTS.

When the squads arrived at the colliery entrances the men they needed were called to the surface, there identified, and at once placed under guard. The last of the men captured yesterday did not come from the mine in which they were working until 6 o'clock last night. There were three in this bunch, and among them was one man who was wanted, and wanted badly, and who, it was feared, had escaped the dragnet which had been thrown with such care.

The other twenty-two had been captured by 3 o'clock in the afternoon, most of them having been located between 10 and 11 o'clock. As soon as they were captured they were placed in charge of squads of the constabulary and brought to this city, where they were given preliminary hearings before Alderman Carkhuff.

All of them were placed under $1,000 bail on each of four charges and in default of this amount they were committed to the county jail. As a result of this sudden influx the jail was swamped with prisoners and four or five were lodged in each cell.

They will be given a further hearing at 2 o'clock this afternoon, when additional charges will be presented against them individually, based upon the evidence already in the possession of the district attorney. At least one of the men will have to answer to the charge of carrying concealed weapons, for one of the last three to be arrested was found to be carrying in his working clothes a long stiletto as sharp as a razor and almost as delicate as a needle.

WITNESSES WILL BE WATCHED.

The blow dealt in this wholesale arrest cannot but have a paralyzing effect on this particular line of industry among the Italians of the county, for they chiefly are engaged in this business, but in order that the case may not fall through by the death or disappearance of the principal witnesses, they are being closely watched all the time by armed guards and will be placed under bail for appearance as witnesses.

District Attorney Salsburg and assistants Dando and Butkiewicz worked until late last night preparing the data for the case and maintain that they have an even stronger case against the prisoners than was presented at Scranton against the members of the Carbondale society and resulted in long terms of imprisonment for them. It is expected that the case will be bitterly fought and it will probably occupy a large share of the time allowed at the April sessions of criminal court.

The men arrested are: Antonio Lagharina, Salvatore Polpe, Guiseppe and Andre Baterrmuatro, Charles Congaya, Guiseppe Gatante, Guiseppe Sabmero, Stephen Latori, Salvatore Lucisies, Peiro and Guiseppe Loreking, Dominick Gabbarera, Charles Damiaiera, Ferdinando Lobruno, Frank Zerbino, Giochinando Cinland, Vincent Lobruno, Guiseppe Tonacino, Dyminch Esposito, Salvatore, Nicholas and Charles Bufalino, Sam Carlen, Charles and Joseph Carmell.

DYNAMITE HOMES OF FOUR MINERS AT PITTSTON PA.

Front Portions of Houses Blown Out and Occupants Tossed from Beds; No One Injured

PITTSTON, Pa., July 13.— The homes of four miners were dynamited here early today. Among them was the home of Alexander Campbell, a leader of the insurgent element of the United Mine Workers of America in the Pittston section. He is also a member of the scale committee which is negotiating with the coal operators at Atlantic City. The front portions of the houses were blown out and the occupants tossed from their beds, but no one was hurt.

The first blast occurred at the home of Campbell, and other blasts followed at the homes of Charles Aiba, Michael Dezaly and Joseph Martinetta.

Campbell had returned from Atlantic City in an effort to aid in the adjustment of a strike at No. 6 and No. 9 collieries of the Pennsylvania Coal company. He is chairman of the general grievance committee of the Pennsylvania Coal company and the Hillside Coal and Iron company and president at a meeting of strikers last night.

The feeling of many of the strikers, it was said was to the effect that a general strike of the 10,000 men employed by these companies should be called. Campbell is said to have disapproved this proposition and to have told the men that their leaders would seek to arrange a settlement with the operators.

The dynamiting occurred three or four hours after the conclusion of the meeting.

SECOND EFFORT BY BLACK HAND TO KILL LUCCINO

BUFALINO BROTHERS' SALOON WAS WRECKED BY DYNAMITERS WHO HAVE NOT BEEN CAUGHT

After a long period of inactivity, the notorious Black Hand mafia suddenly came to life early this morning, when it is suspected of having made a dastardly attack on the lives of the three Bufalino brothers, dynamiting their saloon on Railroad street. The attempt on the lives of the three men was a failure, but the saloon and many homes in that neighborhood were damaged by the explosion. The homes damaged are owned by Mrs. Harry Bennett, Charles Consargo, Alphonso Forleni, Frank Connell, Thomas Armstrong, Mrs. Touiselino. No arrests have been made

It was just a few minutes past 2 o'clock when the explosion occurred. The sound was heard for blocks around, and soon afterwards hundreds of people from all over the city flocked to the scene. Charles Bufalino, who occupies the apartments over the saloon, was the first on the street, and he was later joined by his two brothers, Calvatore and Nicholas. The three men, accompanied by others, started out in different directions in search of the would-be-murderers, but everything was so carefully planned that the men who set off the dynamite saw to it that they would have plenty of time to make a safe getaway before it exploded. Later the city police joined in the search, which ended without any trace of the alleged Black Handers being found.

Family Escaped.

That two young boys who slept in the room directly over the saloon escaped without being injured is considered miraculous. The boys were thrown from their bed, and aside from being badly frightened, they escaped without a scratch. The other members of the family occupied rooms in the rear of the building, which were not affected by the explosion.

The men who were assigned to "pull off" the job were evidently well informed as to the use of dynamite. There is a concrete step leading into the saloon, and this was used as a foundation to prevent the dynamite from taking a downward course. The concrete base was found to be weak. When the explosive went off, it tore a hole about a foot in diameter through the step, and dug another large hole in the cellar. The explosion spread, instead of going upward, and two large front windows in the saloon were demolished, the woodwork being smashed. The interior of the barroom was also badly wrecked.

The houses on the opposite side of the street suffered greater damage than the homes on either side of the saloon. Every front window in the home of Alphonso Forleni, directly across the street, was smashed, and there were but few windows left unbroken in Charles Consargo's home, adjoining the Forleni property. The Bennett, Connell and Armstrong dwellings suffered minor damages.

Heard Men Running.

Several people living on upper Railroad street reported having heard four men running up the street, toward Browntown, about five minutes before the explosion. They were in the middle of the road, and did not make as much noise as they would on the stone sidewalk.

The three Bufalino brothers have been in Pittston many years, and have acquired much property. Salvatore conducts a grocery store in the old Banker Block, at the corner of Railroad and LaGrange streets, while Charles and Nicholas have a saloon business in the old Jenkins property, a short distance up the street.

Salvatore, the eldest of the three brothers, this morning said that he had not received any Black Hand letters demanding money, and he also denied having had a quarrel with certain of his countrymen a short time ago, which was generally rumored today.

The case is almost identical with the Black Hand plot to kill Joseph and Charles Rizzo by dynamiting their home in Jenkins alley about six years ago. Three different attempts were made to blow the men to pieces, but each time only a small portion of the house was damaged. However, the Rizzo brothers, through fear for their lives, were compelled to move to South Main street

SUFFRAGIST SAYS MILITANCY NOT DESIRED HERE

Harrisburg, Pa., Sept 8.—Miss Louise Hall, secretary of the Pennsylvania Woman Suffrage association, said today that the association would not stand for any militancy on the part of Mrs. Pankhurst, if she came to this country. She stated that Mrs. Pankhurst had apparently arranged a tour which included Philadelphia and Pittsburg, but that she would change it on requests, and that the association would not countenance any militant methods.

JEROME APPEARS FOR TRIAL ON GAMBLING CHARGE

Conticook, Sept. 8.—When William Travers Jerome, the New York attorney, reached here at noon from Montreal, his counsel indicated that he would be ready for trial this afternoon before Judge Mulvena on the gambling charge against him and that he expected to be speedily discharged.

A. C. Hanson, attorney for Wilfred Aldrich, who made the complaint against Jerome, was quoted as saying that the act charged against him constituted no offense in the Canadian laws.

Feeling is very bitter here against Jerome, while Thaw just now is the idol of the erstwhile sleepy little village. But the authorities profess to take as a joke the rumors that Jerome may be attacked. The report had it that a coterie of Thawites who caused Jerome's arrest, has planned to shoot him in the court room. Thaw was quiet today. He was still in the immigration detention room at the railway station and it was thought possible that he might be kept there until after his hearing on Sept. 15th.

ENTERTAINMENT BY HOLY NAME SOCIETY

A pleasing entertainment has been arranged by the Holy Name society, of St. John's church, to be held next Thursday evening in the chapel, when the winners of picnic prizes in Valley View Park, will be determined. There will be no admission fee charged. The members of the Holy Name society and their lady friends will take part in the program. St. John's orchestra will furnish the music.

As all the returns from the picnic will be made by Thursday evening, the exact amount realized by the Holy Name outing will be made known a few days after the entertainment. Over $2,500 has already been accounted for, and it is believed when complete returns are made that amount will be increased over $500. Rev. James McHugh, who has charge of the society, and under whose personal directions the picnic was carried on, is more than pleased with the showing made by the recently organized society. The money will go toward a fund now being established to pay for the remodeling of the parochial residence.

DOMINICAN SHELLS ENDANGER AMERICANS

ASSASSINS KILL TWO MINE UNION LEADERS IN PITTSTON'S FEUD

Alexander Campbell and Peter Reilly Riddled With Bullets As They Motor Home After Conferring With Alleged Slayers of Frank Agaty.

PITTSTON, Pa., Feb. 29. (AP) — Running down every clue that might throw light on the identity of the slayers of Alex Campbell and Peter Reilly, insurgent faction officers of Pittston, who were murdered from ambush last night, police authorities of Luzerne county today concentrated forces to bring the killers to justice.

Had Conferred With Alleged Slayers.

Campbell, acknowledged leader of the insurgents, and Reilly, recording secretary of Local Union No. 1703, U. M. W. of A., were returning from the Luzerne county jail after a conference with the alleged slayers of Frank Agaty, district officer, when they were slain. A volley of shots from a passing automobile brought almost instant death to the two men who were occupants of Reilly's machine. They were dead when police arrived.

Death Toll Growing Higher.

With the murder of the two men last night the death toll attributed directly to the feud at No. 6 colliery of Pennsylvania Coal Company mounts to four. Thomas Lillis, close friend of Campbell, was killed from ambush in January and only two weeks ago Frank Agaty, organizer of District No. 1, U. M. W. of A., was shot to death in the district offices in Miners' Bank building here.

Campbell Was Raising Funds.

Sam Bonita, Steve Mendola and Adam Moleski, all officers of No. 6 local union, were charged with the murder of Agaty and are in Luzerne county jail awaiting action of the grand jury on March 12. Campbell was head of the committee arranging funds to defend the trio at their coming trial.

Account of Killing.

Campbell and Reilly were passing up East Railroad street in an automobile when they were shot to death by the gunmen who had been following them up in the automobile. Both men were instantly killed, having been riddled with bullets. The gunmen who committed the horrible crime escaped in their car.

Auto Overtakes Them.

Reilly and Campbell were riding up East Railroad street in the former's Hudson sedan when, according to the most reliable reports available, they were overtaken by an automobile which carried the killers. Reilly was driving his car and he and Campbell were both in the front seat of the car. They had reached a point on Railroad street about one hundred feet east of Vine street when the missiles of death were sent

(Continued on Page 20.)

Theatre Party On Birthday.

Miss Betty Matthews, of Treckow entertained a number of friends at a theatre party at Wilkes-Barre on the occasion of her birthday anniversary.

ARE HAPPILY MARRIED: YES, THEY LIVE APART

NEW YORK—Up rise Robert W. Bell, stage director, nephew of Alexander Graham Bell and Josephine Hutchinson, actress, who is Mrs. Bell, to deny they have separated.

They are happily married, but have separate establishments, because one works in the day and the other at night.

LEWIS SILENT ON MINE MURDERS

Declines to Make Comment When Asked About Slaying of Union Leaders at Pittston

WASHINGTON, Feb. 29. (AP)—John L. Lewis, president of the United Mine Workers, withheld any statement today on the situation at Pittston, where mine union officials have been killed but it developed that the mine workers' international officials had been called into the situation.

Lewis was said to believe that any statement from himself or from any of the executive heads of the union would only create difficulties in a situation that the union considers particularly tense.

Any action by the chief of the mine workers toward supporting or replacing the union management in Pittston, it was indicated, would only be taken after careful consideration and would probably be announced first in the territory by such agents as may be there representing the general organization.

Want Lewis At Pittston.

PITTSTON, Pa., Feb. 29. (AP) — John L. Lewis, international president of the United Mine Workers, was today urged to come here in an effort to bring peace in the war between miners' factions at Pittston, where two more union leaders were shot down on the street in the last 21 hours.

Mayor William G. Gillespie, of Pittston, dispatched a telegram to the international leader at Washington, D. C. His plea for official intervention was voiced in "the name of the tens of thousands of terrorized citizens of the community" who are pleading for relief from the present reign of terror.

Gillespie's plea was made while state police, county detectives and city authorities were holding a conference in an attempt to learn the identity [illegible]f the men who late yesterday shot and killed Alex Campbell and Peter Reilly on a Pittston street.

The bodies of the victims were removed to their homes today after being held in a morgue all night.

The message to Lewis from Mayor Gillespie follows:

"In the name of the tens of thousands of terrorized people in this city and vicinity, I appeal to you to come here at once and use the great influence and power of your office as

(Continued on Page 20.)

New Yorkers Face

ONE YEAR EACH FOR THE ELEVEN BLACK HAND MEN

Judge Halsey Today Gave Them One Half of the Maximum Penalty Prescribed for Conspiracy.

PRISONERS DID NOT EXPECT THEY WOULD BE TREATED SO LENIENTLY

Special to The Truth.

Wilkes-Barre, Pa., July 11.—One year in the Luzerne county jail, a fine of $25 and the costs of prosecution—this is the sentence that was imposed by Judge Halsey today in the case of the eleven Black Hand men, who were convicted on charges of conspiracy, after terrorizing the community in the Browntown section of Pittston for over a year.

As the maximum penalty is two years, there was general surprise in the court room when Judge Halsey pronounced the sentence that sent the eleven men to jail for one-half the period for which they might have been sentenced.

The judge told the men that he recognized the fact that they were strangers in a strange land, and were unaccustomed to conditions here, and what was required of them. For this reason, he said, he would be lenient, and he expressed the hope that when they got out of jail they would become good American citizens.

All of the sentenced men showed plainly that they were exceedingly grateful over the unexpectedly light sentence they received. There was none of them who did not expected to receive the full penalty.

CLAIM ALIBI IN BLACK HAND CASE

Counsel for Defense Tries to Prove That Prisoners Are Themselves Victims of Conspiracy and to Discredit Rizza Brothers

From a Staff Correspondent.

WILKES-BARRE, Pa., April 29.—Additional charges, voiced by District Attorney Abram Salsburg, that witnesses for the prosecution had been tampered with enlivened the proceedings today, when the defense opened its case in the trial at this place of the thirteen alleged Black Hand leaders in this county. The District Attorney intimated that before the end of the trial he would show that the influence of the Black Hand had been brought to bear upon at least two of those whose testimony today did not sustain certain minor details of the story told on the witness stand by the Rizza brothers as to the dynamiting of their home in Browntown Christmas Eve, 1905.

The defense scored several times during the day, but it confined itself largely to trying to discredit the testimony of the Rizza brothers, and by putting on the witness stand four of the defendants, all of whom made sweeping denials of having been identified with the Black Hand or of having been connected with the outrages charged to it in this county.

Frank A. McGuigan, one of the nine attorneys representing the defendants, and a candidate for the judiciary in this county, presented the case for the defense. He declared that it would be shown that the prisoners, instead of conspiring to extort money, on which charge they had been indicted, were the victims of a conspiracy themselves. He said the defendants would establish an alibi, and that no matter how many threatening Black Hand letters had been circulated in this county, or how many homes had been fired upon or dynamited, that they would be proven innocent of any complicity in such occurrences.

Hopes to Riddle Defense

The course pursued by the defense had been anticipated. District Attorney Salsburg is confident that he will not only be able to riddle whatever the defendants themselves may testify to, but that the witnesses he will call in rebuttal will enable him to develop further sensational evidence that will shatter whatever case the defense may construct.

Mr. McGuigan began his address when court reconvened this morning by declaring that the defendants were not guilty. He appealed to the jurors to consider the case from a standpoint free from prejudice or sentiment.

"We will show that the defendants were not idle members of a Black Hand," he said, "but hard-working, respectable men, who earned a livelihood for themselves and their families in the mines. We will show that some of the defendants did not even know one another until after they were arrested. We will show that Vincent Loubouna and Salvatore Luchinna, whom the prosecution charge with being ringleaders of the supposed Black Hand band in this section, did not become acquainted with one another until they met in the county jail after they were apprehended. We will show that when Joe Giorg gave Charles Gongazas $26, he did not do so because he feared the Black Hand, but because he had offered to aid Gongaza to pay a debt.

"I do not wish to cast any reflection upon former Chief of Police Loftus, of Pittston, whom I regard as an honest man, but I believe that when the chief saw Giorg hand Gongaza the money he was merely witnessing the consummation of a scheme by which Giorg, from sinister motive of his own, wished to entrap Gongaza.

"We will show that the Rizza brothers did not tell the truth when they described what occurred when their house was dynamited and fired into. We shall prove not only that the defendants are not leaders of the Black Hand, but that, instead of being blackmailers and thugs, they were industrious, law-abiding citizens of this community."

Room Too Small for Meeting

Charles H. Kennard, a photographer of this place, was the first witness called by the defense. He testified that he had photographed the home of Vincent Loubouna, one of the defendants, at Browntown, and that he had measured the interior of it with Attorney P. F. O'Neil, one of the counsel for the defense. He said the room in which one of the Rizza brothers testified to having seen a score or more of Black Hand thugs assemble in one night was but 11 by 14 feet and but 6½ feet in height. The defense tried to show by these dimensions that it would have been impossible for such a gathering as described by Rizza to have been held in the room.

Charles Domenican, one of the defendants, was then called to the witness stand.

Continued on Second Page—Second Column

Mary Bufalino Loses Her Job

Larry May Hired By Wills Register

Miss Mary Bufalino, 47 East Columbus Avenue, Pittston, yesterday was dismissed from her $3,324 a year position as an assistant clerk in the office of Register of Wills Edward W. Lopatto.

She was employed by the county 19 years, most of which were as an assistant to the marriage license clerk.

Lopatto announced Larry A. May, 102 Sambourne Street, had been named to fill Miss Bufalino's job, effective today.

Stork Club in Detroit Destroyed by 40G Fire

DETROIT, Oct. 18.—The Stork Club, East-Side night spot, was destroyed by fire attributed to a carelessly tossed cigarette after closing hours. Damage was estimated at $40,000

Spot was operated by Eddie De Mercurio and the several Bufalino brothers who have been prominent in the juke box and other music fields here.

road street and barber shop next door owned by Angelo Volpe.

KILLS ONE MAN, WOUNDS ANOTHER AS DYNAMITERS

Brother-in-Law of Pittston Man Whose Home Was Blown Up Seeks to Avenge Act

One man murdered, another possibly fatally wounded by the same slayer, and property damaged to upward of $10,000 is the outcome of the early morning dynamiting outrage at Pittston of last Saturday, detonation of which was echoed in a brief paragraph in the Record, which was about to go to press at the time the dynamiting occurred.

The murdered man is Rocco Martello, aged 45, a mine worker and prominent union leader, employed at the No. 6 Inkerman colliery of the Pennsylvania Coal Company. He leaves a wife and four children, youngest one month, and oldest aged 9, residing at 51 East Oak street, in the Browntown section of Pittston.

He was shot and instantly killed at 4:50 o'clock in the afternoon, in view of hundreds of persons seething in excitement about the corner of Main and Railroad streets, where earlier in the day an explosion of dynamite had wrecked the butcher shop and dwelling of Pasqualle (Patsy) Lavuilo, at 9 Railroad street, as well as two adjoining buildings, and damaged by its concussion a dozen other buildings in the neighborhood.

Tony Murisola, aged 45, a miner, married and father of four children, residing on Oak street, Pittston proper, two blocks from the scene, is under arrest as Martello's slayer. His second attempted victim, who although a bullet went thrown his abdomen and out the back has a good chance to recover in Pittston Hospital, is Capaldo Cosentino, aged 24, a boarder at the murdered man's home. Lavullo is a brother-in-law of the prisoner.

Murisola did not attempt flight from the scene after the slaying, but calmly awaited the arrival of Chief of Police Leo Tierney, County Detective Thomas Allderdyce and Lieut. James Price of the Pittston police department, who but a few minutes before had left the locality after having spent the greater part of the afternoon questioning Lavullo, and other victims of the dynamiting in an effort to obtain clues to the perpetrators.

Chief Tierney last night stated that Murisola will be arraigned to-day before Justice of the Peace Thomas English charged with murder. The prisoner claims that he grabbed up the two loaded revolvers in the wrecked Lavullo home, on hearing that Martello and Cosentino had joined the crowd down at the corner of Main street, and were heard there openly boasting that Lavullo "got what was coming to him," for failing to heed demands made upon him in letters.

Lavullo has turned over to the police eight letters, which he says he has received on and off during the last four months, each demanding payment of sums ranging from $500 to $2,000. The first letter in June, he said, in submitting it, and the entire eight since seem to prove his assertion, demanded $500—"or your shop will be blown up!" And as they continued to come, since then, and hugged to his frightened breast, they reached Saturday's climax—because the last letter was a demand for $2,000 payment, or the alternative was to be:

"Your eyes taken out so you can't cry. Your hands cut off so you can't scratch."

Translation of the letter gives it that way. It was in mortal terror of this last threat being fulfilled that Lavullo and his wife went to bed Friday night, and such information as Murisola had, the police say, that sent him a raving murderer into Railroad street, and down upon Martello, surrounded by the corner crowd, for an end to it all.

Chief of Police Tierney said last night he thinks this slaying will end for a time the series of dynamiting outrages that began last June, including an attack on the home of Alex Campbell, the mine leader, in the same neighborhood.

In the record of the murdered man it is seen that he figured in a shooting at Oswego, N. Y., two years ago, but escaped punishment when brought to trial, due it is said, to witnesses being frightened away from the town. He lived for some years at Utica, N. Y., and to-day his body will be taken there for burial.

The building adjoining the Lavullo butcher shop and dwelling, which like one on the other side, was partially wrecked by the dynamite blast, is used as a barber shop and is owned by Ignatz Cipola, and another part is occupied by Angelo and family. Mrs. Volpe gave birth to a baby on Friday, and she is in a serious condition, suffering with shock.

The building directly opposite, occupied by Charles Montione, had all the windows broken. The Ford drug store and the Perrone building, out on South Main street, together with other smaller buildings in the locality were all somewhat damaged through windows being broken by the blast. Damage, it is said, will run over $10,000.

Consantino, who had been rushed to Pittston Hospital immediately after the slaying of Martello, is reported to have a fair chance for recovery. Drs. Underwood and Dixon attended him on the operating table a few minutes after he was brought in. Probing for the bullet they found it had passed through his body, puncturing organs that mean he has a battle on for life; but the prompt attention given him makes his chance good.

Chief of Police Tierney and also County Detective Allderdyce went to the hospital during the day but found Consantino too weak to be questioned. They both will appear as prosecutors against Murisola in Justice of the Peace English's court to-day. On Martello's body were found a pay envelope and a sixteen-inch stilleto. He always carried this weapon, his friends claim, and never a revolver.

MANY ATTEND FUNERAL OF NICOLO BUFALINO

There was a large delegation of sorrowing friends and relatives in attendance at the funeral of Nicolo Bufalino, widely known Italian resident of this city, which was held this morning at nine o'clock from the family home, 49 East Railroad street. Members of the Montedoro Society, of which deceased was a member, attended the services in a body. Flag carriers were Joseph Galante and Ralph Battaglia.

At 9:30 o'clock in St. Rocco's R. C. Church, Rev. Vincent Bonomi celebrated a solemn high mass of requiem. He was assisted by Rev. George Marenco, deacon, and Rev. Dominick J. Lombardi, subdeacon.

Honorary pallbearers were Santo Volpe, Charles Bufalino, John Grow, Peter Montante, Louis Consarga and Eugene Bufalino. Active bearers were these nephews: Attorney C. J. Bufalino, Russell, William E., Charles, Joseph and Angelo Bufalino.

Interment was in St. John's cemetery.

NICOLO BUFALINO

Funeral of Nicolo Bufalino, uncle of Recorder of Deeds elect Attorney Charles Bufalino was held Saturday morning at 9 from the late home, 49 East Railroad Street, Pittston, and was largely attended.

Members of Montedora Society of which he was a member attended in a body. Flag carriers were Joseph Galante and Ralph Battaglia. Mass was celebrated at 9:30 at St. Rocco's Church by Rev. Vincent Bonomi, assisted by Rev. George Marenco as deacon and Rev. Dominick J. Lombardi as sub deacon. Burial was in St. John's Cemetery.

Honorary bearers were Santo Volpe, Charles Bufalino, John Grow, Peter Montante, Louis Consargo and Eugene Bufalino. Bearers were Attorney C. J. Bufalino, William E., Charles, Russell, Joseph and Angelo Bufalino, all nephews.

ACKNOWLEDGMENTS

It took a lot of convincing to embolden me, as a first-time writer, to tell this story. For their encouragement and support, I want to thank my radio/TV mentor Tommy Woods, Joe Ranielli of Bocci Alley fame, Serrie La Torre, my nephew, my brother Nick—who surprised me by giving the project his blessing—and the many other friends who lent an ear but kept my secret close.

I started my search for a publisher by asking the guidance of a longtime workmate, Tom Tosi, whom I only recently learned had been leading a secret double life as an independent film producer-director and author of *The Curse of the Crummy Mummy*, the latest installment of his Green Hill Academy Chronicles. (Boy, you think you know a guy . . .)

Tom generously took it upon himself to introduce me to his mentor: writer, broadcaster, teacher, film historian, and raconteur Nat Segaloff, who has TV and literary credits out the wazoo and fourteen published books, including Kensington publications *The Exorcist Legacy: 50 Years of Fear*, *Say Hello to My Little Friend: A Century of Scarface*, and *The Rambo Report: Five Films, Three Books, One Legend*, among others. Nat patiently listened to my pitch, generously awarded me a twenty-minute master class in preparing a book proposal, and steered me to his editor, James Abbate at Kensington Publishing Corp.

James Abbate's enthusiasm for the topic and advocacy probably did more to sell the idea to Kensington than my proposal could have ever done. His editorial prowess and knowledge of the genre have helped keep me on track, and his never-waning enthusiasm kept me chugging along.

I should further thank members of the Kensington team who took on the project and performed all of the tasks necessary to design (love that cover), assemble, print, publicize, and distribute the work, and my literary agent, Frank Weimann, and his team at Folio Literary Management for their representation and support.

I reserve special thanks for you, the reader, for your interest and forbearance.